THE BROAD LAND

The Life and Times of
Stephen Fuller Austin

BY
RUTH GRANDSTAFF RASBURY

DORRANCE & COMPANY
Philadelphia

Friends of the
Houston Public Library

*To my dear daughters, Marietta, Ruth, Jr.,
Patricia, and Greta and my patient husband, Walter*

CHAPTER ONE

Stephen Fuller Austin peered out the window of the *Louisiana Advertizer* with little interest at the moving black umbrellas along the narrow streets of the Vieux Carre—moving like ants toward the open French Market near the batture. Mr. Hawkins watched Stephen, knowing that he had made a decision against his will.

"You've never really had much faith in your father's dream, Stephen."

"To say the least, it certainly has no precedent, and to fail at his age would be a shattering experience." Stephen turned from the window, from the black clouds scurrying over New Orleans, from the dark pall hanging over the French Quarter, but not from the anxiety he felt over his father's colonizing of Texas.

Stephen had found employment at the newspaper when other young men were willing to work for a place to live and enough to live on. He had learned New Orleans from the marine house that Dominque You had built for Napoleon on Chartres Street, to the Ursuline Convent said to have been built in 1734, where the nuns served for ninety years, before it became a meeting place for the state legislature. Thereafter it was the Bishop's Palace . . . and Stephen knew that the old clock had been made in Paris in 1638. Stephen loved New Orleans, loved everything about it, including the yarn—perhaps with a bit of truth in it—concerning Marie and her voodoo.

"You don't believe in breaking the ice?" Mr. Hawkins said while he leaned back in his leather chair, and his busy fingers twiddled with a pencil. "It isn't the first time he took colonists. What about the folks he brought with him and Marie from Virginia to St. Genevieve in the Territory of Missouri? He had petitioned for a land grant from the Spanish government and received a grant of land of three square miles—which included Mine A Burton in the wilderness. But then, you know all this."

"Oddly enough, when we landed at his grant, a lead mine it was, I was five and Emily was three. Naturally, we don't remember much about it. But one thing I learned about my father: he never

1

lived in the past; only the future concerned him—the new land, the strange river, what might be over the next mountain. We were sent away to school, both of us at a very early age. My brother James E. B. was born at Durham Hall, our home at Mine A Burton."

Mr. Hawkins let his eyes rest on Stephen, now twenty-eight years old, unmarried, and as handsome as any New Orleans blade to grace a ballroom. He wore his dark curly hair away from an exceedingly high forehead. His manners were gentle. Stephen had been a territorial legislator of Missouri until 1819. He had served in the Missouri militia with adjutant's commission by Governor Clark. Due to the failure of the Bank of St. Louis, of which Stephen was a director, he and his father explored the Texas possibilities.

So in 1819 Stephen established himself at Long Prairie on Red River in Arkansas, laid out a town he called Fulton, and established a mercantile business, and the first man to drive up to become a land-owning inhabitant was a tall fellow clad in coonskin cap and buckskins, named David Crockett. David was then about thirty-five years old. Working together, they became close friends.

Seeing the town of Fulton growing apace, Stephen went in search for a second resting place, which he found down the Arkansas River and staked it out—really never expecting it to be anything more than a stop-over for the colonists he hoped for. This became Little Rock, a resting place for immigrants yet only a dream.

Then came hard times and Stephen, while his father still worked to consummate his Texas project, found work with Mr. Hawkins in New Orleans.

Likely the whole thing would come tumbling down over their heads. Likely they'd have to give up the idea of Texas as had Aaron Burr and Wilkinson, Maggee and Guerterez and James Long—Dr. James Long from Natchez, Mississippi. As far as Stephen knew the Mexicans had Long. He hadn't been heard of in some time. And that was all right. A man going into another man's country ought to remember he's just a guest at the sufferance of the host, and conduct himself accordingly.

The rain let up some after a while, but booted feet or bare splattered the mud and carts rumbled over cobblestones or brick headed for the French Market, paying little or no attention to the almost daily showers of summer. Stephen debated whether to wait or to make a dash for the ship's office. It was after all a new suit he had just had made. The door of the newspaper office was closed

2

against the rain and the room was humid, stuffy and his whole body was soaked from perspiration.

"I'd better get on to the wharf . . . to the requisitioning of a schooner for father's colonists." It was becoming difficult to breathe. Mr. Hawkins was on his feet. "Just a moment, my boy. I'll go with you if you have no objection. I know the manager." They hunched under the one umbrella. "Mr. Gravois can be unreasonable."

"Thank you, sir. Glad to have your company." They passed along Chartres Street where Dominique You was still waiting for Napoleon, who was already dead on St. Helena. "I've been meaning to ask you about the method of interment here . . . I mean all on top of the ground."

"I suppose it started when the first one fell. . . . You've no doubt heard about the city being built on cotton bales. I wouldn't go so far myself, but one spade of dirt is no sooner out than the hole is full of water. Personally, I have to agree that if I am to have a watery grave, let it be in the ocean or Gulf or what-have-you."

"That would be reason enough, I'd say," Stephen said chuckling softly. "You have a vault over in the St. Louis Cemetery, Mr. Hawkins?"

"Oh, yes. It's old—one of the first, you know. Many of my family were pioneers and they all have their own vaults so that our family will be lost rattling around in ours, there. I guess father expected a dozen children. . . ."

They climbed the slanting levee and walked along the batture watching the boats maneuvering. Shrimp boats, fishing yawls, seagoing clippers. A few steamboats, Shreves and Fultons. It was a busy place and interesting. Fruit boats from South America, and the islands, and Mexico's Vera Cruz. "Well, here we are, Stephen!" Mr. Hawkins exclaimed exuberantly opening the Marine door. "Bon jour, M'sieu Gravois!" A bald-headed man drawled out his greeting, much annoyed by this interruption. He left the desk and a sheaf of papers on which he had been employed. "Damned ship's log. Never come out right. Half the time I make heads nor tails of their scribbling."

"I don't see Mr. Gravois."

"No and that ain't all. He's dead—died day before yesterday and left this office in a mess. Better off I'd be to set fire to it and start out all over again."

3

"Damned if you're not in a mood!" Mr. Hawkins said from the one side of his mouth.

Stephen thought it might be best to state his business now, for Mr. Hawkins was well on the way for a conflict. In the year he had been working for Mr. Hawkins, he never once saw the big fellow back off.

Stephen rested his elbow on the high counter and spoke softly but distinctly. "I'd like to charter a schooner, please."

"When would you be needing it?"

"About the first week of November. And is there accommodation for storing supplies I'll be collecting for the trip to Velasco?"

"Texas?" The manager ran a work-hardened hand across his bald head in disbelief. Stephen nodded. The man levelled his dark eyes on Stephen, and then slid across to Hawkins. "I can't charter no boat for you. Ain't nothing but a fool would try to get into Texas right now. Ain't you heard about that Long fellow from Natchez? Well, I can tell you he got the rollers put under him. Trying to take over Texas! Imagine!"

"I assure you I'm not going to try that. My mission is quite peaceable," Stephen explained patiently to the irate fellow.

"Don't tell me. Tell the Mexicans. They ain't lettin' nobody in!"

"This letter may clarify my position. My father is Moses Austin, Hazel Run, Missouri. He has been granted three hundred thousand acres in Texas for three hundred families. American families to settle out there. About half of them will be travelling in wagons, but the men from Arkansas coming down on a flatboat, will need the schooner for the rest of the way. That means to Velasco."

The man scanned the letter. "I see it's signed all right by the governor." He then asked, "Empressario? What's that?"

Stephen explained, "A person in charge of locating and settling persons of high calibre on land provided by the Mexican government. In this case, my father, Moses Austin."

The man said nothing more, but filled out the paper. Stephen signed.

"Well, now that is done, if you collect anything you can always store it in the back of my building. Come on, Stephen, and let us celebrate over a supper of cold boiled crabs and beer. I know the best place in town. You see, there's just enough of spices and red peppers, a suggestion of bay leaf and sassafras to suit my taste."

"I'd like that. Anything cold." Hawkins headed their direction toward the Absinthe House, newly refurbished. "Old home week,"

Steve exclaimed seating himself at a red-checkered-cloth table. "This very table was where Andrew Jackson, Sam Houston and Henry Shreve were the afternoon I reported in with my load of lead. General Jackson looked at me with a twinkle in his eye and reprimanded me. 'Well, my boy,' he said, 'tis better late than never, although I've no idea what to do with a boatload of lead. You see, the war's over!'

"And Sam Houston said as if to verify what the general had said, 'Pakanhams heart is already in a rum keg full of rum and on the high seas for burial in England.'"

"They couldn't very well ship the body back. . . . I believe it's traditional." Mr. Hawkins, doing justice to the platter of red-blue crabs which he expertly tore apart from long practice, began laughing.

"Clumsy, aren't I?"

"What took you so long from Mine A Burton to New Orleans—down stream all the way?"

"My flatboat capsized. We struck a sandbar hidden by a raft of snags and it just eased over in slow motion. Had we known or thought quickly enough . . . which we didn't, the lead shifted to the low side, . . . It's rather a long tale, and perhaps I'd better begin at St. Louis. . . ."

Nine hundred miles below the little town of St. Louis where Stephen was with only Elmer Smith, "Lasses," to help him get the load to New Orleans, was the large town of Natchez in the Territory of Mississippi, carved three-four years earlier along with Alabama and Georgia from the vast country called Georgia. He realized that Georgia had been developed as an English colony, but that Natchez was predominately French.

The town of Natchez lay along the rim of a two-hundred-foot bluff, with the boat landing on the bank of the river. Travelers re-arranged their stuff here, the merchandise being brought from boat to Red River cart for the exceedingly difficult and steep, deeply rutted road leading from the river to the town. In time, a tavern was opened there, and grog shops dug out places for themselves in the bank. Soon it was known, especially to river men, as "Natchez-under-the-Hill." So it became the place where the action was, with dance halls and that sort of thing giving it purpose. Lanterns swung from every post on every house and signs lit the night.

Stephen was simply aghast at the many and sundry vessels tied

5

up there. The Mississippi River is a mile wide at the crossing from Louisiana and a hundred feet deep, with a current stretching out for the big bend just below so that it slowed down and hadn't been a problem at all. Indeed, it was so gentle that cargoes of bananas and other tropical fruits could be brought up the three hundred miles from New Orleans. The trade in rice and other commodities was brisk.

Lasses Smith tied the lead boat to a willow a little off to itself, for there at the wharf was no room for another boat, much less a flatboat. "You want me to stay with it, or can I go up, too?"

Stephen, who had been watching the river's current, saw the houses on the rim of the bluff facing the lovely, spectacular view. "Of course. We've earned a night on the town!" Stephen replied. "You know, this is a treacherous stream, Lasses. It probably won't be many years until the whole bluff up there will be sucked into the river. Mark my words."

He waited for Lasses to pick up his jacket and they bent to the sharp angles of the deeply rutted trail, into Natchez. They passed the Devil's Kitchen, bane of the natives, but eldorado for the bandits who could so easily destroy their victims by dumping them into this green caldron which appeared to have no bottom. They merged finally onto the crest of the hill, and turned to see the land from there. Stephen had not realized that the hilly country was all east of the Mississippi River, or that he would be facing a land flat as a smooth-surfaced lake. Flat. Flat. Flat, cordoned in the far-off distance by a margin of green, with swamps, low. Low.

"I've never seen any town with so much going on!" Stephen said, still puffing and breathless from the climb. "Small wonder it's on everybody's tongue." He was impressed with its obvious prosperity with not the least bit of ostentation, as that snobbish St. Louis. Here in Natchez all the people were lighthearted and gay, with Spanish, French and American mingling their voices and happy laughter. They just walked about the up and down streets, the crazily winding streets, seeing homes that put the most pretentious in St. Louis to shame. There were white dove cotes, and summer houses, and two-, three- and four-storied houses, palatial. "Lasses, let's examine those high-wheeled carts. I've never seen anything like them before."

Lasses's hand felt around the wheel, touched the thongs the details of which he could reproduce when they returned to Ste. Genevieve. "They'd be great in Missouri!" The Red River carts

6

had twelve spokes, an iron rim over a wooden circle, and green leather tied it securely to axle. The bed was watertight, and high. It had no seat. "Hey," Lasses exclaimed," that's how they go acrost the rivers and come up dry. No foolin'."

He was enjoying his speculations when a voice from behind them rapsed out, "Get away from that cart afore I make two of you come four!"

"We've never seen a cart like this before, sir," Stephen replied. "We're from Missouri."

Lasses drew up by Stephen's side. "We're taking a load of lead shot to Andrew Jackson down to New Orleans. Spending the night tied up down under."

"Well, now," the man said, sticking out a rough hand to Stephen, "that makes us both on the same side. That's where I'm headin', too."

"It's about supper time, Mister . . . er . . . ."

"Bowie, Jim Bowie. I live acrost there in Vidalia. I say, where was you when that earthquake struck? Two weeks of the damnedest shaking. Took our house—at least, left it setting out on an island. Rezin and me, we swam acrost to the road, and it was gone, too. The river was purely wild. Changed from its old channel, and got in between us and the settlement. Yessir, damnedest thing I ever saw."

"Mr. Bowie," Stephen said, "we were upstream about a week."

"Well, likely you know more about it than we do here. They're acallin' it New Madrid, on account of that was the center of it."

"New Madrid?" Lasses and Stephen both exclaimed. "Why, that's the part of the country we're from. What about St. Louis?"

"We have not heard what happened in St. Louis, if anything. But who may you be?"

"Why, I'm Stephen Austin, and this is Lasses Smith. I was about to ask you about a good tavern where we might get supper," Austin said, adding, "Won't you have supper with us?"

"Why not, Mr. Austin? After all, I'm headed to Mobile. A few hours one way or tother won't make a bit of difference." He caught hold of the bridle and walked along with the horse, barely able to hold back the load it hauled. Connelley's Tavern was the best—best food, best whiskey, best of anything and plenty of it. Jim Bowie rated his favorite place at Natchez-Under-the-Hill.

At a small table at a window with a view of the river, they talked of many things, but Jim Bowie got worked up powerfully: "Them British now, you know what they been adoin'? Why, I'll tell in case you're not familiar. They attack our merchant vessels on the high seas, and force our sailors to come aboard their ships and purely work 'em to death—fighting their own people, the Americans. If they don't man a cannon like they are ordered, they just get blowed off the deck, food for the fish!" Jim, vicious in his mind against the British, made quick work of a thick steak, and potatoes and string beans and hot biscuits. The gentleman had no appetite.

"I suppose it won't be long before they're attacking Washington. Things are in such a state of flux," Stephen said. "Trouble with the British, trouble with the Creeks . . . Andrew Jackson's got his hands full."

"Yeah, he's in command of all the Gulf country," Bowie said.

"Now, if you're headed New Orleans way, just roll on the flat-boat," Stephen said.

The Red River cart was tied down and the horse unbridled. They slept on the flatboat as was their custom, wrapped in blankets, taking turns at the sweep, for the river was staggering under its load of planters and sawyers afloat in the river. With a fair current, they hove around the bend at Baton Rouge with the dawn.

"The Oumas and Istroumas are Indian tribes living along here. You see, in time of trouble they send woods runners from village to village of their own tribes and friends. The way these friends and relatives gave reply was to set up a pole and paint it red. That meant 'we are with you' or 'we'll make war on your side' or something of that order. This bluff can be seen for a long way, and the red stick. When the French, whom the Natchez hated, saw the red pole, they cried out the warning, "Baton Rouge! Baton Rouge!" which meant to the French that the various Natchez tribes were on the warpath and that vacillating tribe of Choctaw Indians you couldn't depend on and that the French had better get lost." Jim Bowie was in his element.

"Baton Rouge means Red Stick?" Lasses asked, "I don't see none now. Mr. Austin, you want we should draw up to the bank?"

"Since we really are in no need . . . how you feel about it, friend?"

"Why, I'm all for seeing New Orleans and my business soon's ever we can," Bowie said. And Stephen waved on, on. They saw the bluff, not so high nor so steep at Baton Rouge as at Natchez, but an important post. By mid-afternoon the next day they arrived at the wharves of New Orleans. Jim Bowie took the cart off toward the French Quarter, a block or so away. Stephen would not see Jim again for years. . . . But he wondered what Jim Bowie had in his Red River cart that he watched over so carefully.

"And you're still wondering what Jim Bowie had in his Red River cart. I can tell you. Guns and ammunitions—for Andrew Jackson."

"I wonder why he never said!" Stephen said.

"You were telling me about your education, yours and Emily's."

"Oh, yes. There's really not much to tell. Emily graduated from Hermitage Academy in New York, and promptly married James Bryan. But he's a fine gentleman, and loves Emily devotedly. . . . As for me, they sent me first to Bacon Academy in Connecticut, and then to Transylvania—which is more Presbyterian than anything else." Stephen grinned impishly a moment, then added, "My cousin Mary Austin lives there, which made the time just fly. She's my first and only sweetheart—since we were just kids." Stephen was now twenty-eight years old.

"That's funny, Stephen. Let me give you a quick run-down on you from my point of view. You first had to go to school. Right? Then it was the legislature in Missouri, right? Then you were director of the bank in St. Louis, right? Now all this time what did you expect your little playmate to do? Then it was the Mine A Burton out there close by Ste. Genevieve, right?"

"Right. Then came the crash," Stephen said by way of defending his laxity toward his only love. "Then I'm in New Orleans looking for a job, and then I found you. Of course, there was always father."

"He is a most remarkable man, Stephen. Good blood flows in your veins from him, as well as your lovely mother."

"It has been quite an evening, sir," Stephen said rising. "I am bound to leave now, and get my saddle bags organized to meet him in Natchitoches, sometime next week.

"Transylvania was the first college west of the Alleghenies. You perhaps know that it has not always been where it is now; it was first built in Danville, when that was a thriving place," Stephen said.

"Presbyterian oriented," Mr. Hawkins remarked. "I really can't say I believe in all Calvin preached—or the others of like convictions. It seems to me, if I remember correctly, Calvin believed in the divine origin and authority of civil government, that under no

9

circumstances may an individual citizen actively revolt against existing government. But Calvin's strong emphasis on God's sovereignty meant that no human sovereignty could be absolute. If the ruler commands what is contrary to God's will, the citizen must passively refuse to obey. Even more democratic in its ultimate implications was Calvin's teaching that lesser magistrates, such as Estates of the Realm, or Parliament, might actively resist and curb a tyrannical ruler."

"In other words, if a monarch violates his contract—depose him!" Stephen said, enjoying himself. He had so few opportunities to. So few people understood. This was like a meeting of minds.

"Take transubstantiation. There are those who believe this to be traditional—the actual blood and the actual body of Christ. . . . I believe it is a miraculous change—not to substance, but to spirit."

"Of course the mystery of transubstantiation and the Eucharist probably shall ever so remain—a Mystery."

It was time to leave, but Stephen would remember "If a monarch become tyrannical, depose him!"

CHAPTER TWO

It was warm in Natchitoches that July of 1821 and a blacker day Stephen Austin had never experienced. Fog mists hung above the oaks and willows and the endless canebrake, hung above the trees and Red River with little movement, caught up in an uncontrollable vortex, and held Stephen suspended as a feather blown by the wind. He walked along the river bank of the ancient village of the Natchitoches Indians, desolate and blank-faced since the smallpox epidemic. Not even a hungry hound was scrounging around the deserted taolis. He had walked farther than he had wanted, knowing full well he could never walk away from it no matter how far. So he sat down on a log near the sluggish muddy river, opened his mother's letter which Mr. Hawkins had himself brought to Natchitoches only an hour before. He had brought it himself, Mr. Hawkins had, seeing the carefully folded sheet waxed and noting that with trembling hand she had edged the letter in black.

10

Stephen's eyes watered up, blinding him as he reread his mother's letter:

> He called me to his bedside and with much distress and difficulty of speech, begged me to tell you to take his place and if God in His wisdom thought best to disappoint him in accomplishing his wishes and plans for his family, he prayed Him to extend His goodness to you and enable you to go on . . . with the business in the same way he would have done. . . .

The business was three hundred thousand acres in Texas, which Moses had been granted, for three hundred colonists. This was why Stephen was to have met his father in Natchitoches. He pulled a small writing pad from his pocket and made answer to his sorrowing mother:

> I shall go out and take possession of the land and arrange for the families to move in the fall . . . so that I still hope great good will result from my father's astonishing perseverance and fatigue of last winter.

Stephen headed back into town then, up Front Street to rejoin Don Joseph Juan Erasmo Seguin and Don Juan Verimendi, Spanish commissioners who had come to escort him and a party of sixteen men to San Antonio de Bexar. Both men wore black broad-brimmed hats and black broadcloth suits with Saltilla serapes in bright colors stark against their black clothing. But their horses were so burdened by silver trappings Stephen wondered how they could carry it all. He was impressed. These gentlemen coming to meet him greatly relieved his burden of apprehension about this fantastic enterprise.

Mr. Hawkins was standing on the gallery of La Costa's holding onto the horse he had ridden up from New Orleans, and held out the bridle as Stephen approached. "Here, Stephen, is my contribution. My horse, and don't tell me later that for the want of a horse, a kingdom was lost!"

Stephen smiled then, a deep meaningful gentle smile . . . so like him, and took the horse with thanks. "I was about to trade off that wheezy thing I rode up here on. But are you taking the river down?"

"Yes indeed. Ought to be back at the *Advertiser* in short order. Downstream all the way." The friends went then to the boat that was already steamed up and loading and Mr. Hawkins shook hands with him.

11

"Go out, Stephen, into the land that was promised thee, and take possession!" and Stephen replied, "I haven't found it yet!"

His own party of colonists, sixteen in all, were mounted when Stephen returned from the boatlanding and joined in waving adieu to the boat and Mr. Hawkins, whose face was lost amongst the other passengers and stacks of deer hides from the Yucca Plantation, and bear, raccoon, and mink from local trappers—trappers who worked the river as far up as the Great Raft at Grand Ecore, and as far down as the rapids. This was the shipping point, the end of navigation and the last town toward the Spanish frontier.

The party moved through a forest of virgin pine, the Kisatchie Wold, the Hills of Surprise and passed the ancient mission to the Adaes Indians, of the Caddo Federation; and then on a high wind-swept hill stood Jesup, bulwark against the Mexicans and but fifteen miles from the Sabine River, which means River of Cypress, and Texas. They did not tarry here but passed on into Texas, San Agustine, but five miles or so over the border, and Nacogdoches, also an Indian village called after the white Indian of the Caddo Federation, across many streams—the San Jacinto, Trinity, Neches, Brazos, St. Bernard, and the Colorado (of Texas). Stephen said, "Oh it is a beautiful land, and so broad, that landline and skyline merge in the gray-purple that only distance brings."

"The wonder is that there are so few Spanish ranchos and they are along the Gulf nearer the Rio Grande. . . . I like the country myself. It's my family holding me back from becoming a stock-man." It was Don Seguin speaking, a handsome young fellow about Stephen's age.

"You have a family, also, Don Verimendi?" Stephen queried over a plate of beans and boiled coffee—not that he was really interested in the commissioner's marital status, but to make conversation.

"Ah, yes, Senor Austin. I am also the proud papa of the most beautiful little girl. She makes my heart leap just to remember!"

"You figure some day to stand at the front door with your gun?" Don Seguin said facetiously.

"Her husband shall be of her own choosing. Between us we say, Ursala she pick the man. None of this pre-arrangement for us."

"You're a family man, I take it," Don Seguin said, addressing Stephen.

"No . . . not yet. But I've picked her out. We were children to-gether." Stephen decided now would be a time to roll up in his

12

blanket and sleep. But sleep would not come. The men were agitatedly talking and one ear cocked itself to hear. Now and then he could hear his name, . . . "Since childhood?"

On the fifth day they stopped on a range of low hills and looked down into the valley of the San Antonio River. The mission bells were ringing from their various stations calling the hour of prayer. Dons Verimendi and Seguin dismounted and knelt on the sand as the Americans looked on at this unusual behavior. A moment later they were again mounted. Then only, Don Seguin spoke, "There's the most beautiful city this side of Mexico City, which is the most beautiful city in the world!" His hand pointed to the river zigzagging through the valley. "The Indians call it 'The-drunken-old-man-going-home-at-night.'"

"Aptly named, I'd say," Stephen remarked. The party moved down the bending hillside and passed on until they reached the Governor's Palace.

Governor Martinez's welcome was warm and gracious. "But where is Senor Moses Austin? Was it not for you to meet him and give escort to Bexar?" he asked his two commissioners, Seguin and Verimendi.

At once they both explained that the senor had passed away and turned to Stephen, who had not yet had a word. "Allow me to present young Stephen Fuller Austin, who bears a letter from his father transferring the land grant and the responsibility for his colonists. I assure you, sir," Seguin said, "you shall have no regrets in allowing him to take over." Governor Martinez remarked, with a great showing of white teeth under his jet black mustache, that it would be most agreeable.

A plat of the country was given Stephen. "Now between the Rio Colorado and the Brazos would be preferred country, Senor Austin. Look over all of it, should you care to, and let me know soon in which you are interested. I bid you good day, gentlemen. I await news from you, Senor Austin. But let me insist that before you go exploring, please to find your father's good friend—the Baron de Bastrop."

Stephen with Josiah Bell of Arkansas and others from Missouri, nine in number, left San Antonio the next day to locate the land grant. The other fellows returned to their homes to prepare their family and business in Missouri and Arkansas. They had liked what they had seen.

13

Stephen looked back at the low white building framed in bougainvillea and black bars over the windows. Tropical plants transformed it into a garden and the patio, with no trace of the fact that a former governor, Salcedo, had been hacked to death there—by Guterrez-Magee, who was attempting to take over. But Texas is a broad land . . . with many facets, the two learned the hard way.

It was at the tail of July or the first of August when with nine picked men Stephen began his study of Texas. The two whom he knew best were Lasses Smith and Josiah Bell. The air was becoming hot and burdened with blowing sand, so that soon he had his bandana up to his eyes, while the fellows spit and coughed and carried on to show an impression. Stephen was more concerned with what he saw emerging as a black line which could portend only a storm. As they rode the miles, a cabin would show up by and by, near the trail, off a mile or so, under a clump of trees, right out in the broiling nothingness. The men wanted to know what had happened to the people who were living or had been living on those ranches.

"About 1813, they say, when Mexico was embroiled in its fight for some freedoms, the emigrants who had crossed the Sabine River without a grant or much of anything but guts, were cleared out, by order of the government or from fright of the Mexican army. A few, it seems, did come back. That now poses a problem for me as to their status." But Stephen's eyes were tracing the density of the oncoming cloud.

"There's one, right yonder," Lasses called out, pointing to a clump of oaks. "See it?" They swung in, for the wind was coming in gusts and a white wall was gaining on them. They unsaddled and threw the saddles in a pile on the funny little gallery, four-maybe five feet wide, and the white wall coming across the prairie hit the cabin. Stephen peered out the door. He was barely able to see the animals, who had turned their rumps to the rain.

Fetching in his saddlebag, Josiah Bell said, "Let's get some fire there. Looks like it's still in fair condition."

The boards or planks of the floor had curled at the ends, probably laid without nails. The grass was a pale yellow-white struggling for life under the cabin, which like most cabins had been set on stumps of some two feet in height. Josiah yanked a few of the planks off, from one place and another wherever he found them loose. A fire started on the mud and straw fireplace with spits still anchored into the sides. Josiah slapped his hands together, exclaiming, "Now for a good cup of coffee." From his saddle bag he drew out the smoke-bottomed pot, went out to the gallery with it and held it under the eave. By now the quick-burning pine boards had flared themselves out, not slow as hickory or oak, and Stephen racked a bed for the coffee pot. The coffee boiled mightily and the glint of tin cups could be seen as the fellows got ready for it.

They talked of many things over their meal, waiting as well for the storm to pass. There had been the priest of Dolores, Father Miguel Hidalgo, who had resented the viceroy's edict that priests were not to grow grapes, not to make wine, not to give a paying wage to the peons. It was he who began what developed into a battle with Spain for Mexican freedom, for which he lost his head. Others took up the cross and the instruments of war, many also losing their heads, but as many as fell were matched by replacements. "You see, Mexico, although an ancient land and civilization of Mayan, Toltecs, Aztecs, and then the Spaniard, is a new government . . . still in the maze of finding a footing because it is the first time that the people must rule. The people. In just two-three years . . . still so new and untried."

After a while the men began yawning. It was late in the afternoon. The rain had wept itself out—passed and gone on east. The men sprawled over the floor away from the heat of the fireplace. It was just as well they withdrew from the fire. Rattlesnakes cannot abide heat (just five minutes in the hot sun kills them), and they were emerging from the side of the fireplace in a mad rush to fall through the planking for fresh air and a cooler place. But not so with one young bull. In defiance he coiled up, ready to strike. Missourians have a saying that an uncoiled snake is not dangerous. Don't you believe it! Stephen, who was not asleep, was watching a spider in the unceiled cabin, swinging from its anchor and weaving a web. Ah, Robert Bruce, you may have had inspiration from a spider, but I'm not learning a thing from this one, except that she never gives up. Well, on second thought, that was all he needed. "Never give up!" he said aloud. Lasses awoke and whispered, "Hold still!" and made a lunge over Stephen with his long knife. Following his flight, Stephen saw the rattlesnake coiled, his red forked tongue shooting out like a warning . . . with his rattles like a mariachi with gourds like a sprung spring. And then its head rose up to meet the enemy.

15

Stephen had not heard it, because the rattles had only begun and Josiah Bell, who was snoring like a bull alligator in mating time, had turned over, exclaiming that his throat was dry and he needed water. He lit the lantern just as Lasses's knife struck the snake in the head. It writhed for a while and then was still. But Lasses was holding his wrist where it had come into contact with the fangs before the knife had pierced it.

Bedlam broke out then, the men having been awakened from sound sleep.

"Did it get you?" asked Stephen, seeing the face muscles work as if it were the end of him, and his eyes filling up. "Hang on to me," Stephen said. "Out on the gallery!" And Josiah ran ahead and set the lantern down, shouting to the men to get the hell out of there. He put his hunting knife in the coals for a moment. Then Stephen, holding a tourniquet, his bandana above Lasses's elbow, watched Josiah carefully follow the line of the red marks, looking all the world as though he'd been pricked by his ma's sewing needle. The gash made, Josiah set his mouth so as to draw out the venom. He spit it out and drew more. Actually, it had been a young snake, with four, maybe five rattles still loaded with deadly fluid. After repeating this until it was only pure blood that was flowing, Josiah called for the whiskey, and rinsing his mouth and deluging the saddles with it, he held it up for a bit of added strength. Then, after his own treatment, he poured a quantity over the wound, which was pretty big for lancing a snake bite.

"You can let go the bandana now, Stephen," he declared, taking another swig from the bottle. "He'll be all right. You know I'm the best damned rattlesnake hunter in Arkansas!"

Stephen, always so quick of mind, with amazing reflexes, turned from Josiah and Lasses to the edge of the small gallery and was very sick. The men had snatched up their blankets and stuff and torn out, forking their unsaddled horses, holding in their arms whatever they could grab. Josiah drawled, "Look at 'em. They've purely had the hell scairt out of 'em." He took another swig at the bottle, shook it and growled. "Is this all?"

But Josiah Bell, after washing out his mouth, pulled his cud of chewing tobacco and bit off a right generous chunk, wallowed it around a bit in his mouth, then observed, "We sure as hell can't stay here, Stephen."

"We'll get our things and Lasses and the horses saddled."

"And then wait for the sons-o'-bitches to come back for their saddles?"

"No use letting a small incident in a man's life ruin it, Josiah. They were afraid of snakes—well, so am I."

"Yeah, but didn't run off and leave the victim to make it by himself. There's a helluva difference!"

"Most are new and untried. If you want to know about how a person will react, Josiah, just ask Lasses about the trip down the Mississippi with a load of lead. That was when the earthquake struck, but I never had experienced an earthquake, and I couldn't imagine what was happening. There it was, the river leaning like crazy, up on one side, down on the other, and when that took place, the boxes of lead broke their moorings and slid off into the Mississippi. Not the half of what was going on with Lasses and me trying to hang on to the up side, when suddenly, the thing upended on us and away we went, clear out. We dogtrotted, trod water, and, man, we could not find it. Lasses, a good swimmer, went under, and I lost him for a while, for the flatboat decided it was a turtle and struck on a sand bar, just eased over, up side down. And heaven only knew where Father's lead shot had gone."

Josiah stopped still. "Did you ever make it?" and Stephen replied, "Six weeks later, and by the hardest. Lasses is quite a man."

CHAPTER THREE

Stephen and his party reached Natchitoches in late fall, when the sweetgum was blazing from red to gold, and the virgin pine forest of the Kisatchie Wold soughed in the Eternal West Wind . . . soughed zither-like high above Stephen's head, while the hooves of his horse made hardly a whisper on the thick carpet of brown pine needles. It was a strange and eerie feeling that encompassed him as he rested at the little falls of Kisatchie. It reminded him with its tinkling, of rain splattering on a corrugated roof.

With his back against the bark of a giant tree, he took from his saddlebag the writing materials he always carried and began his report to Governor Martinez, outlining the boundaries of the land he had chosen. He felt that what the Mexican government had offered was more than generous: a man was to receive 640 acres for himself; 320 acres for his wife, 160 for each child, and 80 for each slave. There was to be a charge of twelve and a half cents per acre to each colonist as payment for surveying and general expenses. Special provision was made to professional men, merchants, mechanics or those who rendered some special service to the colony.

Governor Martinez approved the distribution of land as suggested, and appointed Stephen civil commandant of the colony.

There were two permits Stephen issued for grants in his colony before proceeding, One was to his old friend, Josiah Bell from Arkansas, October 6, 1821; the second was to William Kinchelae, part owner of the schooner *Only Son* on October 16. These two men were to assist in supervising the first colonists with locating and surveys.

October was flamboyant with fall colors—the green of the oaks called Evangeline now, and the yellowing cypress shrouded in threads of dripping gray. "Right here's where I want my land grant, Stephen. If the choice meets with your approval."

"It does, indeed!" Stephen let his eyes wander down the bank of the turbulent Brazos and decided Josiah Bell had made a wise choice. At this, Josiah Bell dug his fingers into the black soil and threw it to the wind, spaded a shovel and dumped it.

Josiah looked at Stephen then with a happy and contented expression. "It is equal distance between the calm St. Bernard and the raging Brazos and about eighteen miles up from the Gulf."

The land lay flat with not even a suggestion of a hill, and hundreds of oaks, ancient even then, were spaced as though planted in that manner. Of course, Stephen thought, only Indians knew this wilderness. Split-offs of the Caddo tribe of white Indians with the Head tribe living on Red River near Caddo Lake. They were the true pierced-nosed people who worshiped the sun. They had never spilled a white man's blood, they claimed, and always wore clothes.

"Yes," Stephen said. "I think you'll be safe here, and a waterway to the Gulf and New Orleans or Vera Cruz. . . . That's enough of Spanish ritual, Josiah . . . at least it's enough for me." Stephen laughed at Josiah, who said, "I was wondering when you'd tell me to stop!"

"You'll get along fine with the Caddoes, but they tell me that a fierce tribe of Indians called Karankawas live on south of here, mostly on the island of Galveston."

18

"You aim to settle William's today?" Bell, asked poking the tools into his saddle.

"No. I'm headed to New Orleans," replied he.

New Orleans was balmy as Indian summer. The sky was blue as the waters it dipped into, and Mr. Hawkins with Stephen was at the Marine depot to make a purchase of a boat. *The Lively* was the schooner settled upon, with Mr. Hawkins assisting financially. Now arriving at the wharf were the eighteen men who had just bashed to pieces the flatboat on which they had made the journey to meet Stephen.

They were mostly young and mostly dressed as farmers as they were and mostly in search of a new life in a new country. Missouri would sustain a family if all worked from four in the morning, arising in pitch black of night, until they could no longer see the furrows. They all had bags made of old carpet. Durable things they were and easy of handling.

"There's our boat, fellows," Stephen proudly waved his hand toward *The Lively*. "Get aboard for I must go over the rest of the way with you."

"You're not coming with us?" one young fellow exclaimed as if he were already missing his mama.

"No, I'm going back to Natchitoches. It's already the first week of November, and I'm expecting others to meet me there."

Standing on the deck of *The Lively* with the wind tousling his wavy hair, his hat in his hand, he said: "Sail on west until you come to the Colorado river. Go on up that river until you find a suitable landing place. Build a stockade first. Now listen, I said first. Get your plowing done and corn planted. Then, and only then, are you to begin the erection of your homes. Lots of timber for the taking. We'll meet you just as soon as we can. But as soon as you are housed, send for your families, or go back and get them."

In Natchitoches Stephen traded his horse for a team and a wagon, paying too much, but he, too, must have supplies. He drew up from the roped corral to the hitching post at Criswell's General Store. The place was dark, heavy with the smell of rawhides, and coffee beans roasting in a back room. Stephen passed the time of day with Mr. Criswell and gave him a list of supplies. It was for lime, flour, pork, beef, lard, Heno tea, whiskey, butter, beans, dried fruit, loaf and brown sugar, fresh currants, cavendish tobacco, London mustard, sperm candles, gunpowder and shot of all sizes.

Mr. Criswell said while his hands kept busy with the order, "Be you the Mr. Austin them emigrants be waiting fer?"

"I am. And these supplies are for myself—not for them."

"Lucky you got here when you did. They about cleaned me out but a boat got in this morning. Be there more to come?"

"Not this year, sir," Stephen answered, tongue in cheek.

"Well, it's a wonder to me, with Mexico jest gittin' free from the yoke of Spain they'd be willin' to fart around with you." Criswell hawked his throat. "Meanin' no disrespect, Mr. Austin."

"Where you keep your farm implements?" Stephen asked, seeing them at the back of the room. "I'll need plows and such."

"Right there. Just set aside what you be wantin', whilst I collect this order." Mr. Criswell opined, "There appeared to be nigh a hunnert people on that wagon train. Never seed so many all at once."

"Nearer to two hundred," Stephen said. "All together, there'll be three hundred. Others have gone on to Texas by schooner."

"Where'll be settlin of them?" and Stephen said, "On three hundred thousand acres of beautiful land. I aim to conquer it with the axe, the plow and the hoe."

Natchitoches was old with but one major avenue and that was along Red River. The buildings were set back leaving a wide space between the wood galleries with hitching rails and the river bank. In 1714, three years before New Orleans was founded by Iberville first had a barracks and post they called San Juan Bautista, under the ruling hand of St. Denis. This fort served for almost a hundred years at which time Governor C. C. Claiborne saw fit to rebuild the fort and placed it on the north side or west of Red River, Fort Claiborne. During the war with Britain another fort was constructed in the town called Camp Salubrity, and following that conflict in which a young Lieutenant Selden served, another fort was created atop a high promontory in the bend of Red River at Grand Ecore—Fort Selden. This served until a need arose for a cantonment out in the disputed strip of land lying between Red River and the Sabine, for with the Purchase of Louisiana at San Ildefonso "With the same extent it had" when there had never actually been a line of demarcation between French Louisiana and Spanish Texas, that area became the hideout for all manner of villians. And so Stephen rode into a dispute between these peoples of long standing.

In the Hills of Surprise, high on a windswept hill was established the cantonment of Jesup. Colonel Many was commander. Many men served at Jesup whose names would in time become household words, but now they were endeavoring to keep the peace between their respective countries. So that Colonel Many saw Stephen Fuller Austin approaching with his colonists in utter dismay. Stephen said, "This is likely to be the last lap of the journey." He declined to ask why had they come in toto. It was all right, he thought, just something he would not be faced with later, and they have their men with them. He was pleased that their spirits were high.

Young Colonel Many said, "I'm at a loss, Mr. Austin, to know why you are taking such a wagon train through this treacherous land. I'm perfectly willing to give you an escort; we always do give an escort, or did, when immigrants, trappers, or what have you, needed it. But I'm sorry. The border is closed, if you've not heard."

Stephen Austin handed Colonel Many his papers, that Empressario Austin with three hundred families were to be passed into Texas. . . .

Colonel Many extended his hand. "Let me be the first to offer congratulations on being the first empressario to be granted land in Texas. You'll find it rather larger than you anticipate."

"I've been over it and I quite agree with you. It is a broad land." Stephen listened as Colonel Many ordered his horse saddled. He escorted the caravan down the long bending hill with Stephen by his side, and the white canvassed ribs rolling, slanting, creaking as through the swamp with the horses or mules bogging to their knees.

But they made it—slowly, to be sure, but the Sabine lay shimmering in the sunlight, snaking its silver-gold way to the sea.

"We must turn back now," Colonel Many said, raising his hat. "It would never do for an American soldier to be seen on that side of the Sabine. You watch out for the man-eating Karankawas. Savage as can be. Naked as a jay bird even in winter, and eat roots and such things, but they prefer man flesh." So Stephen bade Colonel Many good-bye and thanked him and his escort. "I'll see you again."

Stephen waited beside the San Antonio Trace, or Kings Highway, or El Camino Real, which meant the same, for the end of the long caravan to pass. He then would be better acquainted with his colonists, having seen them. Many of the men rode saddle horses, or bare back. Some were on big strong Missouri mules. Stephen surveyed them, a fine-looking aggregation, and then he thought about the Missouri mule. Of all the animals coming into Texas, he would be most proud of them, for they are dependable. A smile on Stephen's face told of the remembrance of a tale oft told by his

21

father, Moses: A Missouri mule will live to be a hundred, if it takes him that long to kick your teeth out.

Drawing up beside him was a man with red hair, the reddest hair, and with his hat off, the sun glinted it to a burnished gold. He would be about six feet, Stephen figured. It was hard to tell about height when a man was in the saddle, or bare back as this one was. He was riding a tremendous Missouri mule.

"Mr. Austin, you don't remember me, I reckon. But my wife, Lisa, and I are from Ste. Genevieve. She is a product of Mother Duchesne's Parochial over in St. Charles. But I went to the Academy of Ste. Genevieve. It was not a public school, but its charter, as you may remember, required that the poor and Indian children be taught free."

"I was not in Missouri at the time of its founding, "Stephen said, "but father told me it had been established in 1808."

"Say, I sure take a lot for granted—like you remembering me or Lisa. I'm Bill Blanks and that wagon just drawing up is my family. Lisa, who's not much bigger than the kids, is with our oldest boy on the seat, and he's driving, good with animals, and there are six more inside."

Stephen laughed, "It would seem that you and Lisa aim to populate Texas all by yourselves—that is, if you keep going. . . ."

"It's not my idea. Lisa has religious scruples about that and of course it's against nature to fit your urges into some monthly regime of being well or unwell. It never is when you are ready!"

"I don't know what you're talking about, Bill," Stephen said, pulling on the bridle and turning the horse up the road. "I'm not a married man."

"You're not?" Bill exclaimed. "Hell, how could you know?"

That evening they crossed the river and camped. Stephen saw Lisa at close range as she went singing and pushing her pots and coffee pot around on the red coals of their fire. Her children were all washed, their hair combed, and looked well-cared-for even in their road-soiled clothing. They would eat out of the pots as all others in the caravan did to save unpacking the barrels of dishes snugged away in the wagon. And the tin plates and cups were dipped into the river and wiped and stored. Stephen walked over after his supper, which was earlier than the Blankses' and was charmed with Lisa, her gentle attitude toward her children, as each was to her a gift from God, and Stephen felt a twinge of loneliness, a real void in his life. How he would love to have what Bill and

Lisa had! She said, "Won't you have supper, Mr. Austin—or coffee, since I noticed your man has already fed you?"

"You're most kind, Mrs. Blanks. I shall be happy for the coffee." Stephen straddled a log and at odd moments studied her, her white hands, long slender fingers. They had no help that he could see. And as if reading his mind, Bill said, "She uses cows milk and cream—on her face, too. Actually, she smells like a calf. I tease her about it."

December was ending as they neared the Brazos. They camped on a little creek January 1, 1822. "Well, here we are at last!" Stephen said walking by the stream. Then a voice out of the group cried, "Wheeeee. Let's call it New Year's Creek, on account this is New Year's Day!"

"This is the way to begin a new year, a new country, a new life." Stephen observed while he laid the pencil drawing of Texas on the back end of a wagon. Men, having been given their plots, were already chopping down trees, being careful that the trees should not be too large. They all pitched in and built a cabin up so far, then another, and so on so that their cabins were all finished simultaneously. The women cooked for all, and they all ate around a great bonfire, for the woman scream of panthers had ripped the stillness along the creek and back into the woods. They were happy. They were busy, and so Stephen hastened away to meet the eighteen men who had sailed from New Orleans. He wanted now to unite the two groups.

He arrived at a river he took to be the Colorado and made camp and here he stayed day in and day out for weeks. He finally was eating catfish and wild onions, and glad to get that. He was exposed to weather, which was variable. He had lost so much weight that his clothing hung and he finally was compelled to consider *The Lively* lost. He started out for San Antonio to report, and on the way paused at La Bahia to rest, and there met his brother James and a number of men. James had come south to assist Stephen, and so they all traveled together to San Antonio, arriving there March 15, 1822.

"There's been a change in policy, senor," the governor said. "You must go on into Mexico City and there seek renewal of your grant."

"A change in policy? Just because a number of colonists were lost?" Stephen asked.

"You do not know under what conditions your schooner was lost.

23

It could very well have missed the Colorado Rio—and the Karankawas live along there. Indeed their main stronghold is in the eastern end of Galveston Island."

In the meanwhile, *The Lively* missed the Colorado and found itself sailing along at a good clip going through Galveston Bay between Bolivar Point and Galveston Island, stopping at Bolivar.

Strange it was and certainly unexpected to find a lone white woman and her little girl. "I'm Jane Long," she said, "and this is my child. We are waiting for my husband, James, Dr. James Long, to return from Mexico."

"You better come aboard," the captain said. "You're in a bad place here. Indians."

But Jane Long explained that her husband had left her there, and there he would find her. "If you could spare us a little food to tide us over, why we'll manage." She was a determined woman.

The captain ordered food and medicines to be brought ashore and then he said with much wonder, "Have you spent the winter in that?"

"It's been a mild winter, Captain—in fact, we've rather enjoyed ourselves."

"I hate to leave you all here, Mrs. Long. But then, you know best." And Jane thanked them and stood on the beach gazing after the schooner *Lively* as long as she could see through tear-dimmed eyes.

Returning, they again sailed by the Colorado in the dark, and landed next morning at the mouth of the Brazos instead. The port of entry was called Velasco. However they searched near and far for Stephen Austin, and did not find even a small trace. In sheer desperation they began building dugouts and loaded their cargo and began the long haul up a most angry river. They did not know that Brazos de Dios, meant the "Arms of God."

Some sixty miles up the Brazos from its mouth, they came upon a very unusual bend. Here they pulled ashore, and here they decided to stay. They called it Fort Bend, being a natural place of fortification. But Stephen knew nothing of this.

He was seeing in what a beautiful wooded area San Antonio so pleasantly was placed. There were springs at the southern edge of the Central Texas hill country. It had long been a favorite of places for Indians of the region and was the site of an ancient Indian village. He learned about these things from a priest. In 1619 the

Spanish became interested and in 1718 established a mission there called San Antonio de Valero. This was followed by the ever-useful presidio for the protection of the padres, the Alamo. In time there grew up a resting place in this pleasant valley farther on, called La Vallita, or little village, with stores and cantinos and such about 1731.

The civil district was called San Fernando de Bexar and the first colonists were Canary Islanders. This project failed. The Indians rejected them and posed likely not to allow anyone here.

Floods were major disasters along the Brazos. It was more difficult for a cavalry column out of Mexico in 1830, to reach the Damn Creek as it flows into the Brazos, than to stop the Anglo settlers and to induce Mexican families to settle there. Now Lt. Col. Jose Ruiz, commanding troops to rid the land of the foreigners, began to think it was hardly worth all the trouble. He felt the area needed settlers regardless of what country they came from—"even Hell itself!"

Sterling Robertson's group arrived with a contract from an earlier Mexican government, so Ruiz wrote to Mexico City for instructions. In the intervening months Ruiz got to know the men and the other settlers who followed. Mexico City orders finally came: Drive the settlers out! Ruiz replied that the settlers had never arrived . . . that they were so scattered all over the territory and that his horses were in no shape to go looking for them. Meanwhile the plan for Mexican settlers collapsed and Ruiz and his troops went home to San Antonio. Ruiz eventually cast his lot firmly with the settlers, and both he and Robertson later signed the Texas Declaration of Independence.

From its source, the Brazos River is 840 miles long, from Double Mountain Fork, to the Gulf of Mexico. There were wildflowers, birds, white-tailed deer . . . where the mockingbird's song is heard . . . and the dismal wail of the coyote. It is all the land . . . Texas so big, so wonderful . . . so broad.

There were the forever feuds among the Waco, Tawakoni and Cherokee tribes, so that it was a fearful and hazardous place for settlers to be. In 1797 Philip Nolan's trading expedition found peaceful Tehuacana Indians farming the fertile land. These Indians, a Wichita tribe, were destroyed by the Cherokee in the early 1830s. Stephen Austin sent scouts who always arrived too late, with too little.

CHAPTER FOUR

Stephen, always with an eye to the future, prepared to make the journey to Mexico City. The project had advanced so far that no stone should be unturned. "You stay here in San Antonio, James, and learn to read and write Spanish with correct grammar, and to speak it fluently. I shall need all you avail yourself of in the next few months."

"You're not aiming to go alone, are you, Steve?" James asked, obviously discouraged on his own prospects of Mexico City.

"Oh, no. I shall have Dr. Andrews, my interpreter, and Tom Jones . . . ," Stephen said as the three men mounted and set away to Mexico City.

Out of nowhere Dr. Andrews exclaimed, "My God, man. It's twelve hundred miles!"

Tom Jones said, "It ain't the miles that bother me, it's the blisters on my butt, to say nought of the Apaches or Comanches we most likely'll meet."

Dr. Andrews laughed. "Why, Tom, that sits a saddle most of the time . . . "

"But never no more'n a hundred miles, never a thousand miles, it ain't."

And Stephen, not to be outdone, said stoutly, "To say nothing about the robbers." With all their affected bravery it was a rump-blistering ride. "You just never know what'll happen around the next mountain."

April was blithely passing into May when they reached the Valley with the two white mountain peaks rising above, which he would come to know as Popo and Sleeping Woman. But at this point in time, it was enough to say that is my capitol. How spectacular from where they were. In the missions, bells were ringing Jesu decus Angelicum. They were not real—snow points in the azure distance. They rode on for a long time before entering the City of Mexico, where they finally located the seat of government.

Augustine Iturbide had been proclaimed the emperor May 18, 1822, just two days before! What a confusion in the city. There was, Stephen thought, and always would be confusion in this Mexico. Always two sides and always battling. First one would be on top, then another. It was here and now that Stephen wondered about Texas, so far away.

A block away stood the emperor's palace, a peon pointed out. He was a man of about twenty, bare-footed and in tatters. His blouse was shreds of ancient cotton and his once-white pants a dingy grey worn off to his knees. But he had a nice face and smiled humbly at Dr. Andrews, Tom Jones and Stephen. "I see you are lost, senor," he said in a Spanish hard to translate by Dr. Andrews.

"Well, you see," Andrews replied in the Castilian he had learned in school, "we're from Tejas . . . Texas? . . . and have just arrived in the city."

"May I be of some help, senor?"

"If you can point out the emperor's palace, you surely can be," Andrews said, while the peon's face clouded.

"The palace, senor? Ah, si . . . a block away," and he moved away from them while his finger still pointed in that direction.

The emperor's palace was built in the eighteenth century and was where Iturbide lived then (1821-1823). The three Texans walked slowly toward it with eyes bugging out on stems. There was a large central patio with many strange plants, lush, tropical. They could barely take their eyes off the highly ornate structure—such splendor. Such a history!

"Are you expected by someone?" a soldier asked politely.

"I really can't say," Andrews replied. "We are Texans and have ridden this twelve hundred miles on mule and horseback to see the Emperor Iturbide on a matter of great importance."

There it is, he thought, the scene of all Mexico's revolutions. Through its doors have walked emperors and governors, viceroys and presidents.

Built of rose-colored stone and soft red tezoutle, the same porous volcanic rock which the Aztecs used in their cities, the National Palace has undergone many changes through the years, the first and most extensive one having taken place in 1694 after a mob had nearly destroyed it.

Over the main doorway hangs the Bell of Independence which Miguel Hidalgo y Costilla rang in his parish church of Dolores on September 15, 1810, to call the Revolution of Independence from Spain. He really had no idea of the turn of events. What began as his private rebellion caught on and flared throughout the country . . . before he was killed for striking the match, it had become a war for freedom for Mexico against Spain. Stephen was reminded of this the first September he spent in the City of Mexico. The church bells began ringing furiously at eleven o'clock at night, long after he had gone to bed. Bedsheet went off and his feet hit the floor running to the window. People were having a wild celebration in the zocalo, celebrating their long-sought FREEDOM.

But Stephen wondered what kind of freedom they had. It was somewhat like swapping the devil for the witch, for Iturbide was already pressing down, especially on the peons who had so little. He could still see the face of the Mexican who had offered to help and if what he read there was true it would be no surprise whatever. . . .

While waiting to see if they would be received, Stephen said, pulling from his wallet some pesos he had acquired along the way, "Run back and see if you can find that peon . . . we must repay him."

Some time later, they were ushered into a palatial room with flags and flowers and everything was highly polished, and moving toward them was a dark blue uniform with enough brass buttons on chest and sleeve to begin a business. Stephen said in his mind, "nouveau riche."

Stephen was welcomed by Iturbide and when he had stated his business, Iturbide with an apologetic smile replied, "I am so new as an emperor. . . . You have no idea how many departments are involved in running this government. We have a department, we must have certainly, that manages such details."

"Which are they—and where are they located? This is quite a building, you see, sir; we've been lost twice already." Stephen was so dead serious that Iturbide smothered a smile.

No one knew anything about his department. "Naturally, senor, we have only begun. Come back in a few weeks when we are better acquainted with our duties." So that was that.

The National Palace is an enormous structure taking up the whole block on the east side of the zocalo. It was built by Cortez on the site of the palace of the Aztecs and built by Montezuma I. Since the Conquest it has been the seat of all the forms of government Mexico has known. Stephen said in his mind that the two oldest and most important buildings, National Palace and the Cathedral, faced on this zocalo. Six hundred years old.

No one knew how to handle a simple land grant. He presented his memorial through the Minister of Foreign Affairs, Internal Relations, José Manuel Herrera, to the Emperor Iturbide, who was unacquainted with this department of state.

Stephen wanted his deceased father's land grant made valid, and the reason he had ridden twelve hundred miles to present it in person. Finally, his claims were acknowledged and the grant confirmed. But that was February 18, 1823. Months later. Stephen was getting embarrassed, and so it was a good day. He prepared to leave Mexico City and return to Texas. There was a nightmare of revolution in the streets. "Iturbide dethroned!" Hysteria ruled. Gladness and sadness rode the night. It depended on whose side you traveled. "Banished from the country!" Now where am I? Stephen asked himself. Not so long he had to wait. While they had waited for Iturbide to validate his land claim, Stephen met several important characters.

City of Mexico! City of Eternal Spring! Stephen had read Maurice Keatings's English translation of Bernal Diaz del Castillo. . . .

When we saw so many cities and villages built in the waters of the lakes, and other large towns built on dry land, and straight, level causeways leading into Mexico City, we were amazed and we said that it was enchanted things related to the book of Anadis because of all the huge towers, temples, and buildings rising from the water, and all of masonry. And some of the soldiers even asked whether things we saw were not a dream. (Circa 1800)

The Spanish explorations along the coast, march inland after burning their ships, horses, bloody encounters with Indians, the magnificence of Montezuma's palaces, his capture. Cortez's retreat on the "Sad Night," his return and long seige and final destruction of the Aztecs.

While Montezuma encouraged a taste for architectural magnificence in his nobles, he contributed his own share towards the embellishment of the city. It was in his reign that the famous Calendar Stone, weighing probably in its pristine state nearly fifty tons, was transported from its native quarry, many leagues distant, to the capital, where it still forms one of the most curious monuments of Aztec science.

So it had been in the building of Cheops's Great Pyramid which covers thirteen acres, containing 2,300,000 blocks averaging two and a half tons. Conscripted laborers and farmers idled by the flood reared it without iron tools, the wheel, or the horse.

Stephen found the months of December and January quite cold, but then comes May and the rainy season begins. Come June there is a daily downpour, beginning about four in the afternoon and ending suddenly about six in the evening. The rains peter out around September and are quite gone by October. One thing Stephen could always depend on, however, were the mornings, clear and bright and sunny. He often marveled at the time of the rains —he could set his watch by their arrival, if he hadn't pawned his watch to give aid to a colonist.

The city seemed timeless, although it had been founded 1325 A.D., he had been told, but at that time Tenochtitlan or "place of the tuna cactus" was the home of the Aztec kings.

Another bit of information was that the great Cathedral of Mexico City had been built over the rubble of the principal pyramid of the Aztecs. For fifteen or twenty thousand years wandering tribes came down from the Southwest above the Rio Grande upon the Valley of Mexico which was covered with lakes, dotted with islands, the surrounding mountains dark with great forests. Tribes of one kind or another came and went, leaving behind something of their way of life. The first were the Chichimec and the last were the Aztec, who reached the valley around the lakes, and when they saw an eagle with a serpent in its mouth, according to their legend, this was to be their home. Centuries before they had known massive cities, the main one Casa Grande, which Father Font wrote ecstatically about on seeing the ruins. Another was Casa Grande in Sonora. . . .

"I'll get you audience," Santa Anna said. "He wouldn't dare refuse me!" From the young man's attitude, Stephen decided to go back. He had already been there too long. "The door to the far right leads to the office of the president," he said, not giving Iturbide the signal honor of being addressed as "emperor."

Iturbide gave every indication that he had done with the Texas matter. Handing him some notes to consider, mostly directives, he said, "Senor Austin, you must visit our cathedral before you leave us. It is quite the largest in the Western Hemisphere, I understand."

Actually, Stephen wanted his grant validated; he wanted to get back to Texas. There were several things he wanted but this government, if indeed you could call it that, was as slow as molasses in the winter time. And he informed Santa Anna so.

"Iturbide has always been a royalist, Senor Austin; even back in 1810 he was a lieutenant in the regiment made up in his native Valladolid (Morelia) displaying such valor that in 1816 he rose in command of the Northern army. In 1820, there was much exasperation among the clergy, and they selected Iturbide, making him commander of the army of the South. So he formulated a plan, called the Plan of Iguala, with Vicente Guerrero, for the unification of Mexico. The whole upheaval happened cataclysmically, and the signing of the Treaty of Cordoba in August of '21 acknowledged Mexico's freedom and independence and proclaimed Iturbide Augustin I. Immediately he showed such arrogance and cruelty. We may have to get rid of him."

Stephen thought about Iturbide that March night 1823. . . .

Jade here is almost always nephrite, but the jewels found at Monte Alban were indeed jade. Opals and amethysts are genuine and come from Queretaro. Turquoise is widely used with silver by the Indian silversmiths and Stephen was enchanted with the deft manner in which they handled the silver, or shaped the turquoise.

He watched them making baskets of which he noticed two kinds. The most ordinary type consisted of flat woven strands of reeds or palms. These were left flat to make the little mats or petates— sleeping mats. They were gathered up, forming large shopping bags, in the daytime. The stronger baskets were made by using willow reeds, stripped to bare wood, around which palm strands are wound like twine or wire. These bound reeds were then tied one above the other, forming the wall. These finished products were called hampers.

"Really," Stephen said to the artist, "my donkey won't be able to carry all that I want to take home with me."

"Then what you need, senor, is one of these hampers on each side of your ass to keep the weight even. Now, you take everything you desire." The man was washing his hands in air, thinking no doubt, of all the American dollars this Texan would leave in his palm.

Stephen meandered under the arches, so like pictures of the Alhambra he had seen, and here he stopped, for the lacquer work is similar to that for which China has long been famous. But here the original native lacquer was made from chia oil, extracted from wild sage, and from the boiled remains of plant lice called aje. To this mixture of these two extracts, the natives added powdered

31

dolomite, a mineral common to Mexico. From this surprising combination came a lacquer as smooth, hard and durable as the finest Chinese lacquer—which is made from the sap of a tree not found in Mexico.

Now he went to the stall where there were to be found fine hand-loomed and genuine wool serapes, used as overcoat or bedroll. The women used this shawl like rebozos, but in these, the cashmere-like wools were best.

His donkey staggered under the load. He must have two donkeys so he headed for the place where asses were sold. He passed by the Church of San Francisco, which sat back from the street behind a massive stone gate, with date 1524, built by the first Franciscan priest to arrive in Mexico. It had a fine churrigueresque facade and baroque doors. Ah, yes, Stephen thought, mosying down the calle, the Moors certainly left their mark on the Spaniards. . . . After a seven-hundred-year occupation, why not?

But it had been the flowers that caused Stephen to meander through the stalls. There were orchids, roses heavily scented, lilies of every kind, it seemed. Jacaranda shaded the avenue in purple and green. He wanted to know if certain of the flowers could be grown in Texas, along the Gulf coast. "Si, some will, some won't— who know until you plant and see, senor."

Stephen turned to Tom Jones, "Tom, you think they'll grow in Texas?" Tom replied laughingly, "Try 'm. Try 'm."

They were one more thing Stephen would send back with Tom and the doctor.

Dr. Andrews scanned the two volcanoes and the Valley of Mexico. "It does beat all, Stephen, how the buildings remind me of the Nile!" Naturally he would make comparisons: On the Nile also, at Memphis was the Step Pyramid of Djoser, oldest freestanding stone structure in the world. It was by Imhotep, the architect "who discovered the art of building in hewn stones."

Dr. Andrews remarked, "And so the wheels turn. . . . " How does one measure time? Would it be predicated on speed, of living? warring? There was ancient Jericho with fortifications constructed almost nine thousand years ago, requiring sustained and specialized labor over a very long time. "You have any idea when the Pyramid to the Sun was built, Stephen?" Dr. Andrews asked shading his eyes to better see it. Down a long avenue was another, Pyramid to the Moon, but to go from one to the other you passed along this avenue, "Street of the Dead."

"Then in the Nile Valley and that of the Tigris and Euphrates said to be the Garden of Eden, first in Egypt and Mesopotamia as well as in the Indus Valley and along the Yellow River in China, people were to live, not against nature, but man against man. Already, Mesopotamia and Egypt had writing, but before this art was acquired history had been evolving since time. Only the color and physiognomy of man has changed. He was created man, and as man he has remained."

"Like a thought or inspiration seems to be carried by the wind," Dr. Andrews said. "In far and near places at the same time. You wonder about that."

"Yes, they think Etienne Bore was first to granulate sugar cane juice into sugar . . . but it had such processing for years in the Carib Islands."

After fifteen months in Mexico City he knew what the Sun Stone "Aztec Calendar" had meant to the Aztecs; it is a carving in the form of a disk and is a votive monument to the sun. He knew that *Nahui Ehecatl* meant the wind; *Nahui Ocelott* meant the earth; *Nahui Atl* meant water and *Quiahuitl* meant fire. Other items that drew his interest were the beautifully carved horizontal wooden drums called by the people teponaztlis; ocarinas he had never seen and felt impelled to purchase for Peach Point; there were conch shells, flutes and turtle carapace drums. In time he learned that Xochipilli was their god of flowers and of songs, of love and poetry, and that Coyolxauhqui was the Moon goddess, beheaded by her brother, the Sun, as he rises triumphant each morning.

It followed that his thoughts would turn to Texas at such times. He missed Tom Jones and Dr. Andrews, who had accompanied him to the capital, but these men had business interests back home and after a few weeks of impatiently waiting for the government to validate Stephen's land grants, left for Texas. In a way, Stephen did not mind, for he had kept the good doctor from his patients, and Tom from his plantation. As matters stood he nor anyone else knew what tomorrow might bring. Duty had always drawn him, compelled him, even as he had been drawn into this Texas business of Moses Austin, his father, who had expired on the threshold of great promise. Stephen rode it out, while Moses would have chucked the whole business long ere this.

Stephen was not a man suited to frontier life as was his pioneering father. His gentle instincts and quiet tastes, his love of order and of the amenities of cultured society, should have found a more congenial atmosphere in Texas, but few and far between were families or gentlemen with whom he felt really comfortable. Here in Mexico City he found these amenities. Something was going on all the time. In due course he met Lorenza de Zavala and through him, others of like calibre. There was young and gallantly handsome Santa Anna, General Cos, who probably was already Santa Anna's brother-in-law. Lorenza de Zavala was also from Yucatan, and was a close friend of Santa Anna. In the legislature or out they could be seen together all over Mexico City. And very often Stephen would be invited to go with them.

It was on such days that their minds turned to the government. "If we just had a formal structure to build on," Antonio Lopez said with a most disarming smile. "But we are so new as a nation. Always, since the days of Cortez, we've been ruled by the king of Spain, through his viceroy. The viceroy's word was law. Anyone disputing his authority was dispatched before a firing squad."

Zavala said now, "That's one way to get rid of trouble-makers."

Stephen thought, they each know what the other is about. They had learned that he had had experience in the territorial legislature of Missouri, and certainly knew the Constitution of the United States, and all that appertained to governmental law.

So he said, "It is a simple matter, to form the structure of a good and lasting government. It should be a lasting one, you know; otherwise, the whole nation, including Texas will just bounce around like a boiling kettle."

The day was simply magnificient with bright sunshine and the city but a garden in bloom. Shortly after the hour of siesta, Santa Anna joined him for another sight-seeing tour.

"Today, Stephen," Antonio Lopez said, "we go to see el Arbol de la Noche Triste."

"My Spanish hampering me, I've no idea what you're talking about." They walked on. Antonio stopped under a gnarled tree.

"This old Ahuehuete tree is where Cortez is said to have wept on the night of July 20, 1520, after his disastrous battle. Now, according to his diarist, Bernal Diaz, Cortez and his men were forced to get rid of all their gold and to plan their escape from the Aztecs whom they had robbed. Diaz states:

"As it was somewhat dark, cloudy and rainy, we began before midnight to bring along the bridges all the baggage. . . . while this was happening the voices, trumpets, cries and whistles of the Mexicans (Aztecs) began to sound. . . . When I least expected it we saw so many squadrons of warriors bearing down upon us, and the lake so crowded with canoes that we could not defend ourselves. Had it been in the daytime, it would have been worse, and we who escaped did so only by the grace of God. To one who saw the hosts of warriors who fell on us that night and the canoes full of them coming along to carry us off to our soldiers, it was terrifying."

"When they reached this old tree, the fleeing Spaniards paused, and one of them cried out to Cortez, 'Senor Capitan, let us halt, for they say that we are fleeing and leaving them to die at the bridges, let us go back and help them, if any of them survive' But according to Bernal Diaz, not one of them came out or escaped!"

Many days went by while he was waiting for his grant to be validated. And many of these days were spent with Santa Anna and Lorenza de Zavala, the youthful governor of the state of Mexico. But on this day Stephen went out early . . . before the stalls were crowded. He saw some exquisite pottery. The fellow said it was from Oaxaca, a pottery he explained that is made from black clay which contains lead. Stephen's ears rose at the word *lead* oxide— just the old miner rousing up. This distinctive pottery, often coated with a green glaze, is strong—so strong, in fact, the man said, "they are used for mezcal, made from the maguey plant, senor . . . which is saying a lot. Have you tasted mezcal?"

Stephen let a smile wrinkle his mouth . . . oh, yes, he had tasted mezcal. Only once! So he purchased two pots for Rob . . . who did the cooking in his log cabin at San Felipe de Austin.

Certainly, he would be returning to Texas any day now. But Stephen had no idea what lay ahead.

John Austin was born in New Haven, Connecticut, November 17, 1801. He received his elementary education in his home town; in early manhood he attended Yale College. At the time many youths were attracted to the sea. John went to sea, making a number of voyages up and down the Atlantic coast. One voyage took him into the Gulf of Mexico, where he reached the port of New Orleans in 1819. This was just at the time Dr. James Long of Natchez, Mississippi, was calling for recruits to enlarge his expedition, for his plan to "free Texas from Spanish rule."

Among those who, with more vigor than brain, joined in Long's contingent were John Austin, and Ben Milan and others as daring as themselves, going directly to Galveston Island where Long attempted to enlist the services of the notorious privateer, Jean Lafitte. But Lafitte had received orders from the United States government to abandon his fort. Lafitte burned "Campeachy Camp" and sailed away to Yucantan.

General Long made his camp at Bolivar Point, opposite Galveston Island, in the summer of 1820. Leaving his wife, Jane, his daughter, Ann (born at Natchez, November 26, 1816), and the servant Kian, with a number of men at the fort, he continued his attacks and succeeded in capturing La Bahia. He was forced to surrender that settlement, after which he and some of his men were captured. They were escorted to Mexico City, where a short time later Long was released, only to be murdered.

The remainder of Long's expedition, unaware of their leader's fate, was taken to Monterrey. The group of Captain John Austin and Ben Milam were hauled off to Mexico City, arriving there *just the time Mexico had won its independence from Spain.*

In the spring of 1822, Stephen Fuller Austin arrived in the City of Mexico, seeking information of his father's grant. Being attracted by their mutual name, "Austin," they began a lasting friendship, and so when Stephen returned to Texas, Captain John Austin accompanied him. He became constable of District of San Felipe, and as reward for his untiring efforts in Stephen's behalf, July 21, 1824, he was granted title to two sitios or leagues in Harrisburg (Harris) County; and on August 24, 1824, one labor (about 177 acres) in Brazoria County. Later on, John built a log cabin at the confluence of Buffalo Bayou and White Oak Bayou (Foot of Main Street, Houston). That was when he bought a cotton gin from George Huff (July 3, 1825). It was then only six months later that John Austin formed a partnership with James E. B. Austin, in the ginning of cotton. This gin burned.

But now Stephen was coming home. The settlement, without name or number, would see to it that he should be hailed in the manner he should be, as a conquering hero. Certainly, the dispatch he had sent on from Mexico City gave them news for which they had been waiting so long. Guests to welcome Stephen should be representative of the people, and residents of long standing. So they invited Colonel Piedras, who lived in the Red House; Thomas F. McKinney; Mr. Barr of the House of Barr and Davenport; Peter Ellis Bean; and so many others. Six beefs had been barbecueing all night. In fifteen months one can learn a great deal, especially if one has contact with knowing politicians. He was learning Spanish at an amazing rate. One day these men of political power confessed they knew little of constitutions and wondered if he might consider assisting them formulate one with which they could build a stable government. He would indeed. Now was his own personal Gethsemane. Could he remember the Constitution of the United States well enough to use it as a pattern, as was the desire of the Mexicans?

In January 31, 1824, the constitution he had helped to write was adopted. It was a meaningful date for Stephen all the rest of his life. The Constitution of 1824.

The party reached Monterrey the middle of May and by June he, armed with unheard of powers over his colonists, arrived at San Felipe de Austin. He explained his long delay in Mexico to his friend and Josiah Bell relayed it to the settlers of the Brazos.

Stephen found Mrs. Jane Long and Gail Borden, Godwin Cotton, Thomas Pilgrim, Robert Williamson, William B. Travis, John Austin, and so many others. Some he knew well; others were colonists signed by Moses his father. But they were all welcome.

Soon the Brazos had a ferry which was propelled by the current guided by a wire cable. Soon, too, they built a church and Sunday School in which Thomas Pilgrim served. It was a quaint little structure of hand-hewn timbers and rough siding. There also the Masons later met in the upper room. There was in time a cotton gin and a water cistern made of hand-formed brick. Later on wells were dug.

Through Baron de Bastrop Stephen was granted twenty-two and one-half leagues and three labors of land as his very own. It was here he built a two-room log cabin with a hall between, and a cannon provided against Indians.

To celebrate, a big barbecue was held, and speeches were made. They were naming their town in honor of the patron saint of Don San Felipe de Garza and partly to honor Stephen Fuller Austin; hence, the name San Felipe de Austin. At the table among others were the handsome Baron de Bastrop, commissioner; Horatio Chriesman, surveyor; and James, his brother.

During the year of 1824, two hundred seventy-seven titles were granted.

Stephen had as secretary, Sam May Williams. He was also conversant with all grants and other business Stephen had. It was a busy but quiet town, and Constable John Austin, not related to Stephen, kept it so, so that the celebration, while with cock fights and whiskey, had no brawls.

Jane Long was lovely in a wide-skirted, tight-bodiced gown of sprigged muslin. Her long black hair was done in a most becoming chignon. Stephen wondered about Jane. She kept busy giving all men and women an equally attentive moment. Evidently, Stephen said in his mind, she is still waiting for her husband, who'll never come.

It would be comforting to know that Jane Long would be independent and have her own business. The more Stephen thought about it, the more it seemed like a proper thing to do. Both idea and realization came about in an unexpected manner. She opened her tavern in Brazoria. And because Jane was an aristocrat, with flawless manners, she soon became the best known of the hostesses in the county. Supervising, in her quiet way, sticky governmental situations, she had not long to wait, until she became known far and wide as the "Mother of Texas."

CHAPTER FIVE

Stephen's mother passed away in January (1824) at Hazel Run, Missouri, at the home of her widowed daughter Emily Bryan, James Bryan having died in 1822, and now Emily was about to be remarried. In the midst of the sadness of their mother's death, there was also happiness. They all loved and admired James Perry and in September the couple were wed. Mr. Perry was born in

Pennsylvania and was a man held high in the estimation of Hazel Run. They planned to join Stephen in Texas later, so James E. B. returned in November.

There were so many things Stephen was learning about his adopted country, especially the old missions and settlements. Liberty, for instance, was the third oldest town in Texas. The Spanish built a mission there in 1756. And Roma, part of Jose de Escandon's Spaniards, was also built around a mission. In 1770 Port Isabel was settled by Mexican ranchers near Padre Island.

For two years now at the store could be found such items as French quinine, Bulls Sarsaparilla, Mexican Mustang Liniment, Cherokee Ointment, and Sweetpea perfume.

And Stephen leaned back with contentment. Ah, yes, the people, Americans, were accomplishing beautiful things in Texas, a land so broad it took forever just to get to the next town. But in the spring of 1826, Stephen and his brother sat together on the gallery.

"We ought to be running some stock out there!" Stephen said. "Over at Victoria everyone has a good start toward making this known far and wide as the cattle country of Texas."

"Don't you ever think about anything except bringing in colonists and getting them started raising cattle?" James said. "Not that I'm against it, but you ought to find yourself a wife."

"You just keep your own mind clear, brother James. . . . You leave in the morning for Saltillo to confer with the authorities about getting a port at Galveston. I have all kinds of confidence in you."

The next day James left, with quite another admonition for Stephen to find himself a wife. He named off a few possibilities at which Stephen only grinned.

The evening crept on and dew was falling when Stephen decided to write Emily. She was all he had now except brother James, and in the action of writing, he felt close to his family. Like a great rock, she had been there in the deaths of his parents, or rather, they had come to her. He thought about the Bryan children and the Perry children and smiled at the outrages they must have with the other children. He wanted them all with him in Texas. He wrote in part:

Brother has taken a trip into the interior about six hundred miles, and I do not expect him back before January. The constitution of the state will be finished shortly and when I see it I can give Mr. Perry more certain advice as to the prospects of a removal here. If brother succeeds in procuring stock I shall settle down on a stock farm and perhaps follow the example of Mr. Perry and hunt a jolly widow to comfort me in my old age. The truth is that brother and myself are too much unsettled as yet to trammel ourselves with a family, or one of us would, no doubt, have been married before this. . . .

It was a good life. Calm and peaceful. But not for long. Over at Nacogdoches all hell broke loose.

CHAPTER SIX

Hayden Edwards looked at a young fellow riding half on, half off his saddle, casting his eyes to right and left along the Calle del Norte, as though looking for someone, or something.

"Hello, there!" Hayden called, to which horse and rider pulled up to the gallery post of the Old Stone Fort, in which Edwards had his land office.

"Hi," the lad said. "I'm Buck Bassett, of Sleepy Hollow, Cumberland country. States."

"Welcome, Buck," Hayden Edwards said, giving Buck a right strong welcome shake. "I'm a citizen of the States myself, although I am an empressario for the Mexican government. Have been quite a while."

There was something of the trusting backwoods about the boy— the excitement of seeing Texas and a big town like Nacogdoches shone in his large brown eyes. Standing by Hayden, he was of an equal height although Hayden was thicker of shoulders and chest. Hayden decided right then that he would be the kid's friend, whatever it was he was after. Out here with that Sam Norriss, who had sworn allegiance to Mexico and who needed a bit in his mouth, with that trouble between American and Mexican element he'd need more than a fly-by-night friend.

"You looking for somebody, Buck?" Hayden asked, all the while

helping Buck untie his saddlebag, and loosen the saddle cinch.
"Yes, sir," he said over the horse's back. "I'm alookin' for Mr.
Sam Norriss, who lives hereabouts."

"He a friend of yours?"

"Well, I don't rightly know, sir, as to his being a friend. I met
him on the road to Red River." Buck took the cup of coffee Hayden had stuck under his nose. "We got sort of separated there. I
wanted to ford the river, looked all right to me. Had a sand bar
nigh all the way acrost. But Mr. Norriss said that was silly on account the path over the top of that Great Raft, he called it, was
plumb safe. Goose grease, he said. And that nag I rode was of Kentucky racing stock. Never could let another horse get more'n just
even with her. She took out across that log jam like a bullet, and
got up even and slowed down. All of a sudden, I felt her bump and
then we both bumped right down into that swirlin' whirlpool at
least twenty-five feet from the top to the water.

All the time Buck was talking, Hayden's face grew red and red-
der as his tale revealed all he needed to know, so that by the time
Buck stopped talking, Hayden's face was like a turkey gobbler's in
rutting time. "And Sam Norriss put spur to his animal, and you and
your nag hit the water. What did you have he wanted?"

Buck's face lit up. "Now how in the world did you know that?"
Buck opened out the saddlebag. "He didn't want nothin' . . ." and
took out a Bible he had wrapped in oilcloth. "I reckon hadn't been
for Colonel Brooks, I'd shore a been a goner. He pulled me outten
the river right in front of the Caddo Injun agency. But Lucy was
dead. Colonel Brooks said her neck was broke."

"What else do you have there? He wanted something you have,"
Hayden said bitterly.

"Why, nothin', Mr. Eddards. I told you twicet. Nothin' at all."
Buck searched the objects he had stashed in the saddlebag. "You
can see for yourself, there's only the Bible and pa's land grant."

"Tell me about your pa's land grant, Buck," Hayden coaxed as if
talking to a child.

"Accordin' to Colonel Brooks, pa's land grant was a island called
Rush on account of all them reeds and stuff on it, right on Red
River the west side it was, but Colonel Brooks allowed it belonged
to the Caddo Injuns, and Governor Esteban Miro's surveyor had
purely made a mistake."

"Judas Priest!" Hayden smirked. "And from a kid!" Hayden let

41

thought drone on for a while. "Let me tell you about that island, Buck," he finally said. "Sam Norriss lived on that island for years, as did several others. But Sam's farm was just across Loggy Bayou, straight across from the Caddo Indian agency. But one day, the soldiers came from cantonment Jesup, and ordered them to clear out. Come to think about it, that was only two years ago. No, three."

"That sounds about right, Mr. Eddards," Buck agreed. "Colonel Brooks, now, just pointed his finger straight out, and said there's the island. It's turrible mixed up, ain't it, sir?"

"I'm sorry about that, Buck," Hayden Edwards said. "No doubt Sam had been in the States to get colonists for Texas. . . . He is the mayor as well, with a detachment of Mexican soldiers to do his bidding. They love him. But you watch out for Sam Norriss, Buck."

Hayden's brother Ben, with whom he was in the land business, appeared at the door. "Get in here, Ben!" Hayden almost whispered. "You must hear this . . ." and the yarn was retold.

"Why, that sonofabitch!" Ben exclaimed. "I'm not at all surprised. He's nothing but a traitor to us Americans."

"Walk down the gallery a way, Buck. The House of Barr and Davenport has a mercantile business. You might get on as a traveling salesman. You know, take a wagon of supplies, such things as the Indians like, and you make the deals. They give a man a fair shake for his trouble. Sometimes they have conflicts, and sometimes it goes real good."

"What happened to the last driver they had?" Buck said, standing there like a young giant.

Judas Priest, he thought, that kid's got everything. Youth, handsome as they come, and he was beginning to see, with all the ignorant sounding things coming from his mouth, there was nothing wrong with his brain. "Yes," he said again, "I think you'll do real good."

"What happened to the last one?" Buck asked again.

"The Comanches got him." But he was talking to Buck's heels as he made off down the gallery to the House of Barr and Davenport.

"Well, Mr. Davenport's in Louisiana, son," said Mr. Barr, who retained the business. "Back in 1813 . . . the Mexicans chased off all Americans. But Davenport had a legitimate reason for fighting with them—his wife was sick and they wouldn't let an American doctor see her." He swiped across the counter, and raising his eyes, said: "Nobody ever blamed him."

"What happened to Mrs. Davenport?"

"Oh, she died."

"Well, do I get the job, or don't I? And if I do, what sort of stuff would I be taking?" So Buck left the next morning for the many tribes scattered out to the north and west of Nacogdoches, and three months later, they saw Buck had returned. They couldn't help seeing and hearing all that went on at the Old Stone Fort. It was a large two-story building with three-four foot walls made of stone native of the country. The gallery extended from one side of the building to the other, and the stairs were on the outside.

There in the middle of Calle del Norte was Buck's wagon, still loaded with hides and pottery and such things as he had traded which Mr. Barr could turn into cash. Standing at their door were the brothers Edwards. Buck was seated on his perch and Sam Norriss had one foot propped up on the wagon wheel. His voice was loud and demanding. "You owe me twenty-five dollars for every tribe you traded with. I told you about the trading license!" He was punctuating his remark by poking his finger under Buck's nose and shaking it.

Buck jerked his face back. "You're a damned liar!" he cried. "You never mentioned a license nor money nor nothin' . . ." and so saying, Buck flung his body from the seat onto Sam Norriss and they wallowed in the dust, fighting tooth and nail, shouting into each other's ears. The blows and grunts were so loud that the horses became nervous and bolted.

From the edge of his eye, Buck saw his team tearing down Calle del Norte. He rose up so furious all caution went to the winds, and his fist made contact with Sam's jaw, knocking the sense out of him.

Buck, satisfied about Sam, took out after the wagon and team.

Hayden Edwards could see that something was about to happen—something big. Sam would never rest, not now, not after this kid had knocked the hell out of him right before his soldiers. It was embarrassing to say the least. "Ben, get to San Felipe, I mean leave right now, and get Stephen Austin to hurry, and bring his cannon with him!" There was no telling what would happen, and Hayden wanted it stopped by the commander of the colony before it started.

But Ben, never one to obey his brother, did *not* go for Stephen Austin at San Felipe de Austin, but directed himself to San Antonio de Bexar. There he laid the situation before the officials, which was a mistake.

Hayden and Ben Edwards had been wealthy planters in Mississippi and now had all their fortunes tied up in this Texas venture. Ben was all for fighting it out with the Mexicans, but Hayden wanted nothing more than to remain in Nacogdoches and make a go of it. His plat covered many thousands of acres. Norriss had a big plat, also.

"Certainly you brothers have enjoyed Texas without benefit to us of citizenship. . . . Now you take Senor Norriss; he's not only a citizen of Mexico, but the alcalde as well."

"You don't seem to understand," Ben burst out, "that he is playing Americans against Mexicans. A game he is bound to lose!"

"You think so, senor?" the Mexican smirked. "From this moment consider yourself an alien in fact; the lands contracts, invalidated. Further more, leave Texas at once!" He waved his hand in a nasty dismissal.

On the road to Nacogdoches Ben kicked himself for a fool. On the other hand, this business between American and Mexican had to resolve itself. Just as well now.

That the soldiers under Norriss had fallen upon the hapless lad and had thrown him into the calaboose with a knot on his head from a pistol butt, Hayden well knew. That night Norriss slipped to the jail in a storm such as the town had not had for many years. Taking Buck a bundle of food, he declared that his, Sam's hands were tied, and that Buck should escape now. The door was left open. All this was taking place in the Old Stone Fort. Hayden Edwards, expecting the commander of the colonists to arrive in Nacogdoches momentarily, had not closed his eyes, nor left his office for the two days Buck lay unconscious. He had wanted to call a doctor, but Sam said it wasn't anything. He'd just been knocked out and would come around. "You stay away from that young'un!" Sam said.

Nevertheless, Hayden kept his eyes open. In such a storm, nothing could happen, Hayden thought, and closed his eyes for a nap.

A clap of devastating thunder brought Hayden to his feet, and in the glare of a flash of lightning, he saw Buck on a horse, riding out of town. At least the animal had been headed that way. While he was putting on his slicker and reaching for his rain hat, he saw a half dozen or so Mexican soldiers on the Calle del Norte, passing in the shadow of the trees on the plaza, taking the same road, armed heavily. They were riding along leisurely so as not to disturb the Americanos. From out of the House of Barr and Davenport emerged the familiar figure of Barr. How long had he had this drama under surveillance? "Have you had enough, my friend?" Barr asked in a stage whisper.

"I sure have!" Hayden replied.

"I sent my man, the Haisanai, around the American colony, so Sam Norriss wouldn't suspect anything; he carried like an order . . . and warned them all to get their guns and be ready for Sam's next move. I've but to raise my hand as we pass the end of the plaza."

"It may be a long drawn out affair. Shouldn't we dispatch a rider to the Cherokee for help?"

"Not a bad idea—unless Austin's already sent word for them to help him!" Barr said. "There's no sense in attempting to do a vast job with a half-vast crew!"

Even so, not waiting, Hayden Edwards and Mr. Barr forked their horses and struck out after them. As they passed the end of the plaza, Barr raised his hand. But the sky was rolling black clouds and no lightning flashed. Barr cried, "They'll never see me in this midnight blackness." They raced on. They had lost too much time. A little way outside Nacogdoches, they found Buck's naked body, hacked into mince meat. His clothing, his saddlebag and his boots were gone.

"My God!" Hayden exclaimed. "I was waiting to hear a shot!" Americans came on at a gallop in a body, having heard the horses go by.

Buck's body was buried in the cemetery, in the night, by the night riders, in a hastily dug grave. Hayden removed his wet hat, and while sheets of rain fell, he said a few words over the grave. Lightning spit on the ground, and thunder resounded. The men sprang onto their horses, bound for the town and revenge upon Sam Norriss and his Mexicans, and came face to face with Stephen Austin's cannon.

Anger so filled these Americans they were unwilling to wait. Hayden saw a formidable group of Americans standing in the street looking into the mouth of the cannon. "Disperse, Americanos!" a Mexican ordered. "I say disperse!"

"Disperse, Hell!" and who knows the finger that pulled the first trigger? Americans occupied the town. Dead Mexicans were hauled off. A few Americans paid, also.

Austin had sent three men to Nacogdoches to advise Hayden and

Ben Edwards of his interest, but to tell them that they should submit their grievances to the Mexican officials under whose government they now lived. Austin was not conversant of Ben's frontal attack in San Antonio. Hayden said, "Mr. Ellis, Mr. Cummings, and Mr. Kerr . . . We shall never concede one inch short of an acknowledgment on the part of the government of their entire free and unmolested Independence from the Sabine to the Rio Grande!"

Austin's cry of "Union and Mexico" only angered the Americans. With about thirty volunteers and Mexican soldiers sent from San Antonio Austin headed out for Nacogdoches. . . . To put down the insurgents!

CHAPTER SEVEN

January was a bitter, cold month, with rain turning to sleet, and no sun. Under command of Colonel Mateo Ahumada the company approached the town of Nacogdoches. The Americans, the Fredonians, after having been denied the Cherokees—Austin had preempted them—and seeing the army, with themselves almost defenseless, abandoned the Old Stone Fort, and fled. It was the last day of January 1827 that the Americans reached the Sabine and safety. But before they fled, that cannon Austin had fetched was dismantled. The lands of Sam Norriss, who having been born American, had to flee for his life, also, along with the other Americans, and the lands under contract to the Edwards brothers, were confiscated.

In February, Stephen heard of the death of his old friend, the Baron de Bastrop. And Stephen worked harder than ever, to keep his mind from sorrowing. Late that year 1828 Austin settled a hundred families on the shores of the Colorado River, at a place where that river is crossed by the San Antonio Trace, and there founded a town for mail, troops, and a stopping place for travelers and also to prevent to some degree the incursions of the Indians in that vicinity. He called his little settlement Bastrop.

That year Stephen estimated his inhabitants as three thousand. There were extensive farms, cotton gins and mills. There were cattle and horses and commerce. Austin remained manager of the Land System.

After the joint venture of J. E. B. and John Austin, when their gin burned, John Austin turned his attention to real estate; in 1827 he laid out the town of Brazoria, which came to be known as the town of the four Austins. Later he married Elizabeth Perry and willed her all that he had, including the property in Harris County (which in due course she sold to the Allens for the city of Houston for $5,000).

Trading schooners plied the Brazos from up river and down, and Brazoria centered the mercantile business going as far north as San Felipe. A weekly mail service was established between San Felipe and Quintana, serving between these points—Orozimbo, plantation of Dr. Phelps, and Columbia, or Bell's Landing, and Brazoria and Velasco.

In this year Stephen was granted the right to settle three hundred families on the reserved lands on the coast from Lavaca to the San Jacinto rivers.

Now John Austin and James E. B. engaged in a coastwide trade in 1828. John had been issued a passport by Commandant General Bustamenta for carrying cargo. They visited Vera Cruz with the schooner *Eclipse*, for the purpose of procuring Mexican register, and hoped that soon they would be able to furnish such products as "beef, pork, lard, bacon, pease, butter, sweet potatoes and such articles as would be wanting for naval supplies."

So many wandering thoughts hovered, so many painful of remembrance, and Stephen, who had been motivated for this trip to Nacogdoches, was saying aloud, "Vanity . . . all is vanity, at these men with such a little time to be here on earth, fighting amongst themselves for elevation in the estimation of men, just to die at last and leave the hard-won victory."

In the wigwam of the Cherokee, he came to be known as the "Raven" and they sent him as their representative twice to Washington, strangely attired in buckskins with a blanket over his shoulder. But on the second visit, Andrew Jackson had had enough of Sam's stage business, and sent him to his personal tailor with directions not to return to the Capitol again in those rags. Jackson footed the bill for Sam's new finery. That was in 1832. But then, Sam had accomplished what he had set out to do. He left Washington with a War Department commission to hold parleys with the border Indians, and riding his bobtailed nag he called Jack, entered the village of the Caddo Indians below the bend in Red River.

"I understand, Chief Tarshar, that the Government of Mexico has invited you to come into Texas . . . it being a well known fact that you are the best farmers in the country. It may be to your advantage to take up that land down there. Lots of game, I hear, and good soil—the best." They continued smoking the fine ceremonial Caddo tobacco.

Tarshar did not reply at once, but let his eyes scan the north, to the north where was what remained of their Temple Mound, but now a vast lake, called Caddo; then to the east along the Great Raft of the Red River, the ancient barrier they and their people enjoyed since time; south to the land to Natchitoches, remembering that the smallpox had decimated his brethren but nineteen which after the epidemic were brought by Chief Sawbe, his father, to live with them here on the prairie; and west toward the River of Cypress, Sabine, to the land to which Sam Houston was asking them to go. Why would this white man press so for their removal? Was it that he wanted their million acres for his Cherokee? Finally, Tarshar replied, "I shall hold council and give you my answer then."

He seemed like an intelligent enough fellow—one he felt easy with, but Sam Houston had never seen an Indian with a hole in the septum of his highbridged nose nor one who wore a silver plug through it. Tarshar had massive earrings, and bracelets and ringidings on his ankles, amulets and his head was shaven on both sides of his heavy jet black roach and there was a long queue at the nape of his neck and a silver tube through which this long length of hair had been secured.

Houston had been of the opinion that most Indians were average people in height, but Chief Tarshar stood equal to Houston and him in his heelless sandals. The man had massive shoulders and a deep chest, but was slim of hip and had long very muscled legs. Tarshar was a handsome Indian—handsome in any language or color, but he was a light brown, that which was visible, for the tattooing striped his body in all seeable places.

"Your Caddo tobacco is most excellent, Chief Tarshar," Sam praised and not without reason. The ceremonial tobacco fields were attended to, he was told, by the braves of high rank. The women worked the vegetables mostly, but men did the hardest labors. The women worked in clay, as Houston had heard, and no tribe in the whole of the land could compare with their pottery. Finally, Houston said, "I must go to Rainey Mountain now to have a parley with the Comanches. We want to make a treaty with them." After waiting for some response, he added, "They're making raids on the colonists out there . . . all the way to the Gulf."

Sam Houston rode away as he had come, a lone man with a purpose.

So the first activity of the unofficial envoy pleased Andrew Jackson no more than the diplomacy of Anthony Butler, for Tarshar had first to consult with the Caddo agent to see if this move could be arranged before he took up the problem with his tribes. Colonel Jehiel Brooks had been for many years the agent, had formerly lived in Washington and knew Andrew Jackson well. The agent lost no time in acquainting Jackson of Houston's prologue, adding some personal observations, like why in hell did Houston bear down so on the Caddo giving up their million acres and going to Texas? What was Houston to gain? How? He was openly playing the game of the American land-speculating clique, now hot for rebellion or revolution. Houston aroused the suspicion of Mexico City so promptly that Andrew Jackson was forced to disavow him.

By the time he reached Nacogdoches and presented himself to Stephen Fuller Austin at San Felipe, he had already been to Rainey Mountain, and already the Comanches had heard of his contact with Chief Tarshar. About this time, Sam decided that if the Indians knew so much without wireless or pony express or other means of communication than by smoke signals, he had better be wary. This Stephen Austin was a stickler for straightforwardness in his dealings with people. With this in mind, he changed his approach—to purchase Texas was right, if the Texans wanted to annex to the States, which was Jackson's plan.

The situation was paradoxical to say the least, for Jackson seemed to close his eyes to the emigrants entering Texas any way they could, armed with guns and ammunition, not ploughs and axes and hoes, which had been Stephen's colonization requirements.

December of 1832 Sam Houston entered Nacogdoches on his bobtailed nag. He had come from Nashville by way of the Caddo village, and San Augustine just a few miles into Texas, and wasted no time after his business was effected, and he was armed with a passport signed by President Andrew Jackson. He also carried a letter of introduction from Leander H. McNeil of Nashville to Stephen Fuller Austin.

Stephen saw him dismounting. He did not know him and decided he must be another empressario wishing to get his grant validated. Houston carelessly flipped the bridle over the hitching bar and with long, comfortable strides, walked noisily across the puncheon floored gallery as a man who knew where he was headed and why. Austin and Houston, born the same year, looked at each other for a moment, but it was time enough for each to take the other's measure. Stephen considered himself above average in height, but this chestnut-haired fellow towered above him. What a wonderfully disarming smile the giant had, Stephen thought, extending his hand. "I'm Stephen Austin."

"And I'm Sam Houston."

Stephen had been away from Tennessee for many years, but who had not heard of the Tennessee governor's troubles of the heart, of the years he had spent in the wigwam of the Cherokee Indians? Sam's handshake was strong and sincere and he looked a man in the eye. No illiterate backwoodsman this. "Welcome to Texas, Governor Houston," Stephen said with great respect.

Producing McNeil's letter, Houston said, "I've a letter of introduction. . . ."

"Then if you'll excuse me a moment," Stephen replied opening the seal.

I am not informed of his views in visiting that country. I think he would be a great addition to our country as a citizen, as he has a great number of friends and acquaintances in the State. I think it would be worth your trouble to try and make him a citizen of your colony. The President of the United States has been in Nashville for two weeks past which has caused a considerable stir here.

James Bowie walked into the two-room log house, and stood in the wide hall which divided it for some minutes as though making up his mind about something. Stephen poked his head out, "Come in. Come in." Jim grinned one-sidedly and sauntered in. "I see you got company!"

"A very select company, too," Stephen said as if pleasured beyond the telling. "Just about everybody knows Jim Bowie, unless it's you, Governor Houston. It was his brother, Rezin, created the Bowie knife used throughout this country with great effect. But Jim here, he's been raised up around Natchez, Mississippi, but on the west side of the river. Bayou Sarah, and Vidalia."

"To be sure. Yes, indeed. I have not before had the pleasure," Sam rose and shook hands with Jim Bowie, "but I own one of the Bowie knives." He pulled it from a leathern case appended to his gun belt. "Fine, keen cutting point."

Jim joined in a drink. "I'm about to leave you, Stephen. I told you about the beautiful senorita I met in San Antonio? Her that's the daughter of the vice governor, Verimenti? Yep. I'm gettin' married. Can you imagine that? Me, that's been everything, me that's been a slave trader, Injun fighter, and one more fool to go in search of the lost San Saba mine. I been here since thirty though. Watched old Stevy digging his heels in Texas soil to get a foothold. Damned if I ever saw a man could work so hard, and sleep so little and get so many sonabitching jobs done."

"What's her name? The girl you're marrying?" Houston asked.

Stephen already knew and was not in the least surprised for Jim of a fact was a man wholly and completely in love.

"Miss Ursula de Veramendi. Her father will be the next governor, all things being equal," Jim replied. "But I tell you, Stevy, you and me, we been loners so long that now I'm aleaving the club, you and Governor Houston join me in a sort of Christmas and farewell dinner kit and kaboodle, over there at Peyton's Tavern."

"When are your folks coming to Texas, Steve?" Jim asked over the wild turkey and wild rice and steaming black coffee.

"Soon. Very soon. They'll live here in San Felipe until their plantation house is completed down at Peach Point. I always did think that the very prettiest ridge in all of south Texas. I know my sister Emily will love it too. But, Jim, you remember out about center on the Colorado, the rolling hills, the lakes, where I told you I'd like to spend eternity. Well, of course, after I'd lived there. I mentioned then I wanted a seminary of learning there?"

"Sure do, Steve. I'll remember it too, when they cart off your bones."

"My!" Sam exploded. "How gruesome . . . and it Christmas!"

He lifted his glass, "Here's to the good girl!" he toasted Ursula, bride-to-be.

"It's terribly warm in here," Steve muttered, feeling the blood pushing up his face. "For a cold day in December, that is."

His was not the only red face, for Houston hoped with all he had that Jim Bowie had never heard nor would ever hear the rest of it: "Here's to the good girl—not too good, for the good die young and we don't like dead ones."

After dessert of mincemeat pie and more scalding coffee, Jim said, "Governor Houston, let us ride over to San Antonio so's you can get better acquainted with this state of ours, for I hope you'll like it well enough to make it your home. Not to mention the fact I'll be right proud to introduce you to my senorita."

The last Stephen saw of Jim he was waving a big wide-brimmed hat he wore as protection against the hot, at times blistering, Texas sun. And by his side was Houston on his bobtailed nag he called Jack.

Sam Houston continued on his rounds of Indian villages, speaking with the chiefs, but without much success—they must hold a council before they could sign a peace treaty. That Andrew Jackson wanted and needed these peace treaties was academic, thought Sam as he rode over the endless miles of Texas. Soon after he returned to Nacogdoches, he went over into Louisiana and from Natchitoches sent his report to the Commissioners of Indian Affairs, not wishing this information to leak out in Nacogdoches.

February was a cold, sleety month, and the Red River still struggled against the planters and sawyers, but he heard Shreve would soon arrive to clear the Great Raft from the stream. The letter:

Addressed to the Commissioners of Indian Affairs at Fort Gibson.

Natchitoches, Louisiana
February 13, 1833

Gentlemen:

It was my intention to have visited Fort Gibson, and to have reported to you my success, so far as it was connected with the Comanche Indians; but at this season, as I may expect a great rise in the waters, and the range for the horses on the direct route is too scarce to afford subsistence, I will content myself with reporting to you the prospects, as they are presented to me, of a future peace. Since my report from Fort Towson (on Red River) I proceeded through Texas as far as Bexar (San Antonio) where I had the good fortune to meet with some chiefs of that nation, who promised to visit the commissioners in three moons from that time. This will make it the month of April before they will be enabled to set out for Fort Gibson, and perhaps defer their arrival at that point until the month of May next.

I found them well disposed to make a treaty with the United States, and, I doubt not, to regard it truly and preserve it faithfully if made. It was necessary for them to return to their people, and counsel before they could send a delegation I requested that they should endeavor to see both tribes of Comanches, as well as the Pawnees and their bands, that when a peace is made it may be complete and lasting between all tribes that meet in convention. I presented a medal of General Jackson's to be conveyed to the principal chief (who was not present) with the proper explanations. I do not doubt that it will have an excellent effect in favor of the wishes of the commissioners.

You may rest assured that all the information in my power shall be collected and presented in such character as will be most useful to your commission. I am at a loss for means to enable the delegations to reach Fort Gibson; but, so far as my resources will enable me, nothing shall be wanting on my part to realize the wishes of my government, and bring about a general peace. If anything can defeat the present expectations it will be the indirect influence of the Spaniards who are jealous of everybody and everything; but even this, I trust will not prevail.

Your Ob't Servant, etc.

Sam Houston.

In less than a year, Sam Houston had an active law office in Nacogdoches and was already admitted to appear before the Court of the First Instance, presided over by Judge Juan Mora. In this work Houston became acquainted with such men as Phil Sublett of San Augustine, and Frost Thorne and John Durst, and of the Adolphus Stearne, a rosy little Rhineland Jew whom Houston liked tremendously. All of these men were of Nacogdoches. There were others of equal stature, but Adolphus Stearne, because of his long residency in the town, could give Houston details of the trouble-makers, Aaron Burr, Philip Nolan, Magee, Dr. James Long, Hayden Edwards, and Sam Norriss, who had attempted to take over Nacogdoches back in 1827, and whose attempt was stopped by Stephen Austin, who lost his one and only cannon. The thing was dismantled somehow—Austin now had nothing to grace his wide hall! It became like a game to Sam Houston, and in the game, he discovered that Austin could be a powerful adversary. Hayden Edwards and Sam Norriss had lost their lands and their citizenship, and had to flee the town. There was a great length of that land. No? Oh yes, from there to here, and from here to there . . . thousands of acres. Well, well.

As he and Phil Sublett figured out things, there came to his office a Mr. Swartwart of New York who desired Houston to represent the newly-formed Galveston Bay and Texas Land Company of New York. Since the Law of 1830 had closed the door to immigration, it was a moot question about colonizing further. There were, of course, those grants of Hayden Edwards and Sam Norriss.

David Burnett, after transferring his grant of land in East Texas, to the Galveston Bay and Texas Land Company, left for Cincinnati and returned with a wife, establishing their plantation home, "Oakland," on a tract of land which he obtained from Nathaniel Lynch, facing on Burnet Bay, where he lived from 1836 to 1858. Santa Anna burned the first house on his firebranding of Texas.

Stephen realized that the Texans were moving out of hand, and recalled the twelve hundred miles he made on the back of a mule! He had written that if he could get a state government and the 6 of April law repealed he would be perfectly satisfied and well paid. He was hopeful, yet fearful of the outcome because of the aggressive and impulsive nature of his people—they were hell bent to destruction—and he wrote Mr. Perry:

If everything had remained quiet until now our chances would have been better, but as the current is in motion, it must flow on, and if we cannot get a state by peaceable means, I shall then unite with the hottest to get one by other means. If we are to have war, we must all go together, there must be no division amongst us, but I hope that calamity will never fall upon Texas.

CHAPTER EIGHT

James E. B. Austin and Miss Eliza Martha Westall were given a lovely wedding in Columbia—Bell's Landing. Stephen was elated. "No one in all this country," Stephen said to her, "would have pleased me half so much as you." He kissed her on the cheek. James, grinning, peering over his brother's shoulder, said, "I didn't marry her to please you, brother Steve!" and kissing his bride amorously added, "I hope you do as well."

"I hope so, too," Stephen thought as he spoke. He would be very fortunate indeed to find that kind of girl. He had been casting a wistful eye on several, Jane, for one, although she was a bit older perhaps, at least about his own age. But she had a little girl and would no doubt never find another she could love whole and of a piece, as she had loved James Long. Then there were the girls on Caney Creek—he must not overlook that possibility. He wondered if this wedding might not be contagious, like smallpox or some other. . . .

That same night, after the dancing and the banqueting and all the wonderful festivities, for everybody in the whole region had come, Stephen wrote to Mr. Perry, and of course, to Emily, relating all about the day and the girl and detailing the exciting happenings. There was nothing left to be said. "I must arrange for James to go into business so that he may have more time to spend with his lovely wife. . . ."

The business was partnership with John, no relation, Austin. They had been in business before in earlier days, with a cotton gin the first in Brazoria country, on James's land grant. But it had burned.

James's home was in a new town they laid off on the Brazos River, fifteen miles from its mouth, and three miles below Bell's

Landing, or Columbia. There was certainly no town like it. "I'll move here as soon as I can divorce myself from the perplexities of colonizing, which are many, I can assure you."

The town of Brazoria was laid out on a labor of land (177 acres) which had been granted James by the Mexican government through S. Austin on August 24, 1824. Later, Stephen had added two hundred acres to the original town site. It was on an elevated area of laurel or peachland, and considered to be a most healthful climate. Ideally situated, it was near the Velasco Port of Entry. Some ten miles south of Brazoria, Stephen set aside a tract of land on this peach ridge which extended to the Gulf of Mexico for Emily and her family. He called this heavenly spot "Peach Point" and right beside her he would develop his own little world. But this world tumbled around him.

James had gone to New Orleans to buy the merchandise for their new store, and was stricken, while there, with yellow fever and died there in August after an illness of only a few hours.

Stephen, not well himself, had elected to keep Eliza and the baby company during James's sojourn in the city and so was there when the news came from New Orleans that James was dead. He took up the infant, who bore his own name, and, cuddling it, said, "Never you worry, my precious . . . Uncle Steve will always take good care of you."

There was so much to do. James's body must be brought home. "I must hurry to New Orleans, dear Eliza. . . . James must be buried here. Then there are his business interests."

"He's already buried, sir," the courier said in a tired voice. "You don't keep dead bodies around in August. If you can call being pushed into a vault on top of the ground "buried," then he's already buried."

"But where?" Stephen cried.

"In the St. Louis Cemetery."

"I don't understand."

"Some friend of yours whose family vault had an extra space, sir. Mr. Hawkins it was . . . he knowed you years ago he said, and to tell you your brother James didn't suffer none. Just sick three hours."

"Oh, thank God for friends like Mr. Hawkins. . . . Yes, I worked for him in New Orleans before coming to Texas."

And he tried to comfort Eliza all in vain.

CHAPTER NINE

Always honest with himself, as far as realization, Stephen wondered concerning the anxiety he felt about providing a land grant to Mary Austin's brother, Henry. Was it possible that the old flame was only smoldering? He had faced the fact that she had married Mr. Holly . . . had wished them a life of happiness most sincerely, and no one knew of the torture he felt, or the tears that seeped onto his pillow, of the sleepless nights when he walked the floor. She would never be his, not ever. She was lost to him—and he only to blame!

Stephen rode on through the swamp with a light heart. Too light. Just to be near her brother was a poor substitute. He met Henry on the road by the bayou and they rode on toward the land grant together.

Henry said presently, "Sad news has reached us, Stephen. Mary has lost her husband. The letter was short and gave only the details of the funeral. She had thought it was an attack of indigestion, but when the doctor reached him, he pronounced it a heart attack. He died in just a few minutes. We have written for her to come to Texas for a visit . . . take her mind off her sorrow."

It should have caused Stephen to feel the tragedy of her loss. But it did nothing but clear the clouds away. All he could think of was that she was free now, thank God, "and I'll never let her leave me again!" Ashamed of the tenor of his mind, he said, "It probably would be a good thing—a change of scene, with no sad reminders."

"That's the way we figured it, Stephen," Cousin Henry said. "How much farther is it?"

"At the end of the bayou."

While looking over this new land with Stephen, he saw through the forest of oak and other kinds of fine wood, a magnificent place glistening in the sun of high noon: a great two-story house with a dove cote and other outbuildings. Barns, stables. "My word!" Cousin Austin said with his eyes bugging. "Who lives there?"

"That's Orozimba, home of Dr. and Mrs. James Phelps. You'll meet him soon, I guess. He's a Mason, too."

"What a plantation. What a layout!" He saw riots of crimson roses and bright red salvia and white honeysuckle vines clambering for a permanent foothold up the tall white columns. Wisteria covered the summerhouse and the perfume that swept across the Brazos River was startling.

"Be a great place to bring up my six children," Cousin Austin said as they rode back to Columbia.

It was late in November when Stephen again visited with Henry. He had come to see his cousin, Henry's sister, Mary Austin Holly. She was visiting Texas, she said, to gather material for a book.

"Bolivar" was all that Henry, who had a marvelous imagination, had envisioned. Mary Holly met Stephen at the door of the high French cottage, built up so that in times of high water, they would be perfectly safe. She was wearing a lavender frock with her golden curls pulled up into a cluster on the back of her head. Stephen saw the color of her eyes were a deep purple under dark brown eyebrows, arched so that it seemed to him there was always a question. And her dark lashes swept into them when she raised her eyes or lay upon her cheek when she lowered them.

"You're too serious, my dear Stephen," she said and laughed. It might have been the lilting music of her voice, of her laughter, who knows exactly what it is that made of Stephen a willing vessel? They talked of Texas, and other things, but objectivity soon faded off into personal things, with Stephen saying that he wished with all his heart she would remain in Texas, and her saying she would like nothing better but she must finish her manuscript. Along the line he realized that she was the ideal—companionable, intelligent, lovely as a magnolia, with a gay disposition. What a life they could have together.

Stephen remained three days at "Bolivar" and by that time, they had become constantly in conversation. They had planned their home, next to Emily on Peach Point," to build us a cottage rural, cottage comfortable, and splendid . . . the splendor of Nature's simplicity." What a dream. As he mounted to depart Bolivar and return to Peach Point, Mary stood by his side. "Laugh cares away," she said.

Steve was so elated he didn't even remember passing by familiar plantations, so anxious was he to get to Peach Point and find the loveliest spot on the ridge for Mary's home and his. Glorious feeling would consume him, and die down, and again he would be flooded with this amazing feeling of being drunk. . . . *Crazy* would be a better word. He felt, after deciding on the place to build the house, rather relieved. Now he could write his keynote address and so by the window of his room at Emily's, he wrote it all out, and was pleased. "The banquet is to be at Jane's Tavern," Stephen said, dressing with unusual care, brushing the brown hair from a receding forehead. He was now ready to go. Emily kissed him on the cheek. "You look younger tonight than you have in years!" He hadn't told her about Mary.

CHAPTER TEN

The new village was to be some miles down river and Bill Blanks had left Lisa and the children to go with Stephen, as most of the men folks had, to cut some trees and generally prepare for the new colonists. They had been there several days and already a wide clearing was easing outward with each day's cutting. Raw stumps and brambles littered it.

The fellow had ridden in a gallop to reach them. Foam rimmed its black mouth, but the rider did not dismount. "Mr. Blanks! Yoohoo! Your wife's terrible sick. The doctor said you should get there quick as you can." Bill threw the axe down and went for his mule.

"No. No, Bill. Take my horse, she's already saddled," Stephen exclaimed. "You hop down and have a cup of coffee, and let the horse graze a few minutes. You've done what you could."

"I've no time for that, Mr. Austin."

"You'll need the strength. So will the horse. She's about ready to keel over!" Stephen took a johnny cake off the skillet and said, "Here take this to go with the coffee."

Sonny Tilden slumped onto a stump, swilled the too-hot coffee, and choked on the cornbread. "She's yellow's a punkin, Mr. Austin. Swamp fever the doctor said. But he ain't got nothing to treat it with."

Two weeks or so ago before the fellows started out for the clearing, Lisa and her seven children were some yards from the house picking up hickory nuts and wild pecans that lay thick on the ground, and having filled her sack, she decided to take these back to the house without the children, who were laughing and

59

having fun running from one to another of this windfall of pecan trees. Suddenly, from the direction of the Gulf, a cloud of mosquitoes had swamped her. She was literally swathed in their dark casement, and in a mad tarantella she had fought them, screaming, flailing her arms to dislodge them. They would swarm away a foot or two, and on signal, regroup for the next tackle. Still screaming, she dropped the gunny sack and fled toward the house when quite suddenly, the millions, seeing the horses in the scattered enclosures, took off in their direction. Bill had seen her running, and had reached her by the time she fell in a swoon on the puncheon gallery. Her face, already swelling, looked to Bill as though a million needle pricks covered her, arms, hands, and face, and by the time he laid her on the framed bunk bed nearest the water bucket and disrobed her to her chemise, her legs were puffed out over her shoe tops. Bill could think of nothing but soda so hastily he filled a basin and dumped a box of soda into it and began drenching her from head to foot. He removed her shoes and sopped the soda water there and when he looked toward her face, her eyes had swollen shut.

If the mosquitoes did this to Lisa, what chance would the children have? They would never be able to stand it. This was something they had never had to experience in Missouri. Mosquitoes, yes, but never in black clouds. Lisa had not been against the move, but then she was never against anything he suggested. He was uneasy.

They had tackled the horses and mules and San Felipe people ran yelling in the road with coats, aprons, anything over them. There was no stopping the animals as they tossed their heads with manes flying and, wild-eyed, raced toward the river, where they dove in, neighing frightfully. Corral fences lay in shambles, barn doors kicked off. Through all that disturbance the children came skipping along, gunny sacks bulging, singing, "Skiptomaloumadarlin." Oh for innocent childhood.

"You be quiet now. The mosquitoes been stinging your ma," Bill said. "Nigh about kilt her. Look she's swelled up fit to burst!" Lisa stirred. "She'll be all right. She fainted, I reckon."

"You see!" exclaimed the six-year-old red-headed Tommy. "I told you I heard ma screamin' and yelling, but you wouldn't listen to me. But then, you never do."

"If you didn't allus be amakin' up things, Tommy! I heard her too, but I reckoned it were a painter." Little Bill was twelve, a living image of Lisa. "They sounded the same to me." Thus he denied the blame, which, of course, was no one's.

"What's done, is done," Bill explained. "Our problem now is to keep quiet so's she can nap a bit. We can see about some supper, and do the chores."

Little Bill, peering out the back door, cried, "Where's the mules?" Bill, right on his heels, saw the fence down and no sign of his animals, cows, pigs. "They must be around somewhere! he gasped. He went back to the bunk and taking a fresh pan of soda water, began all over again to soak her in it. "This soda water ought to help."

"Soda water?" Little Bill asked. "What good will that do?" They were all strung out around the bed. Baby Ann, right up in her mother's face, began to cry. "At's not my mommy!"

"If soda water will make crawdabs puke out their insides, it ought to take some of the poison from those stings. You don't bother now—go fetch the doctor. Jim, you can go look for the animals."

Mary, who was ten and blessed with golden hair and brown eyes, touched her mother's face gently. "I'll fix supper, ma."

"Yeah," they all said at once. "Ma dumped a whole basket full of crawfish in a tub of soda water, and such a bubbling looked like a explosion goin' on!"

Stephen and Sonny left the clearing in less than ten minutes, Stephen riding Bill's Missouri mule. They reached San Felipe as the sun blazed a red canopy across the prairie, rendering a pinkish glow. Sonny rode on down the lane to his house, and Stephen cleaned up a bit before he, too, would know how it was with Lisa. Surely he knew that she had lost the swelling by the next morning, declared she was just fine and sent Bill on with Stephen to the new site. All or most of the men of San Felipe were helping as they had done each time Stephen expected a new colony from the States. The women cooked up everything in sight for a celebration at their arrival and settling in. The children were in other cabins of San Felipe on orders of the doctor and Bill and Lisa were alone. One glance through the half-open door told Stephen that indeed she was as yellow as a pumpkin, the pillow case was dark with wet, yellow sweat. Seeing them there, with Bill on his knees by the side of the bunk, Stephen decided she was an extremely ill person.

How could anyone fade away in so short a time? Stephen asked himself. Her long white fingers combed Bill's red hair. The scene was too intimate for intrusion. Still, if he made a noise he would break the spell of their meeting. He dared not go in, and he feared to step out on the puncheon floor. Lisa was softly saying but with the greatest urgency, "I want . . . I wanta . . . Oh I'm glad you're home. I've been needing you, needing you. Don't you understand my need for you?"

Stephen was confounded and confused daring hardly to breathe. She was dying, there was little doubt of that, and so he thought about the man who was hanged in St. Genevieve for horse stealing. So clearly it could be observed in the man's linsey-woolsey pants that he was experiencing orgasm just before the trap dropped. Could it be, he wondered, that the primordial instinct of man was to perpetuate the human race, that there is great and uncontrollable urgency at the end? Lisa had seven children, and she was a wonderful mother, always happy and singing as a woman fulfilled and comfortable, "and the twain shall be one."

Bill cradled her head in the crook of his left arm, while his right hand slipped beneath the coverlet. Her face, tear-drenched, he kissed devotedly, snugly. Her voice was no more than a whisper, "Oh . . . oh . . ." and a strangely contorted face gave way to a gentle smile while her body went limp.

Stephen had not wanted to witness this most intimate of all relationships, so now he stepped back and knocked on the half-open thick pine door with the great black homemade hinges, calling "May I come in?"

Bill rose then, swiping his eyes so he could see Stephen. "Come on, Stephen," he said as if it were coming from far off. "I must wash my dirty face and comb my hair."

"How is she?"

"Resting."

"I'm glad. She does look so peaceful. I'll be back directly," Stephen said, turning and going out into the twilight. He must try to breathe deeply. His throat hurt.

Stephen's feet flung the dust of the winding road to his two-room cabin and office, and back again to Bill's one room with lean-to. He carried a big brown jug in his hand. Bill was going to need it. And to think, Stephen said in his mind, that I figured old Bill must be a something in bed—and all the time, it must have been Lisa's demands he was answering to. When he stepped through the door, he found Bill kneeling beside Lisa's bunk. He was holding her lifeless hand to his lips.

Stephen recalled a poem he had read recently by Walt Whitman which he was unable to dismiss from his troubled mind:
There was never any more inception than there is now,
Nor any more youth or age, than there is now,
And will never be any more perfection than there is now.

Urge and urge and urge, Always the procreant urge of the world.
Out of the dimness opposite equals advance,
Always substance and increase, always sex.
Always a knit of identity, Always a distinction,
Always a breed of life
To elaborate is no avail, learn'd and unlearn'd
Feel that it is so.

CHAPTER ELEVEN

It was time for Stephen to leave for Saltillo and the legislature, and December came on wild with nothing to break the wind from off the staked plains but mesquite and chaparral. He went by horseback through San Antonio, where he met his old friend, a Catholic priest, Father Muldoon, a mighty man in stature and mind. They had supper together in his rooms, which were bare and showed his poverty, for such was the way of the Franciscan. They were served by a Mexican woman who knew how to make tortillas and a mean pot of beans—if you appreciated red hot pepper.

"Father Muldoon, we need a cura in our immediate territory . . ."

"I must get permission of the president of the College of San Fernando . . . he it is who says go there, or come here. But I can leave as soon as he permits me."

Stephen spent the night with Father Muldoon, and again was impressed for between the two cots in the room, there was no difference, both as hard as a board can make it. Each had one blanket under, and one over. During the night after the fire had become ashes Stephen awakened shivering. He put on his clothes, glancing at the sleeping priest. Well-padded, he thought. He lay back under his blanket ashamed, but he did not take off all the clothing he had put on. The next morning, Stephen met the sunrise headed for Saltillo. And the new Cura de Austin followed in a few days for San Felipe.

Father Muldoon reached his new appointment late in March and worked out from Austin's log cabin. It boasted a rather large fireplace made of hand-formed brick and delighted Father Muldoon, as he could entertain the many colonists who found their way to the log cabin, and he discovered that Stephen Austin had silver of all kinds and fine china and drawn linen. This told him that the gentleman had not always lived in a log cabin. He was proud to be able to reach into a common cupboard and bring forth a silver compote from which he sprinkled his infants.

There were many journeys out from San Felipe and he was welcomed. He loved to visit "Eagle Island," the home of William Wharton, who had married Sarah, daughter of Colonel Groce, who also lived down there. The Whartons had the finest library Father Muldoon had found since leaving Mexico City.

Stephen Austin returned to San Felipe in the midst of trouble. There was the clash between Bradburn and the colonists; the other was between General Terhan and the Galveston Bay and Texas Land Company, which had been organized in New York and which took over the grants formerly owned by Hayden Edwards, then Burnet, Vehlein, and de Zavala. He wanted to know how it was transacted. And by whom.

"I guess it's better late than never," Stephen said to General Teran. "And quite beyond me."

Stephen now had long had a secretary, Sam Williams who knew Stephen's business inside and out. He had to know it. Stephen was absent from his colonists so often and matters had to be dealt with, official or otherwise. The political parties were moving in and pushing out and who knew what to expect of such vacillating peoples.

He considered that when Bustamente became president, he seemed to have recalled the "Fredonian Rebellion," as Hayden's private war was being called, and Sam Norriss also, and they in parts unknown.

It seemed to Stephen the man was bitter and jealous exposing his feeling toward the Americans who had made beautiful and productive plantations in a land the Mexicans had not bothered with. Of course, there could also be another reason—the United States had again offered to purchase Texas, in 1825, 1827, 1829. So Bustamente had one avenue he could take: legislate the citizens out of Texas, so as not to become too strong and so declare for independence.

He may have been new in his office, but he knew too, that the Americans' spirit would not tolerate suppression.

Before leaving Saltillo, Austin, as agent, received a grant of land for his secretary, Sam Williams, and himself in East Texas, where they planned to settle eight hundred families of European and Mexican colonists. He returned to San Felipe de Austin in June 1831, and now had to direct all his immediate attention to the removal of Emily and her family to Peach Point.

CHAPTER TWELVE

Peach Point rose majestically on the ridge Stephen had chosen at the edge of fifty thousand acres of wooded land. Nothing less than palatial was the permanent home of his sister, Emily. It had twelve large rooms, in a time when four were considered pretentious. There too would be a sugar mill and cotton gin and street for his people. For the last year and a half, Rob had been overseer, getting brick made and kilned of adobe soil, some called gumbo. Mixed with sand it made a wonderfully hard and durable brick. The grounds had been planted with all kinds of shrubs indigenous to the Gulf.

Stephen had been planting more flowering trees, and thought, there ought to be a carriage drive circling in and, say, pillars about twelve feet high at the entrance and exit, with wide iron gates—that is, if Emily wants them. It'll be great even without gates. It was as if it were his own home, and his busy hands marked off where the entrances were to be. He was happier walking about this flowering garden with the Spanish moss ghosting from the wide branches of oak, silver filigree veiling the house from where he stood. "Oh my!" he exclaimed aloud, "I know she'll love it."

The Perrys arrived at San Felipe, where Emily's baby was born.

The house completed, and Emily able to travel, they loaded up in several wagons and began a delightful journey to "Peach Point."

"Oh, Mr. Perry, please hold the baby while I go looking and feasting my eyes. Steve, it's more beautiful than I had any right to expect." She ran on, not even listening to "Don't try going upstairs."

"I'd like this room set aside, Emily, with father's old desk and his chair. Fix it as much like his old office as you can." And when he looked at Emily, he saw tears in her eyes. "I always loved his old office. . . ."

"Was it the old office and desk and chair you loved, Steve? Or was it association with one so dear?" she said. She clutched her infant to her breast . . . so little time together. She would go. Steve would too, each in his own time. Oh yes, she would make a home for Stephen with so much of love in it!

Mr. Perry said, "We'll have to get some salt from Mitchell's salt works until I can send to Goldonna in Louisiana. It's so primitive. Imagine extracting salt from sea water!" Mr. Perry got a big surprise when Stephen replied, "But of course. He gets eight or ten bushels a day and sells it a dollar a bushel. Sells all he can make with buyers waiting their turn. Especially handy in the winter at hog killing time. Texas has javilinas, Arkansas has razor backs, but I've noticed the colonists from Missouri brought down a good breed of hog. In fact, I haven't seen such hams since we left St. Genevieve."

Summer waned and fall came on, and then it was time to get the hogs penned up and fattened for winter's kill. With the cold spell, and it seemed that winter had come to stay, Alice was in Hog Heaven. Hams hung in the smokehouse in net bags, and hickory logs burned in the firepit. Later she would dab brown sugar over them, and she would hang them up renetted to smoke for a long time.

Alice always had one chore she did before anything else—she stripped the feces from the hog guts, and rinsed them off, turning them inside out, and cut them into foot lengths. Some would be used as sausage cases, but the rest? "Ummm," Alice would drool. "My, what fine chittlin's dese'll make!"

Rob brought in the reamed out fat and skin and Alice cut them into one-inch squares, and dumped them into the three-legged wash pot, ordering Rob to get a good slow "fhar so's de craklin's be to suit Miz Emily." She laughed. "Dem white folks sho do love mah cracklin bread."

Christmas had come and gone and Stephen was sitting by the fire at Peach Point. The two sets of children had taken to the swamp as if they'd never known anywhere else. It was a good life. Come summer Emily would have a cottage on the beach, which was becoming a favorite summer dwelling for many of the families to escape the dreadful heat and humidity of the swamps. William Joel, Moses Austin, and Guy M. Bryan would grow up as ignorant as the Karankawas as far as book learning was concerned. It mattered so much to Stephen that he got up right then and rode over to see Josiah Bell. He had to have help if ever a seminary of learning was to be established in East Texas. He remained in Columbia several months.

All three grants, Burnet, Vehlein and deZavala, were transferred October, 16, 1832 to the Galveston Bay and Texas Land Company. Sam Houston was their attorney. De Zavala's plantation was located at the confluence of the San Jacinto River and Buffalo Bayou, twelve miles below Harrisburg. And de Zavala lost no time in creating a beautiful and magnificent home where Stephen was always a most welcome guest. Strangely, Stephen lodged no questions at Zavala, but uppermost in his mind was how it had happened—the transfer was accomplished.

Stephen loved to stroll along its picturesque setting and watch the great yellow-red ball dip into Galveston Bay as twilight came on. So much they had to talk about: Lorenza's time as minister to France (he had been persuaded to take on this position by Santa Anna. "But I resigned after a short time, as you know. I had more to do here than there."

"Do you remember Colonel Bradburn, Lorenza?" Stephen asked. "He is an American by birth, but you'd never know it. At any rate, he is now at Anahauc, commander of the fort and collector. . . . Mostly, it's his attitude."

"I've heard he's abusive," de Zavala said. "And that's not all. I understand he not only arrested Madero, the land commissioner, but his chief surveyor. Dissolved the new municipality of Liberty."

"There is so much unrest—fuel for the fire," Stephen said.

"I hear you've been called as a member of the legislature of Coahuilla-Texas. You'll be in a strong position there."

"I hope so."

67

The Calle del Norte and the Trace would merge directly. The land was rugged and cactus grew without much will, and the wind blew all the time, that the trees along the beach bowed inland, and grew that way. The water was not far, a matter of yards, and a long white sandy island lay out like a breakwater. They called it Padres. They, he and Rob, had made excellent time coming up by way of Matamoros and following the coast line, loaded with sacks of fruit they had obtained in the tropical country, were moseying along, enjoying the wide prairie with a few humps breaking the horizontal line to forever. Stephen thought again, how broad a land. But the humps became dwarfed trees, stunted, perhaps from the salt on the wind. And few in number. They would come tomorrow or the day after to the rivers, and tremendous forests of pecan, and oak.

It was clouding up, even as he searched the azure blue, collecting into a black mass. Stephen saw it coming then, dancing over the rugged country, with a long black snout lowering itself—always lowering so that soon it touched the ground. The speed of the swirling mass was impossible to estimate; shock waves resounded in his ears, with a core. He had seen them in Missouri measuring six to eight hundred feet after the tornado had passed, so that they thundered as so many log jams after a freshet, a deafening roar. He realized that they were in danger of being in its path, but direction was always the unknown quantity; such were the vagaries of their temperament. He had seen them back in Missouri dip down and follow a ground path for so short a distance as a hundred feet, or again as much as a mile, or a hundred miles or more. Running was not the answer. It had come on from their backs, and it was remarkable that neither of them had turned. They must find an escape. Already the pull of it had ripped off his hat. Just between the road and island stood a massive boulder, back of which was a wash dug out by the winds. Stephen motioned to Rob to follow, for now nothing could be heard, because of the indescribable roar, and pulled the mule down with him. With Rob falling, they braced themselves under the back of the boulder. Stephen had seen houses literally explode outward under the funnel tip with its tremendous vacuum build-up; it could rip a roof from a large building and draw corks from bottles. Its driving force could pierce tree trunks with a straw, propel splinters through brick walls. Yes, it was the Destroyer, forming suddenly, as a funnel-like cloud. Sometimes they came as a vertical cylinder or a thin, strangely twisted rope, but mostly like a mammoth elephant's trunk. This one was like the elephant trunk. Rob had his hands on both mules' bridles, as he squatted beside them and Stephen. Stephen saw his eyes roll heavenward, "Lordy, pass that thing ober us, deliver us like you did the chirrun of Israel. Pass ober us sinners, case we ain't got no blood to sprinkle on dishere rock."

Stephen heard no more. The tornado, like a giant leap frog, raised itself up, up, up, shaking the earth and rock, and raising the hair of their heads. And the first words he could hear were in thankfulness to the Master God, for letting it pass over. That faithful Rob knew more about the Scriptures than did he, a graduate of Transylvania! He let his eyes rest on Rob's kinky hair. Always quite black, it was now sprinkled with gray. When had it happened that the years had passed so fleetingly?

Then, it hit the water, and it seemed bent on drawing up whatever existed below, and soon, it was a gusher, a fountain, raining fish, crabs, kelp and plankton with other nameless creatures scattered about, but when Stephen saw the gray-white of a porpoise, he stood there in wonderment, with his mouth open as if to speak. But nothing came out. Rob caught his sleeve, "What did you see?"

"I saw a porpoise or a whale, I don't know which, probably dead by the time it was dropped." Nevertheless, there was the weird glow over the sea for the sun shafted, it being now late in the afternoon over their heads and struck the tornado, whose trail from south to east was drawn in sharp lines. To be able to see it! To witness its mighty strength! Stephen was weak in the legs. But Rob had new faith, always renewable.

"We'll likely not get home tomorrow night, Rob. Let us make camp right here."

To the north, a way off, were the unmistakable signs of a thunder storm, so knowing the rivers would be flooded, they went about the duties of each over many, many years.

"I just as soon rest, yessuh," Rob said, and got up and began bringing out fruit, bread and cold roast beef. He filled Stephen's plate and brought it over, then for himself. So often Stephen had told Rob to fill up and eat too, mostly to save time, for the distances were so far, but Rob had fiddled around and after one fashion or another, failed to quite make it. Stephen decided he'd never really know Rob, and so let it pass.

As Stephen lay on his blanket, watching the black sky, he again knew that there were few men and seldom that he loved so much as Rob.

Stephen told Rob about the times the place had been wiped off the face of the earth by tidal wave, cyclone and tornado, and how the people had loved the area so much that the first time it happened, they came back and rebuilt, for nothing had been left, but the second time, many lives were lost, the village wiped out again, and the long wharves they had built a half-mile out into the bay disappeared—not a pile, not a plank. "It must be an awful experience," he said and Rob nodded that it surely must be so. They wandered about the sand and found rare shells, glass floated from Portugal or the Orient and arrowheads, remnants of a tribe of Indians long gone and forgotten.

On the morrow they would come into the squat little adobe village called Corpus Christi. "They tell me that Corpus Christi was founded in 1519, Rob, at the time the bay was discovered and named by a Spanish explorer, Alonza Alvarez de Pineda. I've often wondered why the Spanish-Mexicans did so little with this fabulous country. To think how long Spain owned it, then lost it to the natives, Mexicans, who really are Mixtecs, mixed with your blood and mine—why they might have by this time had magnificent plantations or ranchos, and what have we found? Mud huts squatting without trees, around waterless fountains in plazas with nothing denoting such, save the huts go around a square, and end with the everlasting church which has drained the peons of their life's blood. Why I know of a town in Mexico that maintains three hundred and sixty-five churches!"

"It seem to me, yessuh, that one would have been enough . . . all us chirrun of God hoping for everlasting life in one place . . . I never understan' that . . . nosuh." Rob plowed his kinky hair with long gnarled fingers, shaking his head. "Nosuh, maybe we understan better bye'nbye."

Emily's children would enjoy the citrus. And before him was the Rio Grande, and on across it he would be in Eagle Pass, for it was the gateway, in a manner of speaking. There he had found Rob waiting.

Padres Island is a hundred and ten miles long, hugging the coast of Texas, a natural breakwater. The lagoon was quiet and very blue, but to reach it, Stephen had dismounted, as had Rob, to find a way through the fifty-foot sand dunes which shifted constantly, at times uncovering the wreck of an ancient ship, at times hiding all be-

70

neath a smooth layer of golden sand. The salt on the wind was good to breathe. "Let's make camp here, Rob," Stephen said standing tall and breathing deeply. "What a place. I'll vouch there's not a soul within miles of us!"

CHAPTER THIRTEEN

Stephen was glad to find Father Muldoon at the Whartons'. And where but in their fabulous library? Late in the afternoon, he and Father Muldoon walked along the spacious grounds while before them was Buffalo Bayou and the San Jacinto River and a waving sea of salt grass hiding the deceptive quagmire for it was neither land nor yet sea, but earth in the making. Cattle roamed over the green bending low hillsides under the shade of the wide branches of ancient oak trees to chew their cuds. It was a pastoral scene which Stephen never tired of, and thoughts of his own future infringed upon his mind. Where would he be and with whom when he had built his own plantation and would there be children to gladden his heart in old age? But Father Muldoon, as if translating his thoughts was saying: "Oh, St. Francis, you who went to your reward at the age of forty-three, so young! You who lived to see your humble band grow into a great institution—yet rejected by the Church, for the Church had become a part of the international banking in Italy! Oh, St. Francis, intercede for us, your poor followers who refuse to give up your doctrine of poverty—especially those called heretics, who were burned at the stake!"

"Father Muldoon?" Stephen said. "Who burned the Franciscans?"

"The Church, my boy . . ."

"What happened to the five thousand Jesuits who were taken in chains from their posts as if they too had been guilty of something?"

"Who knows what became of them? Many died from the experience."

"Now I know why Father Miguel Hidalgo rebelled against the viceroy. It surely was not just the injustice of the grape vineyards."

"You might recall that in 1681, there was an Indian uprising in

Santa Fe, when the governor and his people were held down, with their water supply from the river diverted from the villa, so that in desperation they fled the palace and made it down the Rio Grande. While the Spanish fled, the Indians set up housekeeping in the Governor's Palace. These Spaniards were headed to the protection of the nearest fort, called Paso del Norte (Juarez was across the river). So in appreciation of their escape they built the first mission in Texas. Their village was called Ysleta del Sur, so the mission was called Ysleta. Age-old whitewashed adobe buildings are there with their blue painted doors and windows frames—an ancient charm to insure happiness and good luck, but mostly, I reckon, to ward off evil," Father Muldoon, always at his best in imparting information, said. "Descendants of the Tiwa or Tigua, as we say in Spanish, who were loyal always to the governor and who had fled with him, still live at Ysleta."

"There's certainly much to learn of this big country," Stephen said. "It seems that a couple of missions were taken from Nacogdoches and rebuilt at San Antonio. Can you imagine every stone being carted from the village of the Haisinai all the way out there?" Stephen said. "Ox carrettas—heavy enough of themselves, but loaded with stone!"

"Well, like Rome it wasn't done in a day. It took them twenty-one years to build Mission Concepcion," Father Muldoon explained. The Mission San Francisco de la Espada was erected in 1731, 'St. Francis of the Sword' Father Junipero Serra was delighted with the aqueduct he found there. It is, of course, Spanish, built by the Franciscans about 1740, who settled San Antonio River Valley. They still use it. However, there is one earlier, 1720, built by them for the then Viceroy Aguayo, the Mission San Jose de Aguayo, that we call 'The Queen of the Missions'. You must see it some time"—never dreaming how the future would unfold. "It is the most complete mission established in the United States, or Texas . . . as far as I can learn, and built in shops of all kinds as the Senora Nuestra Adais of Louisiana, only much more impressive. They too, had a granary, leather-working shop, a grist mill certainly, the very oldest in Texas . . . and a carpenter shop. It's rose window is already famous in far-flung countries. They also have the barracks for His Majesty's troops.

"The one they carted from Nacogdoches, San Juan Capistrano, 1731, has three bell towers, each with a bell. To my way of thinking, it is the most charming of all," Muldoon said.

Stephen's mind kept going back to Father Junipero Serra. "How long did Father Serra labor among these missions?"

"For many, many years. He had wanted to be a missionary in the true sense of the word . . . far places to spread the Gospel. But while still a young man, he boarded ship, landing here in Mexico, and he labored year in and year out, never going on his muchly desired missionary travels. Then, when he had reached the ripe old age of sixty, when most of us want only our comforts and peace by a fireside, Father Serra was called to replace the Jesuits in Baja, California, and everywhere to undertake the Jesuits' pursuits. Then from that, he was given the presidency of the California projected string of missions."

"At sixty years old?" Stephen asked, really not believing it.

"Stephen, have you never wondered of the names of the California missions? Are they not also the names of the Texas Missions—almost all?

"1226 A.D. That's a long time ago, Stephen, but wounds as these do not heal with time. Francis was canonized only two years after his death and a great basilica was built in his memory. It was staggering to see such a massive masterpiece of engineering, Gothic, I remember, just hanging there on the side of a cliff!" Father Muldoon said. "They with all their poverty had become the richest church in Italy."

"A poor little man who grew rich. Extraordinary!" Stephen said at this revelation.

"Whose very austerities had brought on his early demise. I have already told you he passed on at forty-three. St. Francis who loved the birds and animals and all nature, and lived on the premise that 'Foxes have holes. Birds have their nests—but the Son of Man hath not where to lay his head.' "

"You're certainly in a mood today, Father Muldoon. Are you troubled about something?" Stephen asked.

"Ah, yes, my son . . . I love this country. I love these people, Protestants and Catholics alike. But I have been ordered back to Mexico City. I must leave all this . . ." His hand swung in a wide arc over Galveston Bay and the streams and bayous, the mossy oaks, the near estuary. I shall miss you, too."

Stephen thought he likely would never see the good padre again.

Under the leadership of Alcalde James Dill, Nacogdoches soon regained its former prestige as the largest town in East Texas, and settlers from the United States began coming in increasing numbers under the beneficent colonization laws of the new government of Mexico; but things were much changed. In 1825 Hayden and Benjamin Edwards secured their ill-fated contract as empressarios. When Edwards began to plant his colonists, sometimes on land which had belonged to the Mexican inhabitants and had been abandoned temporarily in the flight of 1813, the friction between the Americans and Mexicans increased. On the northwest of them also had settled a tribe of Cherokee Indians, who claimed the right to occupy a vast territory which had formerly been the habitation of the friendly Texas Indians, the Caddo, tribe of Tawakoni.

This triangular situation bred distrust and antagonism that at last broke out into open warfare and threw the country into the wildest disorder. The coup of Edwards was at first successful, and he and his followers were able to seize the "Stone House" and fortify it; but the citizenship of Nacogdoches and the surrounding country was not behind the movement, and so it was doomed from its inception.

This Fredonian Rebellion resulted in many of the prominent citizens of the town being expelled in 1827—among whom were John S. Roberts, Hayden and Ben Edwards, Adolphus Stearne and Martin Parmer, and Samuel Norriss. The Mexican general, Ahumada, who occupied Nacogdoches upon this occasion, was a genuine diplomat, and with the assistance and advice of Stephen Austin, who came to Nacogdoches with Ahumada, soon had the old town peaceful again. However, the man whom Ahumada selected as commandant here proved to be an unfortunate choice, and Colonel Jose de las Piedras soon aroused the hostility of the American settlers with his high-handed, arbitrary methods, as was the case with Colonel Bradburn at Anahuac.

It all started with Bustamente's Law of April 6, 1830, forbidding further immigration from the United States, while permitting Europeans to come in unimpeded. Juan Antonio Padilla was unwilling to enforce its provisions, and in the latter part of April he was ordered by Don Ramon Musquiz, political chief in Bexar, to be imprisoned and suspended on a trumped-up charge of murder.

The military force was doubled during 1830 and passports of all immigrants going through Nacogdoches for Austin's colony, which was exempted by Bustamente's Decree, were to be signed by Austin in person.

Under the dictatorship of Bustamente the military commandants continually encroached upon the power of the civil authorities, and finally, in June 1832, the settlers at Anahuac rebelled and ousted Bradburn, Piedras arriving too late with troops from Nacogdoches and Fort Teran. Becoming alarmed at the rising tide of opposition, Col. Piedras, upon his return, ordered the people of Nacogdoches to surrender all their arms. This order was followed immediately by an appeal from the ayuntamiento in Nacogdoches, issued in July 28, 1832, to the neighboring communities to present a united front against this action; copies of this resolution were sent to Ayish Bayou, the Palo Gacho, Tenaha, and San Felipe de Austin and met with immediate response from all except San Felipe. Two companies came from the Ayish Bayou settlement, commanded by captains Sam Davis and Bailey Anderson, one from Sabine and one from Shelby, and Capt. James Bradshaw's company from the Neches settlement, while the people of Nacogdoches were led by Alcalde Encarnacion Chirino. On the morning of August 2, 1832, these forces met in the eastern outskirts of Nacogdoches and elected Colonel James W. Bullock as commander-in-chief of about five hundred men.

Colonel Piedras commanded about the same number of Mexican soldiers and proceeded to fortify the Stone House, the old Catholic church and the Red House. An ultimatum from the settlers for Piedras to declare in favor of Santa Anna and the Constitution of 1824, or surrender at discretion to an officer to be selected by Colonel Bullock, brought forth an answer that none of the demands would be complied with, and that he was prepared to fight.

Colonel Piedras advanced to meet the Americans and fighting commenced in the eastern part of town about eleven o'clock. By noon the Mexicans had retreated to the business section, around the Stone House. Alex Horton, a member of the American forces, said:

> We were armed with shotguns and various other guns such as citizens used for hunting purposes, while the Mexicans were armed with splendid English muskets; so we turned north and marched down North Street. As we began our march we heard a French horn. When we had gotten about opposite the Stone House the Mexican cavalry made a furious charge upon us, pouring upon us a heavy fire of small

arms; they advanced to within a few steps of our lines, but were forced back with considerable loss.

This cavalry charge met the Americans' force near the Catholic church, which had been used by Piedras as quarters for his soldiers.

The Mexicans about mid-afternoon were driven out of the Stone House, and the main body of their army was concentrated in the cuartel or Old Red House, the older part of which was built of adobe, and almost as strong as stone. It also had the advantage of several dormer windows on the second floor, from which sharp-shooters could better defend the building. The fighting continued with unabated fury until night separated the combatants. Colonel Piedras evacuated Nacogdoches during the night of the second, under the protecting cloak of a heavy fog, retreating westward toward the Angelina River.

The next morning James Carter, with seventeen volunteers, set out in pursuit of the Mexican army, overtaking them at Durst Lake, and after a skirmish at that point, Carter and his men went further south, crossing the Angelina at the Goodman Crossing, and marched northward to the west side of Durst's ferry to oppose the crossing of the Mexican troops. Here Piedras lost many of his men in an unsuccessful attempt to cross the river.

During the following morning Colonel Piedras surrendered the command to Captain Francisco Medina, who in turn declared for Santa Anna and surrendered to James Carter the entire Mexican force of some four hundred men.

Colonel James Bowie, who reached Nacogdoches a few days after the battle, agreed to convoy the Mexican troops to San Antonio, and in his report stated that there were thirty-three Mexicans killed and seventeen or eighteen wounded—the Americans having three men killed and seven wounded. That is how the current began that Stephen had been caught up in, and he must now go with the current. . . .

CHAPTER FOURTEEN

In 1832 a law authorized the use of the English language and a donation of land by the government for the purpose of establishing primary schools. Finally, a petition for a state, Texas, to be separate and distinct from Coahuila was adopted. Musquiz promptly declared it null and void. Stephen was so discouraged and enraged he replied to Musquiz's communication showing his desperate mood:

I have but little hope of obtaining anything from the Government of Mexico; there is little probability that we may have a stable and peaceable government for some time to come, and I believe that Texas is lost if she takes no measure of her own for her own welfare.

He laid the turkey quill on his desk, while in his mind's eye he could see himself standing before a firing squad. That this would be considered treason he had no doubt. Yet he dispatched it by courier within the hour.

The Mexicans' garrisons were driven out of Texas that year, and Texas declared for Santa Anna and the Constitution of 1824, which Austin had helped create. It all began when Austin was in Saltillo as a legislator. At Anahuac Bradburn and some colonists had a small conflict. But Stephen was back in San Felipe in time for the convention and was not really too concerned. The reason was Emily and her family. He could barely keep his mind on this pressing business of Emily, thinking she would be bringing up her children in a wilderness of unschooled people. He was furious with Musquiz.

There were two large springs on the Brazos which had always been popular with the Waco Indians, whom DeSoto found there in 1540. It was called Ranger Fort at one time, but the name by which it was generally known was "Six-Shooter Junction" because it lay along the old Chisolm Trail, Waco ultimately.

In March of 1833, Stephen had a letter from Jose Antonio Mexia in which he gave the news that Santa Anna had been elected president of Mexico, with Gomez Valentine Farias his vice president. Mexia also suggested that a commission be sent from Texas, as a public testimony of their respect and good wishes on behalf of Texas. Mexia was at the time in the Senate and declared himself the friend of the Texans, interested in their welfare. He wrote that

Santa Anna-Farias would be inaugurated in April.

Yes, Stephen thought, they must carry the badge of friendship, for Santa Anna had indeed been a loyal friend. Now he let his review go back to the First Families, the Old Three Hundred: 1822; Five Hundred in June 1825; a hundred in November 1827; three hundred in April 1828; and eight hundred families in partnership with his secretary, Sam Williams, in February 1831. During that time Mexico's presidents had been Guadalupe Victoria 1824-1829; Manuel G. Pedraza, spring of 1829; Vicente Guerrero, also of 1829, who was bumped by Anastacio Bustamenta 1829-1832. In October of that year was the First Convention of Texas at San Felipe—and now, 1833, Santa Anna was the new president and Gomez Farias his vice-president. Yes, he might go, would go, to honor his friend.

Samuel May Williams had always been a vigorous person, endowed with a great personality, winsome, you might say. There was little difference in ages, and Stephen Austin and he enjoyed a warm friendship. Now, Stephen was planning to attend the festivities; he sat with Sam May Williams going over the land ledger.

Sam looked up from the ledger. "Steve, what gets me is why you feel obliged to attend Santa Anna's inaugural celebration. The way he's carrying on, the next thing we know he'll be demanding a crown!"

"So far, Sam, he has been a good friend to Texas. . . ."

"And, he is a Mason, too. . . . How could I ever forget that!" Sam remarked, poking the pencil between his front teeth. "Now what about this land over here along the Sabine?" Sam asked, now letting the pencil slide along the crudely drawn map of that part of east Texas. It is over and beyond the eight hundred families" (February 1831).

"Use your own judgment, Sam, "Stephen replied. "I must see if Rob has my things in the saddlebags. I'm not looking forward to this, you know, especially leaving you with so much to do."

It was dark the next morning as Stephen mounted and rode away.

Stephen went to the celebration of Santa Anna—for his friend. And General Mexia was so pleased that he brought Austin home via schooner.

General Mexia and fleet anchored at the mouth of the Brazos River about three weeks later. Stephen Austin was with him. They were welcomed and soon Jane Long had her tavern resplendent in streamers and summer flowers, orchids and bluebonnets, galardia in low bowls along the board. She was obliged to set up many more and have several settings, so many people wanted to join in the fun. For music there were three fiddlers, four guitars, a tambourine and castanets. The men were in tight trousers, with lace at the throat of their shirts, and the ladies were in dresses with yards and yards of silks and taffetas, organzas, and voille. They were as colorful as they could be swinging out upon the floor in the square dance and the new dance in three-quarter time they called a waltz. Candles gave soft, subdued light from the sconces, and Stephen loved every minute of it. "It's truly a midsummer's dream," he said to Mrs. de Zavala, with whom he most enjoyed dancing.

William Barret Travis was bright-eyed as a schoolboy as he waltzed with Jane Long, and Stephen wondered about them. He hoped fate would smile more kindly upon Mary and himself.

General Mexia mixed and mingled with the Texans as though he had known them always, and he saw Jane Long desert Travis for a dance or so to keep the general happy. "She is a beautiful woman," he thought. "Almost any man could fall in love with her!" She was a lady of Mississippi, of the aristocracy, and she so obviously had loved her doctor husband, James Long, and the memory, even now.

CHAPTER FIFTEEN

In the spring, Stephen prepared for the legislature meeting as usual in Saltillo. He began thinking of making a will. Was it a premonition? Emily's caution about his health? At any rate, he wrote it all out with James Perry one of the executors of his estate. He was troubled. General Santa Anna had taken up arms against the present administration and just now was occupying Vera Cruz. From what intelligence he could get, that area was in rebellion.

And now in Saltillo, doing what he could for his colonists, news reached him telling of the disturbances in many sections. He decided to write Mary and bare his heart, as he formerly wrote to Emily. He said in part . . . "I long for retirement and quiet and I much fear that, in spite of myself I shall be borne along on the current of events into a stormy and troubled sea. Such is life! . . . I urge you to make all necessary preparations to return to Texas as by that time I shall have returned. It must be a June wedding, my dearest. And for my part, plans are already under way for the building of our own dream home."

Anticipating her joyous company was a tonic, but lurking in the back of his mind was the confused state. With the very spirit of progress crushed, the hope for prospects for the colonists was at its lowest ebb. Emigration was almost cut off from the United States, commerce was strangled, garrisons were established at the chief ports in Texas, and one thousand Mexican troops were stationed at strategic points.

Stephen manifested a sincere sympathy for the Mexicans in their new-found independence from Spain. He excused them for much of their seeming animosity against Texans. If a colonist made some threatening remark, as all Texans were wont to do, the Mexican took it at face value, and like as not he found himself in a calaboose. It was nothing less than "revolution"—it seemed to Stephen revolution was all they understood.

The population was inadequate to maintain its proper status as an independent republic against such overwhelming odds as existed in the Mexican ranks. He wrote a message of encouragement in December 29. "I think the government will yield and give us what we ought to have. If not, we shall go for independence and put our trust in ourselves, our rifles—and our God!"

After the cholera epidemic had subsided sufficiently for work to be resumed Stephen had some words with Gomez Farias. He had already made a statement which he would better not have said to the effect that Texas must be made a state by the government or she would make herself one. Many changes took place in 1833.

Santa Anna hung up the question of making "a separate state of Texas." He liked the idea perhaps of a territory. And so the conflict raged. Discouraged, weary and worn, he wrote Mr. Perry in October, "I am tired of this government. They are always in revolution and I believe always will be. I have had more respect for them than they deserve. But I am done with all that." What happened later to Stephen taught him not to write such things.

Again Texas asked for separate statehood; a committee, of which Sam Houston was chairman, was appointed to draft a constitution for the proposed state to be presented to the government of Mexico for approval. David G. Burnet, as chairman of the memorial committee, prepared the document that requested the acceptance of the proposed constitution, for repeal of the immigration law of April 6, 1830, and for tariff reductions.

Three commissioners were appointed to present this document: Stephen Austin, Dr. James Miller, both of San Felipe, and Don Erasmo Seguin of San Antonio. The convention adjourned April 13. On the nineteenth Stephen bundled his important papers off to Mr. Perry, and a statement of his affairs, a list of important private articles, and his will. Stephen realized what a great sacrifice he was making—Mary was no doubt, preparing to join him in Texas—but, hoping it would take no more than four or five months, he began preparations for the journey. He considered a mule to be a safer animal, but twelve hundred miles on a mule's back made him weary. But of course, they would rest along the way, and the other men who were to make the journey to Mexico City with him were close friends. It would probably not be too bad, after all. Stephen figured this jaunt would cost him in the neighborhood of $2,000. "But," he wrote hopefully to Mr. Perry, "if I can succeed in getting a State Government and the 6 of April law repealed I shall be well paid and perfectly satisfied." All the time he realized the spurious Texans might stampede the carefully laid plans of the convention, pushing things too rapidly. . . . And Dr. Miller could not make it due to an epidemic of what he called a "death-dealing sickness." So Stephen, in a rare fit of depression again wrote his brother-in-law:

> If everything had remained quiet until now our chances of success would have been better, but as the current is in motion it must flow on, and if we cannot get a state by peaceable means, I shall then unite with the hottest to get one by other means. If we are to have war, we must all go together, there must be no divisions amongst us, but I hope that calamity will never fall upon Texas.

He was furious on learning that Mexican troops were to be sent into Texas, and fearful lest there be a repetition of the recent disturbances.

Alone, Stephen set out for San Antonio de Bexar riding his faithful mule early on the morning of April 22. Erasmo Seguin, who at that time had just returned from Matamoros to his plantation located some thirty miles below San Antonio, would be unable to accompany Stephen for private reasons of a business nature. He was sorry, Senor Austin—but the truth of the matter was that Seguin had been saturated with lies concerning Stephen Austin's real object in going to Mexico City. Matamoros was confused, like most of Mexico, and Texas as well. These rumors caused Stephen to hold meetings in San Antonio in which he tried to explain his memorial and the interpretation of the law. The San Antonians said they wished the seat of government to be there, but they manifested no serious interest in petitioning for such measures. He recalled D. W. Anthony's note to him: "I sincerely hope you may not be deceived in the constancy and firmness of the people with whom you have been in conference." Mr. Anthony was dear to Stephen. He was the publisher of the *Brazoria Advertiser*, had seen the convention news in English and Spanish, and was disturbed by "demand complete satisfaction of the grievances and insults first; then if refused, proceed with separation of Texas from Coahuila." True, Stephen thought. Coahuila, seeing some sort of handwriting on the wall, had been throwing land grants in every direction, and he, Stephen, was being blamed for that, too! D. W. Anthony feared that if and when Stephen Austin got himself embroiled with the Mexican officials, these erstwhile conventioners with their mad demands would deny any knowledge of the whole affair!

Santa Anna and Farias were inaugurated April 1, 1833. Nevertheless, Stephen rode his mule toward the capital with his material tucked safely in his saddlebags. Excessive rainfall had swollen rivers, which retarded him. Then there was the sweep of cholera ahead, beside, and behind him, so that his heart was troubled as well as his mind, for he was leaving behind him all that was dear to him, and burdened so, he left Bexar May 10 for Goliad, to Matamoros to confer with General Don Vincente Filisola, the commandant general. Here he learned more rumors . . . enough to try his Presbyterian soul. He would have cause to remember Calvin soon. "If a Monarch become tyrannical, depose him!" Rumors flew, such as these: "Texas had declared independence," "an army is being organized to fight the Mexicans," "Austin himself is the author of the Anahuac expedition and of John Austin's actions."

While in the midst of his work and awaiting the action of Congress, Austin was stricken with cholera. His weakened condition, due to the illness he suffered while in Matamoros and to the trying trip on to Mexico City, made this second attack nearly fatal. At this time the Asiatic cholera was spreading with alarming rapidity over Mexico, exacting an alarming death toll. Approximately eighteen thousand deaths occurred during this epidemic in Mexico City alone. So serious had it become that all business came to a standstill, and remained so until the worst had passed.

Stephen had sent for information from his family time and again with silence meeting his anxiety. Emily and James Perry had buried a little daughter, and many of their people. Death and the stench of death rode the Gulf breeze like a prairie fire, leaving no one family exempt. Whole families! At last a letter came from Mr. Perry dated October 26, 1833, telling of the overflow of the Brazos River, followed by swamp fevers, followed immediately by an epidemic of the dread cholera.

It was a severe blow to Stephen, who had pulled through by taking medicines against the sickness. He well knew there were not enough doctors, nor medications back in Texas. Captain John Austin died who had been brother J. E. B. Austin's business partner since the beginning of the colony. In 1822, Stephen, in Mexico City to get his father's land grant validated, had met John Austin, each attracted to the other by the name, and death only broke the friendship formed at that time. He felt this loss greatly. For years John Austin had been constable at San Felipe. Stephen had given John Austin two separate plots for his services, one in Harris County, the other in Brazoria.

Stephen thought his extreme weariness and general sickness was his usual reaction to emotional conflict, but the doctor pronounced him a very sick man, as indeed he was, and with the cholera. Luckily it was not a violent case, but it detained him in Matamoros longer than he had anticipated. He seriously considered returning to San Felipe, for he would be unable to pass many sections where the sickness was concentrated, so he forwarded his material—the memorial—to President Santa Anna through Filisola. He also decided he would never make it to Mexico City on the back of a mule, so boarded a ship for Vera Cruz, thence on to Mexico City by stagecoach.

General Filisola ordered all things back as they had been, and Stephen, learning of these actions, wrote his Texans to comply with their demands, "for the benefit of the farmers and regular merchants." Still, it was the middle of July before he reached the capital. There he immediately interviewed Vice President Farias and the Ministers of Relations, Garcia and Arispe, on the subject of his mission. He was kindly received. They were already conversant with his business at the capital, having perused the memorial forwarded on from Matamoros. Stephen endeavored to clarify the Texas situation as it existed, giving reasons why Texas sought separate statehood.

"We'll give it every consideration, grant the just requests, insofar as it is within the constitutional power to do so," they said.

That same day, filled with hope, Stephen wrote to Mr. Perry that Texas would have statehood in a short time. This, of course, was the quintessence of optimism. He went on to write that in the event the application was refused he saw no alternative but to organize the Texas forces to obtain such object. Always of a conciliatory nature, something was happening to Stephen, for once he was convinced that it was wiser to follow the opposite method, he was willing to throw all his strength and devote his talents to the plan: war instead of persuasion.

From his window Stephen watched the black hearses bearing the dead to their final resting place. . . . Eighteen thousand died while he was there. What was happening at Peach Point? How were Emily and her children, and Mr. Perry? He regretted this journey more than anything that had ever happened to him. But he was here, and so must make the best of it. No word came from Brazoria, Columbia, San Felipe . . . they must be getting the letters which he poured out every day. The very silence told him his worst fears must be actual.

Uneasy lest the state government not be granted, on October 2, he had written the *Ayuntamiento of San Antonio to take the lead in establishing a local government.* And on December 10, he started homeward and reached Saltillo on January 3, 1834. The minister of war had him arrested. Placed in the charge of a soldier escort, he was returned to Mexico City. Yes, indeed, it had been exceedingly rash!

In Texas, all the larger settlements sent messages to Mexico City, declaring that Stephen Austin had been their emissary and not to blame for anything. During this time, Monclova and Saltillo each wanted the capital for its own, and Monclova, in the North, pronounced against Santa Anna; this left the rival government in Saltillo of the South so that Texas was virtually without a government. Austin advised his people to take no part in either "pronuncio." It was the Monclova legislature, however, that squandered the Texas lands, but Saltillo, fearing to be split off from Texas, was grabbing all she could.

Stephen, feeling deserted by his colonists, need not have felt so, for there were selected Peter W. Grayson and Spencer H. Jack as representatives bearing memorials to President Santa Anna for Austin's release, bearing also a fabulous purse.

It was to "a scene of things that no human being can unravel" and Santa Anna was very unfavorable. Santa Anna was weaving his web. He wanted to be the dictator of a centralized government. It was through the efforts of an influential Mexican, Pascual Villar, that a bond was secured for Stephen's release. It would take three hundred thousand dollars, but this release was not to be immediate. On Christmas Day, 1834 he was given the freedom of the city.

CHAPTER SIXTEEN

Thinking that he had accomplished all that was possible at this time, he started on his homeward journey December 10, reaching Saltillo January 3, 1834. Immediately, he called upon the Commandant General Lemus, who informed him of the order from the minister of war for his arrest. He was, according to this order, to be placed in charge of an officer and returned to Mexico City as a prisoner, charged with having committed an offense against the law by writing a letter to the San Antonio Ayuntamiento, a copy of which had been forwarded to the officials.

It has been seen with the greatest regret and surprise the exacting plea . . . and there is no doubt that the measure which you propose is exceedingly rash.

So Stephen found himself a political prisoner in one of the dungeons of the Inquisition. He was not allowed to speak to anyone, except the guard. One day Stephen looked up and saw his old friend Father Muldoon coming into his cell. They talked hurriedly for as long as time permitted. Then, Stephen began receiving books and paper and materials for writing, and he used them diligently to reach friends far flung across Texas, across the broad land. There were those in official places within Mexican government who knew Stephen was suffering for something he had not done. In the end, representatives took the bit in their mouths, as Stephen had done, and approached the authorities in behalf of Stephen.

He was removed to the Prison Acordada in the City of Mexico in June of 1834. He wrote several letters, to John Wharton and Sam Williams, his partner and secretary, saying that there were those who had set out to ruin him, by keeping him a virtual prisoner, to keep an investigation from bearing fruit. Stephen proposed to discover how Sam Houston had acquired Hayden Edwards land grants for the Galveston Bay and Texas Land Company and then transferred them to those men who now occupied them. Sam Houston had a New York contact by the name of Swartwart who had made the journey to Texas. But one day he would be a free man. Sam Williams had done a fine job of taking care of the colonists . . . he sure had, Stephen thought.

During that year Santa Anna sent out spies to find if the colonists were really in rebellion. Peter Grayson and Spencer Jack arrived in Mexico City bearing memorials to President Santa Anna for Austin's release. He was released under a three-hundred-thousand-dollar bond. While at liberty in the city, he labored for a good wagon road to Chihuahua. An exemption of duties on cotton bagging, iron, steel, and several other items was obtained. Since cotton was in demand, he recommended that premium be given on cotton shipped to Vera Cruz and Tampico. New mail routes would be beneficial. And again he wrote Mr. Perry: "The political character of the country seems to partake of its geological features—all is volcanic."

With the two opposing parties long in conflict, memorials from each pouring into the National Congress, President Santa Anna, who had been elected leader of the Republicans, suddenly deserted his party and joined the centralists. Saltillo immediately declared for Santa Anna and at the same time obtained the support of General Martin Perfecto de Cos, Commandant General of the Eastern Interior Provinces, including Texas.

Stephen had time to think back to Missouri, for at that time, Missouri was the Far West. In the Great Valley, Indians hunted and built their burial mounds. Trappers roamed. The Thirteen Colonies had become the United States, but the mouth of their route to the sea was controlled by Spain. Yet, land-hungry men came, following the trail Daniel Boone had blazed. They came through the Cumberland Gap from southeast and north. Since there were few roads, colonists used rivers and hacked out the wilderness to build their log houses. Many of them were returned emigrants, unpaid Revolutionary War veterans, for the new government had no treasury. But it did have fertile land and virgin in the Great Valley and so the government paid them in land. It was a land fruitful with wild plums, grapes, dandelions, poke salad. Game was there for the taking. Utopia!

Soon, there was a boat landing and the floating stores would find them; trade flourished. They exchanged their farm products for articles their wives and they themselves needed.

So the rivers, the Monongahela, the Allegheny, the Ohio, the Cumberland and the Tennessee, and the mighty Mississippi carried the flow of merchandise to New Orleans for trans-shipment to the world.

Then, in 1800 New Orleans was still under Spanish Government, but when Napoleon demanded its cession to France and threatened to close the port, Napoleon wanted, now that Europe was peaceful, to conquer an American empire. The New Orleans docks were flooded with goods, perishable or not. The western farmers came down upon them rifle in hand to chase off the French. Things were moving fast; James Monroe hastened to France and President Jefferson wrote his friend, Pierre Samuel de Pont de Nemours, a power of influence in France, to apprise Napoleon that Britain and the United States would form a coalition against him. Napoleon had had bad luck in Santo Domingo, would not sell New Orleans, but the whole of Louisiana for fifteen million dollars. Robert Livingston, minister to France from the United States, shuddered. Fifteen million dollars? Where would the infant nation acquire that fantastic sum? What did they need with so much land? The new country went wild. To appease their apprehension Jefferson dispatched his kinsman, Meriwether Lewis, and Clark, a friend, on an expedition to the far west to ascertain just what he had paid to France in the amount of fifteen million dollars.

Stephen moseyed on up the trail leading from Mexico City to his home. The mule's back had long since ceased to be flesh and blood, and had become a mount of solid concrete! How he longed for a jug of Martin Varner's rum. He recalled Varner's tract was of the First Old Three Hundred 1824, and that he had opened his distillery in

1827. Varner was a close neighbor of Dr. Phelps.

He had ridden that mule from Mexico City, up through San Luis Potosi, Saltillo, and four days ago, he passed on through Monclova. He enjoyed the scenic wonders in certain areas of the Sierra Madre Mountains, where large white-tailed deer faced up to him for a moment and like lightning, fled the place. Many and unknown kinds of birds were around with beautiful and recognized songs—and their colors! Brightest black, red, yellow, and blue! Then he saw Piedras Negras, where the farming was so good, and here at the open markets he loaded up the donkeys.

Mission San Jose de Aguayo, "Queen of the Missions," was established in 1720. It was the most complete mission Stephen had yet seen . . . not so old, but famous, even then. The wall of the compound had dwellings for the Indians, a carpenter shop, a saddle and leather-working shop, a mill, certainly the oldest in Texas, a granary, and barracks where the soldiers of His Majesty, King of Spain housed his soldiers—for protection of the resident padres. The escort remarked, "We'll spend the night here."

Padre Muldoon had told him of the rose window of San Jose, and now he was seeing it for the first time. It took no artist to realize why it had taken Peter Huizar seven years to so delicately carve the stone of the rose window. Magnificent!

The next morning they continued on their journey, to Mexico City. Since his Spanish escort was not allowed to talk, conversation was omitted and Stephen let his mind review Texas, the colonists, their desire for separation from Coahuilla—for Coahuilla officials saw the handwriting on the wall, and was squandering the lands of Texas to an unbelievable extent. Surely it could not be Samuel May Williams. He had always been a clever man with figures, but honest. He would swear it. Then there was Sam Houston, who had known William Wharton and his brother John Wharton back in Tennessee. They were thick as hops. Sam Houston had aligned himself with the Whartons, and they were for annexation. Stephen was a Mexican citizen—had sworn allegiance to that government. And so he had quietly gone about keeping his colonists in line. The Whartons were working like beavers constructing a dam, so much so that Texas began filling up with all kinds of men of a questionable character. Stephen had long since looked upon Nacogdoches as a hotbed of insurgents, and Sam Houston in no uncertain charges which hurt Sam's feelings. But Stephen did not retract his charges. As they rode the tortuous miles Stephen remembered that Miss Anna Raguet's father was for one step at a time—could Sam Houston see the folly of his ways in time? Yes, Henry Raguet was for independence—but one step at a time. Henry Raguet did not only have a beautiful daughter, he also had a brain in his head.

Stephen had left directly after the convention for a quick trip to return immediately to Sam Felipe. But Destiny in his suit of armor had other directives for Stephen Austin—two years he would be away. They reached Mexico City and his fate. It was hot and the middle of July, but the city was resplendent in its summer flowery dress. Palm trees waved in the breeze, and bougainvillia swayed from iron trellises. The streets and plazas were quiet, however, for it was the time of the siesta, when everything closed up and all slept in the heat of the day for two-three hours. Even the political buildings closed. But they had not long to wait.

With the few sheets of paper he wrote from his prison to the people of Texas, "I do not blame the government for arresting me, and I particularly request that there be no excitement about it. . . . Keep quiet, discountenance all revolutionary measures or men . . . have no more conventions. . . ."

Sam Houston had changed sides back in Texas. While packing his bags for a journey, he told the people not to plunge Texas into a war when they were not prepared to fight one!

Stephen recognized the place as the dungeons of the Inquisition. Not that! Si, senor. . . .

He had never seen so many emaciated faces from which all hope had long since faded. One cried out, seeing who it was, "My God, Mr. Austin . . . what'nhell have you done that they bring you to this rotten hole?" When Stephen would have replied that it was because he had no better brain than to write when silence and patience might have accomplished the same, the soldier escort ordered, "You are not to speak to the other prisoners. Do you understand that?" Stephen shrugged his shoulders and entered his cell. But he knew that face, and sooner or later he would find a name to go with it. In this dark lonely cell, removed from the sixty or so' prisoners he found there by several cells, he would have liked to write some letters, again wondering if they'd ever reach their appointed destination.

"No, you may not have writing material, Senor Austin. No books, nothing." And the iron bars swung closed and locked. Like a common criminal! He soon heard why. "You have committed a most dreadful thing against your government, senor." Stephen watched the soldier turn his back and walk away and every vestige of hope and strength drained away, leaving Stephen so limp that he was obliged to lie down on the filthy mat on a rat-ridden floor. Oh yes, I have committed a most dreadful thing against my government, he laughed tiredly. I am a "political prisoner" and I can rot in this dismal dungeon.

After many days in solitary he saw the good father of San Felipe darkening the small aperture with his amazing bulk. "My son!" Father Muldoon murmured, letting fall writing material and books.

CHAPTER SEVENTEEN

In the spring of 1833, Sam Houston was riding in from San Antonio. He had had a visit with Jim Bowie, and had taken care of some land matters. Jim was alone, his wife and two children having gone on a visit to her parents in Mexico. Houston considered this journey a most profitable one. The newest and best client of his law office in Nacogdoches was a newly organized concern, headed by Anthony Dey, a banker. The business enterprise was called the Galveston Bay and Texas Land Company. Houston had been unsuccessful with Chief Tarshar of the Caddoes along Red River, living mostly in Louisiana, but there was that Hayden Edwards tract sufficient for his Cherokees. He simply must have the Cherokees in Texas, by fair means or foul, if his aim of obtaining Texas for Jackson were to end satisfactorily. Still, Houston had not become a Mexican citizen. The only pressure he ever had was that his land deals were to be only to Catholics.

Twilight came and with it the March winds cut across the prairie. Houston was aching with the cold. The night was dark, the darkest he could remember, and yet the sky glittered with millions of stars as he thought about it later. An old peach tree he had once had last year burst out with flowers and fruit in a last magnificent display. In the fall it died. He saw a star fall, and he thought how a soul was ascending to meet Jesus, a childish relic, but when the whole heavens gave forth with a firelight so stupendous he might have been able to see a pine needle, cold chills coursed up and down his spine, and the hair on the nape of his neck bristled. And through his mind ran a song his mother used to sing, "When the stars begin to fall. . . ." He hoped that Father Muldoon was still in town.

The stars fell over Texas. They fell and fell, scattering across the sky in all directions as though they would go, and it mattered not in which direction. Father Miguel Muldoon stood on the gallery of Adolphe Stearne's house in Nacogdoches with Senora Stearne and her family. "It's certainly an awesome sight," Father Muldoon said, making the sign while his eyes penetrated the wide sky. It seemed there was no space left . . . that all the stars in the heavens were coming down. And out of the darkness galloped Sam Houston in fright, utterly devastated with one thought in mind—if this was the end of the world, his soul was in no shape to meet God.

"Good evening," he said and they were talking at once, giving an impression of chaos. "Come with me, Father," Sam said, taking hold of the priest's arm. "I need to make a confession . . . and I want to be baptized, if that can be arranged."

"You'll need a sponsor," he replied and called Senora Stearne. "And we must go to the church, where Pere Chambondeau is resting. He is the confessor of Eva Rosine (Mrs. Stearne) and he comes from Louisiana once a month. You might even consider this his parish." That Houston readily agreed to, since it appeared time was of the essence.

Houston's Godmother, Senora Stearne, stood by him as he knelt at the altar, and was properly baptized with witnesses from the Stearne family, and a few stragglers who also had come into the church to try for ablution. Terror reigned in Nacogdoches and the stars kept falling. Houston arose, and kissing Senora Stearne on her ample cheek, said, "Madre mio," while the little red-faced Jew looked on happily. It mattered not why it happened; Houston was now of the fold. It would boost the church treasury—gratitude always had.

"We now celebrate!" the Rhinelander exclaimed. He was the alcalde of Nacogdoches, and whatever he did was all right. So wine flowed like the Brazos after a hard rain, and a feast followed.

"You'd think," Sam Houston observed on the gallery where they were drinking, "there wouldn't a one be left. Why, you don't even miss these that fell." Under the trellis and vines already blooming, the gallery was well-screened from the wind and the fire of the barbecue on which lay many beautiful steaks warmed him. A real red letter day! He had secured Sam Norriss's land grant, and Hayden Edwards's as well. He had joined the church. He was full of wine and excellent food. Yes, this had been quite a day. There was a day to remember. Yet, in the back of his mind, he wondered what Miss Anna Raguet would think.

Anna was seventeen years old, a daughter of Colonel Raguet, a wealthy Swiss merchant, who lived in the biggest house in town. She was of importance socially as well as politically. Miss Anna was talented on the French harp and was a butterfly in pink. And so having the family Stearne squared Sam Houston with Raguet, and no doubt it would make an alliance worth the bother, if he could only court and win Miss Anna's hand. Mr. Henry Raguet was for independence, but a step at a time, not like the spurious leader of the party, William Wharton. So it had become expedient for Houston to join Stephen Austin in the counsel of keeping quiet and not plunging Texas into war before she is prepared for it. Sam had decided to follow the one step at a time, progressing favorably on two fronts: Miss Anna and her father. "Salting the cow to get the calf," people said.

Sam Houston, now a moderate wrote: "All new states are infested more or less, by a class of noisy, second-rate men, who are always in favor of rash and extreme measure. But Texas is absolutely infested by them. What we need is a leader, brave enough for any trial, wise enough for any emergency, and cool enough for any crisis." So Sam decided he was that man.

It was too bad that Stephen Austin was in prison. This situation was all right with Sam Houston. The first ire had died away and the Texans seemed to have forgotten that Austin was in prison in their behalf. What Sam needed was time. So he mounted old Jack for a trip. Oh yes, he would yet rule in the Halls of Montezuma!

Houston visited Baltimore, Philadelphia and New York. In New York he met the stockholders in the Galveston Bay and Texas Land Company, and enjoyed himself socially. With one of these stockholders, Jackson's erstwhile close friend Samuel Swartwart, Houston had some interesting conversations before he left for Texas.

In Little Rock the populace reviewed him. General Houston was one of the most magnificent specimens of physical manhood I have ever seen. . . . I first saw him on the public road a few miles out of town. He was riding a splendid bay horse, and his saddle plates and buckles were of silver and in profusion. He was enveloped in a Mexican poncho which was richly ornamented with Mexican embroidery work. When again I saw him on the streets of Little Rock . . . it was hard to realize that this elegantly appearing gentleman had voluntarily given up home and kindred and official preferment to join himself to a band of half-civilized Indians, and had adopted their dress . . . and habits of life.

In December of 1834 (Austin was still in prison in Mexico City) an Englishman arrived at Washington, Arkansas, an out-of-the-way log hamlet thirty miles from the Texas boundary. He wrote:

I was not desirous of remaining long at this place. General Houston was here, leading a mysterious sort of life, shut up in a small tavern, seeing nobody by day and sitting up all night. The world gave him credit for passing these waking hours in the study of *trente et quarante* and *sept ' lever*; but I had seen too much passing before my eyes, to be ignorant that this little place was the rendezvous where a much deeper game . . . was playing. There were many persons at this time in the village from the States lying adjacent to the Mississippi, under the pretense of purchasing government lands, but whose real object was to encourage the settlers in Texas to throw off their allegiance to the Mexican government. Many of these individuals were personally acquainted with me; they knew I was not with them, and would naturally conclude I was against them. Having nothing whatever in common with their plan, and no inclination to forward or oppose them, I perceived that the longer I stayed the more they would find reason to suppose I were a spy.

This intelligence found its way into Gail Borden's hands, hence into the newspaper he published, as it scattered newswise into dozens across the country. Gail saved a copy for Stephen, who would certainly be coming back to San Felipe shortly; the amnesty date was in July, at which time he would be free to go.

By August 1834 so much had happened they said in Texas, Stephen Austin was a prisoner and nothing would do but for Peter Grayson and a friend to hasten to Mexico City as commissioners

93

from Texas in behalf of Stephen. Others had broken jail and wandered through the waste lands trying to reach Texas and home.

At Nacogdoches, citizens gathered at the Old Stone Fort, at which time Sam Houston addressed them. He called for a general consultation and he was elected commander of the militia at this point. The two gentlemen arrived Mexico City and set about business.

"The people of Texas will never submit to a dictator!" Trouble was on the wind and by August 28, 1835, Mexico had thousands in Texas for the purpose of being on hand when the change of government took place. Already angered by the arrest of Austin and other men the people of Texas declared not to give up any individual to the military authorities and that made the date of the consultation of all Texans through her representatives indispensable and the mood of immediacy. All across the country, "They're declaring out there, war is our only recourse . . . there is no other remedy but to defend our rights, our country and ourselves by force of arms." As Peter talked Stephen had listened in his dark cell.

Stephen could see the plains of March waving in bluebonnets, the coreopsis of April, Indian paintbrush, purple thistle, claret cup, phlox, dogwood and redbud and the weeks merged into months as he sat or paced in his cell and remembered the land he loved and its ever-changing face. He was homesick. "How soon will you know?"

"Tomorrow, I imagine," Peter said. "They listened most respectfully, and agreed it might have been a spurious action on their part."

Father Muldoon was waiting for Stephen at the door of the dungeon of the Inquisition, waiting patiently as was his nature.

Stephen was pale from his long living in his dark cell, and his clothing hung upon his emaciated frame like a scarecrow's. Father Muldoon held his hand while Stephen's eyes became accustomed to the bright sunlight, which seemed to be brighter in the seven-thousand-foot altitude than at sea level in the Gulf land of Texas. In a few moments Father Muldoon explained again to Stephen, Although the officer had already informed him of the latitude he might expect.

"You are still a prisoner, Stephen," Father Muldoon explained. "And the bond your friends went for you was three hundred thousand dollars. But they were not allowed to enter the prison, again and after they went bond for you they were ordered out of Mexico City."

"How long do I remain here, Father Muldoon—or did they say? I'm kept in the dark all the way around, it seems."

"You have the freedom of the city . . . come and go as you will, but see that you don't decide to skip out, or your friends'll be obliged to forfeit their three hundred thousand dollars!" Muldoon laughed with his belly shaking like Santa Claus; it was so silly a remark like that. "But there'll be amnesty provided in a few months for all political prisoners. Have fun discovering the many interesting places here, while you have nothing else to do."

They walked on to the zocala, and soon found a place to have refreshment. "You know, Stephen, that chocolate is the drink here as coffee and tea are to you Texans. . . . Some years ago, the conquistadors found the Aztec of Mexico adding bits of an orchid's fragrant seed pod to their cocoa, Vanilla planifolia; they tried it and found it most excellent, adding much to the flavor of their cocoa. Strange that the plants traveled to Europe, thence to Madagascar . . . so many orchids and such a variety you'd think they would have kept it to themselves. But today the island of Madagascar supplies half the world's needs. The vanilla flower lasts but one day, and must be pollinated by hand, since there are no insects created for that duty."

"What do you hear from Texas?" Stephen asked, sipping on his cup of cocoa and enjoying the delicate flavor of vanilla.

"You may have heard of Elder John Parker and . . ."

"Not one word. Begin at the beginning."

"These people, nine or ten families came to Texas—I presume they'd been run out of wherever it was they had lived formerly. It seems they came from Missouri. At any rate, there was Silas and James Parker of the family of John Parker, Elder John Parker.

"Mormons. Good people." Stephen thought about them and what a trial it must be to be of their faith. They made good neighbors if you could abide their many wives. "What happened to Elder Parker?"

"Dear me," exclaimed Father Muldoon. "You seem to know more about them than I—Mormons?"

"They lived in Missouri until they got into a fight. Some went one way, others another. But what happened to Parker?"

"They built a fort since you've been away. And were doing fine —that is, until several hundred Comanches came down upon them. Just about everybody lost life, save for about five persons, including Cynthia Ann Parker, age nine. Nothing more is known of their fate."

"Why, Sam Houston had a treaty with them!" Stephen said.

He was alone now. Almost he could hear Sam Houston making his speech and remembered the Old Stone Fort with infinite detail. It had been built in 1779 as a Spanish trading post and fort to store supplies for trading with the Indians. It had been the scene of many strange happenings; the oath of allegiance was administered among others to Sam Houston, James Bowie, David Crockett and Thomas J. Rusk. In its four-five-foot-thick stone walls the first newspapers were printed. There had been in its time men who sought to take over Texas—six flags had flown over it; Spain, 1800 Nolan, Magee-Guttierez, Long, Hayden Edwards' Fredonian Rebellion, Republic of Mexico. The eagle and snake waved from its pavilion now. There were four massive Indian mounds where through the centuries, the white Indians had lived and died, children of Nacogdoches, the Caddoan, people so like certain of the inhabitants of Mexico City and its environs that Stephen wondered about them. Tall, fair and blue-eyed they were, with long straight yellow hair, almost the color of the galardia that grew all along the sandy stretches of the Gulf coast. He decided to get to sleep if tomorrow he might be free of this dungeon. The men had certainly lifted his spirits. Just to know his friends had not forgotten him was quite enough. Stephen was satisfied with that.

CHAPTER EIGHTEEN

As the sun sank behind the hills of Chapultepec, mariachi bands, the players dressed in colorful charro suits, began their serenade most often in the Zocalo where the Great Stone Calendar rested. . . . Where had Stephen seen those brightly fashioned charro suits? He delved into his first visit into the land of these people—of course, it was Verimendi and Seguin, the commissioners who met him in

Natchitoches to escort him into Texas. Their black broadcloth and rainbow Saltillo serapes! How would he look in one?

That evening he attended a game of jai-alai, a game brought, they said, over from the Basque section of Spain and played on a three-walled court almost a block long. There were four players using a wicker basket strapped to their arms to catch and pitch the balls which are of skin but feel and sound like wooden tennis balls. About the same game played by the Indians was called pelote.

Stephen was not long in discovering also that Mexico was the biggest silver-producing nation, he reckoned, in the world, considering their fabulous output from nearby mines. But they had only two semi-precious gems, the mauve amethyst and the blueish, green-orange opals. "All the others are imported, senor." There was some real jade in Mexico, but no one seemed to know where it came from.

Stephen felt better healthwise in Mexico. Rain, usually in short afternoon showers, came mostly in June, July, August and September, giving the air a cool, refreshing tang. Climate is determined vertically rather than horizontally. The combination of altitude and tropical location makes it possible to adjust the temperature to the individual taste—"climate à la carte" the natives say. For instance the average mean temperature in Mexico City is 68 degrees F., but at Cuernavaca, 2,934 feet lower, 81 degrees F. Thus one day they were journeying through pine forests, and the next were entering the land of swaying palm trees.

Stephen's mind wandered back to Natchitoches, and to St. Denis, its founder. Such a time ago. Cadillac, in 1714, sent this young officer to establish a post at Natchitoches to stop encroaching Spaniards, to stop them from taking possession of that region. So he placed a garrison of Canadians at Natchitoches and built a fort he called St. John the Baptiste, or San Juan Bautista, the first permanent settlement within the limits of the present state of Louisiana, and three years older than New Orleans. With a few companions he left the fort for Mexico City to establish trade with that country. But the Mexicans seized him, as they had Stephen—and sent him on to Mexico City as a prisoner. Two years later he was allowed to return, not to Natchitoches, but to Mobile. There was never a reason given for his arrest.

One learns many things, a word here and there; put together they come to mean something, that Stephen Austin, the empressario, had declared for separation of Texas from Coahuilla, and of course senor, it has always been so, why change it? Or that the man had shown he meant to direct the ways of Texas—the directives he sent to San Antonio de Bexar, to set in motion the wheels of self-government! And the reply he had received might have told him the seat of government at San Antonio was loyal to Santa Anna and had delivered his traitorous message to the hands of the authorities.

Free at last, Stephen decided to go back to Texas by ship—which would give him an opportunity to visit Vera Cruz and Santa Anna who resided at his hacienda there. Enroute to Vera Cruz, he would travel through some of Mexico's loveliest country, the antithesis of everything he hated so on the more direct route north which was mile on mile of desert, barren wastes almost two hundred years before Cortez, the Aztecs had built a great capital city on what was originally two reed-covered mud banks or islands. Gardens were planted in this rich earth, that little by little these floating isalnds anchored themselves and no longer floated . . . this was the very beginning of the City of Eternal Spring.

What a riot of crimson bougainvillia, roses, gardenias, orchids and camelias, and not so far off was Mt. Popocatepetl, 17,782 feet; and Mt. Iztaccihuatl, 16,060 feet. There was such a variety of foods: corn, rice, sugar, wheat, beans, tomatoes, tobacco, cotton, cocoa, sisal and bananas. He was enjoying the city for the last time, for he was given amnesty along with several others and his passport was for July 11, 1835.

Stephen had considered returning by land, but decided against it, for travel by boat would certainly be easier than jogging hundreds of miles on the back of a mule. He spent his free time visiting the cathedral, museum and university. He walked along the Street of the Dead, saw the pyramids to the sun at close range and the pyramid of the moon. They were at either end of the Calle del Muerta. And the university, a great institution, amazed him. It was old already, having been established the same year that De Soto made his expedition into the Gulf country. Something would come of it, he decided. He would tell the Mexicans exactly how he felt about schools for Texas, and again he was filled with the almost overwhelming desire to build a seminary of learning on the Colorado River, so that he studied the great university with that plan and its execution uppermost in his mind.

The day finally came, July 11, that he went to Santa Anna, to visit Antonio Lopez at his hacienda in Vera Cruz, and from that port sailed to New Orleans.

The dead had been buried and the country settled back into the business of living and working. Mercantile houses reopened, blacksmith shop, saddleshop, taverns, all busy, booming. Yet, Stephen watched the sudden changes in Mexico government with much apprehension. Revolution and upheavals were the rule. General Mexia was in command of the southern area. A number belonging to the central aristocratic party—Bustamente, Aristo and others—were banished from Mexico for life. General Pedro Lemus was appointed to succeed General Filisola.

Stephen had no confidence in Gomez Farias, as a friend of Texas. "Texas must be made a state by the government, or she'll make herself one!" he declared to Gomez Farias.

Farias was greatly angered by the presumptuous demand. "You are threatening the government of Mexico, Senor Austin?"

"No, I was not making a threat—only stating a perfectly obvious fact!" Both men sprang to their feet with Farias exclaiming, "Ah, we have already heard rumors that you secretly work to annex Texas to the United States of the North. And now, you make it abundantly clear such information was no rumor!"

"I meant no threat," Stephen remarked. "I only wished you to know the temper of the people." Stephen extended his hand. "I have always been a loyal citizen of Mexico. I hope we can keep our relations on a cordial basis."

Stephen must have impressed Gomez Farias for the vice president, lost no time rushing this news on to Santa Anna—and which now obliged Austin to clarify

Now to get to Vera Cruz he must travel for miles of tropical jungle—mimosa, birds, parrots, macaws and mockingbirds in indescribable brilliance, enough to make a painter ashamed. Never were there such bright flashes of color. There were great herds of black oxen and bamboo huts inhabited by a half-negro race who lived mostly on what was at hand, bananas and stuff, and all this was a part of Manga de Clavo, the hacienda of Antonio Lopez, the great Santa Anna of Vera Cruz.

Stephen rode on east on the vanilla road—vanilla in its natural form, the climbing orchid, the cream-white xanah and its cultivation. It is the eastern watershed on which rain-bearing clouds from the Gulf dump their moisture and the hot tropic sun makes the vegetation flourish.

The road had climbed another thousand feet so that now at eight thousand feet he felt giddy. When Stephen left Mexico City, he passed Rio Frio, San Martin, over to Cholula to Puebla, and turning left after a view of the beautiful cathedral there, continued on to Vera Cruz, and the Hacienda de Santa Anna. Antonio Lopez and he must have a meeting of the mind if Texas was ever to become the great state it could be. Having known Santa Anna for many years, always as a friend, he could see no reason why they could not discuss Texas and its problems sanely and without ire—its educational as well as political, for always peering over the horizon, almost daily was a new disturbance, the latest being the American-turned-Mexican citizen at the customs in Velasco, the shipping point of his colonists.

The road now was a twisting, tortured, narrow trail, beat down by the natives carrettas and mules.

He would be entering Jalapa on the road to Vera Cruz where he might spend the night. The next morning, the baskets he thought adequate were by now bulging. It seemed to Stephen he couldn't resist the lovely things he found along the way. As he stood on the crest he could see the most impressive of all spectacular views of the volcanoes. After so long in Mexico City he could distinguish them, now glistening. Popo is the gracefully pointed volcano while the Sleeping Woman lies on her bier wrapped in a mantle of eternal snow. Ah, yes . . . Stephen thought, he would never forget them whatever else he may be facing. He had reached the ten-thousand-foot apex of the Sierra Nevada Cordelierra. The church city of Cholula had given him much to think about, for 365 churches, one for every day of the year, was simply beyond his comprehension. As old Rob used to say, "We all aimin' for the same heaven. . . ."

At Puebla he found some magnificent serapes which were made at the nearby village of Tlaxcala, but had to pass them by. Already he had been on the road a week, and glad he was that he had made this decision for a ship at Vera Cruz. His rump was numb as a stone. He went across windy and arid slopes where maguey and cactus were about all he saw. Then the road dropped down into pine forests, and apple orchards, and berry vines bearing heavily. Here he discovered the best apple cider he'd ever tasted. Beyond and below this temperate zone he found coffee and banana plantations.

Now the rain forest gave way to pineapple, mango, and sugar cane. Cocoa palms waved dreamily near the shore of the Carribean Sea.

Certainly word had preceded him, for Santa Anna was awaiting him at the marvelous entrance. He was a man of medium height, with black hair and eyes and pale melancholy features, but his manners were courtly, and Stephen's welcome gracious. Never could it be said of him that he was not conscious of his image. Stephen had seen him so often in the legislature, had known him in many places with admiration, but Santa Anna was never so grand as when he was playing the host at Manga de Clavo. He was simply superb.

Steven explained the incident with Farias.

They spoke of other matters as well. Santa Anna let his eyes wander across the dismal swamp—eyes that seemed to see things not present, seeming to look back instead of forward. "Yes," he said, "the great civilization of the Maya existed before William the Conqueror came to England; before the Crusades moved across Europe; before Charlemagne was crowned and before Genghis Khan conquered China. Before Cuzco was founded in Peru, or Tenochtitlan, the Aztec capital was even begun on the lake and swamps that were to become Mexico City."

The beautiful Senora Lopez, often called Santa Anna, brought out to the verandah, a pot of chocolate, frothy and delicious. She did not remain, however, but told the men good night and left them.

"You see, Stephen, five hundred years before Columbus discovered America, Maya was deserted and in ruins, their great days only a legend, but I'll show you tomorrow about the land of the Maya— not more than one or two of their cities, for your ship will be in soon."

"I'd like that, Antonio, but I shan't have time this trip. I must get organized for the journey home. I suppose I could donate the little donkeys to the children?" Stephen said, and rising, remarked, "I hope you will come into Texas, to San Felipe soon. . . . I should like very much for our people to know you." Remembering General Cos he added, "As a friend, of course."

"I promise you to be in Texas as a friend or foe; in either case, you can count on it." Santa Anna laughed, also rising, but was there a razor edge there, or was he just imagining?

Stephen found Yucatan to be a hot, flat land, blessed part of the time with cool Gulf breezes. They grew henequen or sisal which they made into rope or twine. The plant grows well in that climate. It is a spiny plant, as a century plant of Texas, which is the same family.

There was a maze of underground rivers, Santa Anna explained, which are called cenotes, which probably accounted for the tens of thousands of windmills pumping up water everywhere.

Along the way, for they were going to Quintana Roo which was south of Vera Cruz, quite a long way south, he saw oval thatched huts which were typical homes of the Mayas and had been for untold centuries.

The religious centers were pointed out to him, temples, public buildings, and the huts of many thousands scattered about for miles, for the people did not live in the stone buildings. They sailed on southward, hugging the coast line where possible, and Stephen saw Tulum set high on a rocky point with a breath-taking and somewhat unreal stone sentry tower—one amongst fifty-six such structures, Santa Anna explained. "It is a walled city. There are courts, temples and pyramids open to the sea . . . it is the other three sides where the walls are."

They reached an island of coconut trees, swaying dreamily in a gentle Gulf breeze: ancient, uninhabited, beautiful Quintana Roo.

"It is the one thing that breaks my heart with its beauty," Santa Anna said in a strange sad timbre. "How can mortal man see it, and be the same man when he leaves?" They walked along the sandy beach and came to the maze of lagoons called Xelha, where clear waters abounded with a myriad tropical fish, yellow, red, pink, blue and black—jewels darting hither and thither, sporting happily in the crystal lagoon.

They found a large cave which they peered into. It had an altar at the far end; otherwise it was empty. Orchids in profusion scented the air. Lonely stone towers faced the wild sea and the quiet off-shore, coral gardens where lobster, and pampano, snapper and mackerel were quite at home. Wild turkeys and boars and small game meandered as though they owned the island—which, in fact, they did, being its only inhabitants.

Santa Anna remarked as they set sail northward, "What do you think of what you have seen, Stephen?"

"Words fail me," Stephen replied truthfully.

Two days later the vessel lay at anchor at Vera Cruz. Stephen said with much anxiety, "I hope I don't miss my boat!"

"Don't worry, my friend. They'll move toward New Orleans when I give the word."

The next morning Stephen with the two donkeys loaded up and Santa Anna riding along with him to bring Stephen's animal and the donkeys back to his hacienda, bade goodbye to the lovely Senorita Lopez shortly after breakfast. It was the last time he would ever see her. Santa Anna, holding the bridles of the three animals with one hand, waved with the other for a long while.

Stephen waved too, and wondered in his troubled mind what sort of destiny was governing their two lives—for certainly if he had ever had a friend it was Antonio Lopez de Santa Anna. He began lugging his gifts to his stateroom, if so it could be called, with the help of one porter.

Antonio Lopez . . . is he an ambitious man? Why when saying adieu was there that look of preponderant sorrow? Dismay? There was another Anthony, Marc by name. . . .

The blue-green of the Gulf rose up and swayed downward. Stephen's face was wrapped in a gentle breeze, more or less as the ship sailed on—wrapped in thoughts that he had never had before. The scene of Julius Caesar had not at the time burdened him, but now he remembered it most vividly, for he had decided that Antonio Lopez was an ambitious man . . . that friend became foe when he stood in the way. He was already a dictator! And when monarchs . . . should be deposed. So he recalled the scene which so burdened him; "O Caesar . . ." "Hence! wilt thou lift up Olympus?" "Great Caesar!" "Doth not Brutus bootless kneel?" "Speak, hands, for me!" Casca stabs Caesar in the neck. Caesar catches him by the arm. He is then stabbed by several other conspirators, and at last by Marcus Brutus. Then, Caesar seeing his friend about to stab him, said, "Et tu, Brute? Then, fall, Caesar." Then the people cried, "Liberty! Freedom! Tyranny is dead!" as they washed their hands in Caesar's blood.

Then, Brutus endeavoring to clear the minds of this act, said that he also loved Caesar: "Not that I loved Caesar less, but that I loved Rome more" . . . but Caesar was an ambitious man!

Stephen once or twice caught sight of land. They would be nearing Texas Coast presently, and his joy was mixed with sorrow— Antonio Lopez meant to subdue Texas, and himself, if it came to that. But now the scene changes. Marc Anthony enters. . . . "I come to bury Caesar, not to praise him. The evil that men do, lives after them; The good is oft interred with their bones; So let it be with

Caesar. . . . He was my friend, faithful and just to me; But Brutus says he was ambitious, And Brutus is an honorable man. . . . When that the poor have cried, Caesar wept. Ambition should be made of sterner stuff; Yet Brutus says he was ambitious. . . . I thrice presented him with a kingly crown, Which he did thrice refuse. Was this ambition? Yet Brutus says he was ambitious. . . . Men have lost their reason"

Tears filled Stephen's eyes then as he saw the scene—My heart is in the coffin there with Caesar, And I must pause till it come back to me."

The tears were not for Caesar—they were for Santa Anna, who would strive for Mexico . . . and Stephen Austin. He turned now to his stateroom. Yes, that was the way it was. He must tell his spirit that while it might appear that Santa Anna was ambitious, it may be that he loves his country and does not wish to see it torn asunder by the Americanos. Several days later, his ship glided to the wharf at New Orleans.

CHAPTER NINETEEN

The transition from a seven-thousand-foot elevation with clear crisp air to an elevation of three or four feet above sea level, with its dampness, was causing Stephen no end of trouble breathing. He at last decided that his lungs were filling. He was miserable at night and had to sleep with his head propped upon a number of pillows. But the Supreme Government, through General Cos, issued a command to General Ugartechea demanding the arrest and surrender of Lorenza de Zavala from Zavala's Point, who had thrown his support to the Texans, and William Barret Travis, for commanding the expedition to Anahuac, and Robert Williamson, attorney, for his inflammatory speech of July 4. Judge F. W. Johnson and Mosely Baker were next in order, for having gone as secret messengers for the "War Party" to Nacogdoches. Besides these, there were individuals whom the government charged had abused their government's messenger and violated their dispatches.

Now all this devolved upon Stephen, who had always been the political chief at San Felipe, and he was threatened that if the demands were not complied with, forthwith he should march with all his cavalry, and execute the order himself!

Overtures were useless. They wanted the guilty men. At Nacogdoches citizens gathered in the Old Stone Fort for a general consultation as they were gathering all over Texas, for no one at whatever cost was willing to turn these loyal men over to the Mexicans. At this meeting, Sam Houston was elected commander of the militia at this point. General Cos would certainly obey Santa Anna, whose brother-in-law he was.

While still in prison, before the two Texans arrived and put up the bond for Stephen's release, and when he was at the very lowest ebb, no friends, nothing, he wrote a letter to John Wharton, William's brother, concerning the activities of the Galveston Bay and Texas Land Company and why had he not been released if someone had not been successful in keeping him there! Mostly, it concerned the tremendous acreage of Hayden and Ben Edwards, as well as that of Sam Norriss. He wrote in part: "There's something rotten about the whole business, and I aim to find out exactly how and why. The land was no more theirs to appropriate than yourself or I might get our clutches on it, a vast area of many thousands of acres."

The letter arrived in due time, and John passed it amongst his relatives, including his brother William, then sent it to the newspaper for public consumption.

Sam Houston had resumed his law practice in Nacogdoches and now the curtain rose with Sam Houston and Stephen Austin center front. Sam, without giving it too much thought, sat down and wrote a letter to John Wharton:

Last night I had the pleasure of passing with your brother, William and his company . . . I remained with them until this morning when we parted, for various routes and pursuits. I to my law practice, and they to their land speculations.

From your brother I learned the news of the colony and its politics for really I was ignorant of them. I heard with singular pleasure that you were recovering the use of your arm. I had heard of the occurrence of the meeting, but never the particulars. . . .They gratified me much because they were in perfect accordance with my estimate of you. William showed me his card in answer to Austin's ridiculous letter from Mexico City. I think he has left the little gentleman very few crumbs of comfort. I was provoked at his first letter of August. I must confess that it awakened no other emotion in my breast than pity mingled with contempt. He showed the disposition of a viper without its fangs. He aimed at me a few thrusts, but I will await an interview with him before I make any public expose of his political inconsistencies. . . .

So much had and was taking place. William Barrett Travis with twenty-five men drove the Mexican garrison from Anahuac and proposed to march on San Antonio before General Cos could reinforce it. Nothing came of it, and Travis was widely denounced in Texas. Then came the order from General Cos for the military arrest of Travis and the pendulum swung back. It was September the first when Stephen reached the soil of Texas. All eyes were on him. He would know how things really were. "Is it war?" they asked, "or is it peace?"

"War," he said reluctantly, "is our only recourse."

But he hastened away to San Felipe. Another encounter at Anahuac occurred with Travis heading a small detachment and others, so that now Mexico demanded the arrest of the offenders. Two messages had been apprehended in which Mexico exposed their plan to send soldiers in to quell the Texans. From the start, not one Texan would support a dictator, such as Santa Anna had turned out to be. Stephen agreed never to give up one loyal man, but rather prepare to fight.

He had written Mr. Perry from Mexico City: "There seems to be no doubt that system of government will be changed from federal to central. This has been a very hard trip on me, but I anticipate a quiet life with you when I get home. . . ."

While still in New Orleans awaiting a vessel for Velasco, he wrote his fiancée, Mary Holly. The weather was damp and warm, August weather in Louisiana, and he was quite uncomfortable. He wrote:

I am, as you will see by my date, once more in the land of my birth, and freedom—It is very evident that the best interests of the United States require that Texas should be effectually, and fully, Americanized, that is, settled by a population that will harmonize with their neighbors on the East, in language, political views, common origin, sympathy, and even interests. General Santa Anna told me he should visit Texas next month, as a friend. His visit is uncertain—his friendship much more so. For fourteen years I have had a hard time of it, but nothing shall daunt my courage or abate my exertions to complete the main object of my labors—to Americanize Texas. This fall and winter will fix our fate. A great immigration will settle the question.

After posting the letter to Mary, Stephen boarded the steamer *San Felipe* for Velasco. It developed that it was not so uneventful as he anticipated. Just before reaching the mouth of the Brazos River, the *San Felipe* engaged in a fight with the Mexican steamer *Correo*, which the *San Felipe* captured to the applause of all on board. For some time the *Correo* had been active along the Texas coast attempting to suppress the contraband trade.

CHAPTER TWENTY

Emily was sitting on the beach making a flower lei of the golden galardia, while occasionally she scanned the calm warm waters lapping gently at her feet. A school of playful porpoises swam up and down like a carousel. The children were on the long plank Mr. Perry had built for them out into the water and they were there now with their long strings baited with salt pork, waiting for the beautiful blue crabs to latch onto the salt pork and so later get into the pot of gumbo. The day was good. The sky was a clear light blue with little floating islands of frothy meringue. But Emily felt a weird change in the atmosphere.

She called Joel to her. "Son," she said, "will you walk down to the edge of the point, and scan the sky? I can't see from here if there's a cloud beyond that grove."

Joel sauntered down the beach, whistling and kicking the sand with his toes. A wad of bright little shells caught his eye. He gathered them, cleaning away the kelp. Had he thought about it, he would have known the sea was not as calm as it looked. A conch drew his attention next, a rare find indeed along there. With the shells in one hand, the lovely pink conch in the other, he finally reached the point and gazing to the southwest, he flung the shells away, and raced back to his mother, "It's the blackest cloud I ever saw. Mom . . . You kids!" he cried. "Get off that plank! Run, don't just glare back at me!" He reached his hand down to Emily, "We'd better get back to the cottage. That thing is headed right at us!"

"Oh, dear God!" Emily cried. "They take everything . . . wipe out whole towns." She rushed to gather her children when across the Gulf the water which had been so calm now rose in bewildering swells.

In just a matter of minutes, Emily had her family in the barouche and never had she laid on a whip as she did on their mad race to get to Peach Point. What happened to the beach house was of little concern to her. They turned in at the high brick pillars shortly, and found James Perry saddled up. He held the sweating pair still trembling from the killing run, better than seven miles. "Emily," Mr. Perry said irately, which was not like him, "Mrs. Perry!"

"Yes, Mr. Perry," she replied. "You think I've been abusing the horses. Don't you? Well, my dear, you'd better be thanking me for saving the children. We saw a tornado coming across the Gulf, tide rising that the swells were becoming mountainous."

"Heavens, my dear . . . why did it take you so long to leave?"

"It just appeared quite suddenly. They're no respecter of persons. How did you think they would stop to consider that Mrs. James Perry was enjoying a holiday and that it should head the other way!" She laughed and laughed and then began wailing hysterically.

The Bryan children and the Perry children were all talking at once. Joel explained about the kelp he'd found and mother had worried about the strange change in the atmosphere. "It was still miles away, father. It might not have come inland at all."

The words were blown right out of Joel's mouth, as its snout poked undecidely across the swamp. "To the storm cellar!"

Stephen and Rob loped in on their mules, with Steve thinking, I hope I never am in a hurry while riding one. "My insides," he declared, dropping down, following Perry, who held the door open for them. "That's the second one we've seen on the homeward trip."

The tornado passed them by and they crawled out of the storm pit and went into the house. It was so good to be home. After supper they sat around in the parlor where Emily's piano was the instrument, brought from Missouri and said to have been the first one west of the Mississippi. Emily seated herself and began to play. She was an accomplished musician. After a session with the children singing all their old favorites, they were sent off to bed, and Stephen sat for a long time with his eyes closed and his head resting on his hands, while Emily's fingers touched the keys lightly with several Bach fugues, some Mozart and Brahms and then she turned on the red velvet stool and exclaimed, "My, I must just be carried away. I'm that glad you're home nobody would believe it!" She rose even with James and Stephen demanding she play on, and remarked, "I'll get the brandy."

The painting of Stephen, done by George Catlin, famous Indian artist, sometime during the early years in Texas, or just prior, looked at them from its place on the mantle over the fireplace. But his mind was not on the likeness of himself; he was wondering about the sugar cane and whether the sugar mill was working. How many cattle on Chocalate Bayou or wandering about the swamp? Had they seen any of the Karankawas in the vicinity? Emily gave up and went to bed, leaving Stephen and James Perry plowing through the maze they called business.

Later that night seated at his desk among his books and important papers, he wrote a long letter to Mary Holly. What he would give to have the life of James Perry!

The next day Joel exclaimed, "I'll bet that whooper was four maybe five feet tall, Uncle Steve. There were thousands of them so that the beach as far as we could see was white. They got black legs and a rim of black about the side of the wings and a red head and a long bill!"

"And the noise they make! Loud, clear and sounded sorter like bugles, I watched one of the cranes chasing a horned toad one day, and before I could get to the poor little thing, that crane had got it between that long black bill and run away down the beach. He was gobbling it up as he ran."

Stephen looked across at Emily with arched brows. "You never saw anything like it in your life. There must have been thousands of them!" Emily exclaimed. "And cranes—why, I never saw so many!"

Mr. Perry came in then, having brought up some things from the wagon and barouche, his arms loaded. But he heard Emily saying that the coast looked like a snow bank. "I hear from Doc Archer they have habits the human race could copy with advantage."

"And what may that be?" Steve asked.

"Well, you see, when a whooping crane mates, it's for life. They never look around with an evil eye. . . ." He dropped the bundle onto a chair. "Be damned if you kids don't mess up more clothes!"

"Well, some of those things were clean, Mr. Perry. You've got them all mixed up. Clean and soiled. Oh, Alice!" she cried and slumped onto a sofa. "I guess it's not your fault. It was just that I was getting anxious to get back to Peach Point."

"What else did you do, Joel, for fun?" Stephen asked. He had gone to a deal of trouble to get the cottage finished in time for escape from the heat. It had been built on Perry land, for it extended all the way to the Gulf. Emily was relaxed and lovely with more of a tan than she usually had, and her hair was unruly from salt water.

"Oh, Stephen," Emily said, "the water is warm even in early morning—that's when I liked to swim. But some sort of clear disc kept getting on me, and it was hard to remove."

"Jelly fish, Emily," Stephen declared that the sting was not dangerous, only painful. "Even San Jacinto River has them, I hear."

But Joel and Moses declared for the porpoise. "Whole armies of them. They're the playfullest things we found, and friendly. Why they'd come right up to you and nudge you like they wanted you to get out of the water, or to play—never did know what they were wanting!"

"All right, boys. Off with you to your rooms. Wash up, it's almost time for supper." Mr. Perry said, gesturing with his hand.

With a glance to ascertain if they were alone and being satisfied that they were, Mr. Perry began giving Stephen the news. All of it.

"Samuel Williams is mixed up in some fashion with the lands, and has a bank. I know you had asked for and had obtained a charter for a bank for Columbia, failed to materialize, yet McKinney and Sam Williams are carrying on a banking business along with their mercantile business. And John Austin is serving well yet as alcalde. Oh yes, just a few yards from John's plantation is where the Masons met, out there under an oak tree. John Wharton received the charter from the Grand Lodge of Louisiana. The order was initiated in service in Texas December 27, 1835."

"Who all are members, or do you know?"

"Sure I know . . . there was Dr. Anson Jones; Dr. James Phelps; John Wharton; Alexander Russell; Asa Brigham; J. P. Caldwell, and

Warren D. Hall. But of course, many have since been brought in."

"What else is new?" Stephen asked, glad that the country was taking its place. Having a Masonic Order was a feather in their cap.

"Let's see. It was while you were in Mexico City there was a duel fought."

"A duel? In Texas?"

"It happened in August. And between John Wharton and William Austin. Wharton got his shoulder shot up, and Austin didn't get a scratch. Wharton nearly lost his arm."

"My word!" Stephen said. "How did it happen, the duel?"

"The general cause was jealousy . . . some sort of rivalry. But the more direct cause was a toast given by John Wharton at a gathering —a dinner party, I believe. At any rate, the guests had all given toasts, and so John rose and held up his glass and said, 'The Austins; may their bones burn in hell!' and of course, news of this nature being choice, it was no time at all until William Austin heard about it."

"Of all things. It's I they are striking out at, you know."

"A very bad time for this to happen," continued Mr. Perry. "William had just lost his wife and many slaves and he himself had only recovered from the malady. We were all having our tribulations for we had lost little Mary with it, and also a number of our people. At any rate, William rose from his bed to attend to the burial of his brother, John Austin. After that, he challenged Wharton to the duel. The appointed day came and Wharton showed up with a half dozen of his friends. Austin had only Colonel Warren D. Hall and Tom, his personal servant."

"Austin was not hit, but Wharton was struck in the shoulder," Stephen recapping the dialogue said. "That's very strange. I mean the whole bit."

"Oh, Wharton apologized to Austin," James said. "Later. It seemed there was a matter of the heart that changed their attitudes toward one another. I wrote you about the family of Bertrands all dying from the cholera, all except Elizabeth Ann. The William Whartons gave her a home. Their wedding took place at "Eagle Island" with William and Sarah Groce Wharton acting like they maneuvered the whole thing. Folks said Elizabeth Ann needed a home, and Austin was on the rebound. Just a natural, I guess. Anyway, they're very happy."

"Well. Well. I'm glad to hear that."

111

"I recall that David Burnet, after transferring his grant of land to the Galveston Bay and Texas Land Company, back in 1830, went back to Cincinnati for several months and returned with a bride in 1831. That was when he built "Oakland" near Lynchburg, on a tract he obtained from Nathaniel Lynch. How are they doing?"

"Very well, indeed."

"In the morning I want to go into Columbia," Stephen remarked as they walked down the long hall to the dining room. Emily was already seated with her foot on the pedal which moved the punkah and a soft waving of air served both to keep the flies away and make the dining more comfortable.

The next morning Stephen was on his way to Columbia. The road twisted through an amazing stand of ancient oak trees on a vast prairie and he rode in from the southwest turning with the road and pulled up in front of the newspaper office. He wanted to see Mr. Anthony, W. D. Anthony, publisher of the *Brazoria Advertiser*, before going on to see Josiah Bell in Columbia. There was a strange man sitting at the worn rolltop desk. "I'd like to see Mr. Anthony, please."

"So would we all, sir. He went with the others during the cholera epidemic." Stephen almost reeled but caught himself in time by clutching the counter.

Mr. Perry had not told him. Perhaps it was because of how much he had always loved the man. "I've only come in from Mexico City. I had not heard. How many?"

"About eighty, I think," the man said. "My name's Cox. Selser COX. There was Mr. Perry's daughter, Mary. They live out at Peach Point, not far. And Captain John Austin and one child, and John's sister-in-law, Mrs. William T. Austin. But he married Elizabeth Ann Bertrand not so long ago. Quite a wedding. I covered it for the paper. Out at William Wharton's "Eagle Island" . . . and let me think, there was Mr. Westall, Mr. Neel, Mr. Brady, Mr. John Cox, my cousin of Bernard, and Henry Munson of Gulf Prairie. Yes, about eighty in all."

"Oh, my! Oh my!" Stephen sounded sick.

"Can I get you something, sir? You never did tell me who you are."

"Stephen Austin. I've been a political prisoner for the last almost

112

two years, in Mexico City. I never have found out what it was I'd done. . . ."

"Let me shake your hand, Mr. Austin. I heard you made some sort of threat about getting schools in Texas, and if they didn't supply them, you would, one way or the other!"

"I guess I did say something like that!" Stephen smiled. Was that all it was? Then of a certainty, somebody in Texas had kept him incarcerated. That was no complaint. But he said, "Don't you think we ought to have public schools?"

"I sure do, Mr. Austin. But likely it'll be a while, on account of the mess down at Anahuac. The Mexicans are riled up no end.

"Here have a cup of coffee," Mr. Cox said, already pouring it.

"I'd like to stay longer and talk schools with you, Mr. Cox, but I'm going over to Bell's Landing, Columbia, to see Mr. Bell."

"Did I say that Port Velasco was depopulated by the epidemic? Well, it was." the man said, walking out with Stephen and chattering away while Stephen mounted. "You come back soon, now. I want the full story of your imprisonment in Mexico City."

CHAPTER TWENTY-ONE

Stephen saw the brick foundations, the jug cisterns, the wrought iron fences, and three brick buildings, two of which had recently been built. Many of the fireplaces were of mud and moss over wood frames. Some, like the Perrys' at Peach Point, had a wide hall and beautiful stairs with cherry banisters.

There were so many memories that Stephen searched out places through tear-dimmed eyes. He saw where Elizabeth Perry had lived with John Austin. The child was born to them here in this house. . . . And the cholera taking away both John and the child. . . . But he had willed Elizabeth all that he owned. (Later she remarried to Dr. T. F. L. Parrott, and of her land she sold off 177 acres for $5,000 to the Allen brothers, who wanted to lay out a city [Houston] in the spring of 1836. The land had been granted to John Austin by Stephen.)

There was the home of Peter Grayson and Spencer Jack as represented the colonists to proceed to Mexico City bearing memorials to President Santa Anna for Austin's release. They arrived in Mexico City October 15, 1834. But by the time they arrived, Padre Muldoon had already had him freed from the dungeon of the Inquisition and he spent some time in another, the Acordada; he was confined in a third prison, the Disputacion, when Grayson and Jack came.

Brazoria was a restful town. There was another who wrote from Bexar in his behalf, Ramon Musquiz. He had known Musquiz since the first day he landed in Natchitoches, Louisiana. From him he had learned about the Mission of the Adais Indians. Yes, he had been around a long time.

Stephen went on then to Bell's Landing on the west side of the Brazos where he found Josiah Bell walking a horse which he was about to buy. The men met out under the great oak trees, the moss dripping from their wide branches shadowing the grass. And there were tears in Bell's eyes while he wrung Stephen's hand.

"Two years!" he exclaimed. "Come on in, I've so much to tell you!" And laughing, wiping his eyes, "And I want to hear about your sojourn in Mexico City. That was a helluva thing to happen to you, Stephen!"

"So many have gone. So much has changed," Stephen said, accepting a cup of coffee from Mrs. Bell." But what happened that Austin and John Wharton fought a duel—if you can call it that."

"You must have heard most of it. John Wharton is a jealous man . . . says that the Austins are all over the place . . . got the best land and, well, you name it. But he went too far at a dinner party. Oh, yes, we were there, not knowing too much about the troubled water or how deep it ran. Most of the guests made excuses and left early, most of them fighting mad. Wharton made a toast—I'm sure someone told you about it."

"Yes, I heard."

"It seems that Sam Houston had disagreed with them and said it was all right to aim for the Halls of Montezuma . . . but one step at a time. He also said that if the Whartons had half the good sense that Stephen had, they wouldn't be in such a turmoil."

"Well, now," Stephen said, "I had no idea that Sam Houston felt about the instigators of a war as I did. It's not the way I heard it. You see, I, like a fool, wrote to John, and remarked that someone was keeping me in prison, and suggested that it might be Houston, inasmuch as he had been engaged in land deals with Samuel May Williams while I was out of the country. When I heard about that, I was furious. It concerns a parcel that ends at the mouth of the Sabine River. Choice land, but too swampy over a lot of it."

"He and Sublett bought it together . . . already laid it out," Mr. Bell said. "I had no idea that he was working so hard for the Galveston Bay and Texas Land Company. Mr. Swartwout, that thief, probably has in mind boxing our colonists in."

"Which gave him no reason to call me a viper. I have always dealt with Houston as I might have wanted to be dealt with. But nevertheless, I fired Sam Williams. He's in business with McKinny, a mercantile and bank and what-have-you. Doing rather well, I understand."

"I had no idea that Williams had the money to start such a vast enterprise!" Mr. Bell said. "He was a poor man . . . allus had been."

"We wish him well, at least."

"You wouldn't if you knew he had gone down to Galveston and bought up some land to build him a fine house on!" Bell said. "He's having the hemlock and fine white pine milled in Maine and other places . . . has it all shipped directly to Galveston Island."

At first, Stephen was more hurt than angered. In the name of common sense what would prompt Sam Houston to make such cruel remarks? He had been welcomed to San Felipe, indeed to Texas, with unmerited consideration. Even with aligning himself with the Whartons, and their, at times, warped thinking, no one could accuse Sam Houston of not knowing his own mind and or using ways and means to further his own ambitions. It, of course, had entered his mind that Houston very possibly was behind his continued incarceration, and the two men who came to Mexico City to obtain his release from that dungeon were not of Wharton's party—which simply meant not with Houston.

Stephen let his mind dwell on the death and burial of the laziest man in Texas. It was during a very bad drouth. Only in one settlement had it rained, so that summer everyone was going there to buy corn. Soon the people began saying, "I'm going down to Egypt to buy corn" and the name stuck. That's how easily a name, good or bad, wraps itself around you, and the devil himself couldn't get it off. But the thing that worried Stephen's mind was not so much the name—it was certainly no misnomer—but that the man in question half-dead from starvation, was hauled off to Egypt to accept a cart of corn from his neighbors. The old man raised up his head and asked if the corn was shelled off the cob, and when told no, that it was still in the shucks, he laid his head back and said wearily, "Just drive on the cart, boys."

And that was the way it was in Texas.

"Gail Borden is handling my land grants. Has the printing press there, too. Gail is a hard worker, but never have I seen a more inquisitive mind. He wants to know what makes everything go, how it's put together. No halfway measure with him," Stephen said, walking out to the door. "You know, I've been here almost all afternoon . . . and I aimed to see Sam Houston and demand an apology for the dirty names he called me."

"Oh, for goodness sake, Stephen. You know how spurious he is and big enough to just hold you out and let you wiggle yourself to death."

"He won't attack me, and I don't aim to attack him. What's your worry?"

"He's on your side, now . . . don't spoil it. When he saw how the country went wild over you being in prison, it didn't take a fortune teller to tell him who had the hearts of the Texans!"

"I see," Stephen remarked with tongue in cheek, "if you can't whip'em, join'em."

"Sam Houston's a fine man, a bit emotional where females are concerned, like Miss Anna who up and minded to keep him dangling until she was sure of someone else. Everybody knows it but Sam, and there ain't nobody with guts enough to tell him."

"I reckon," Stephen said with a wry smile. "At any rate, I'm just awfully glad Houston's had a change of heart concerning the political arena."

CHAPTER TWENTY-TWO

Stephen rode along the San Antonio Trace, more apt, where he was at the time, to be called El Camino Real. He was headed to Nacogdoches. He was tired of carrying doubt with him—there were too many questions. He slowed his pace on reaching the Plaza Principal around which the town had been built, and let his eyes search the stores and buildings on three sides without any luck, but on the fourth, he saw the sign "Sam Houston, Atty at Law." He dismounted, and with his sombrero, dusted his black broadcloth pants. He rapped on Houston's office door. "Come on in, it's not locked!" the voice called out, followed by Houston's towering frame.

"Well, how about this?" he grinned and shook Stephen's hand with genuine pleasure. "Am I ever glad to see you!"

Stephen lost no time informing Houston of the trip. "Why?"

And Sam Houston explained, "There was de Zavala, who wanted land, and two others—you know them already. De Zavala has already built a fine house, neighbors to the Groces and William Wharton. Buffalo Bayou and San Jacinto River. You know the area, Stephen."

"I know it well . . . it was the land grant of Hayden and Ben Edwards, and also the grant of Sam Norriss, whom the Mexican government expelled. It invalidated their grants."

"I knew all this. Sam May Williams had given me full details, including your map. Now I was acting as the lawyer in the case; the deal was made between Mr. Swartwart and Sam Williams. Mr. Swartwart is from New York. He had to get back and so left the details to me. You see, I represent the Galveston Bay and Texas Land Company of New York."

"It wasn't the way Sam May Williams explained it to me. He didn't say, but implied that you had more to do with it. He even agreed to make a public statement concerning the land grants. I've all but been tarred and feathered on account of it. Many, including the Whartons, have accused me of pulling off a land deal to end all land deals—but you know I'm innocent; I was in prison. How could I have?" Stephen said.

Sam Houston grunted. Stephen continued, "I was ashamed of the dismal way I had fired him, and even wrote him a letter saying so, asking him to come home."

"Yeah," Sam Houston said. "I heard about you even going over to Quintana to see him, and that McKinney told you Sam Williams had decided to shake the soil of Texas off his feet and left for, they said, Baltimore." Sam drew out a bottle, and poured a couple of glasses. "They had a bank, did you know that? And a store supplying this whole country? But it was your permit to have a bank, they tell me, that he was using. You ought to kick the bastard's ass clear up to his gullet!" Sam paced the floor with his itchy fingers doing the job his mind was seeing.

Stephen drained his glass and got up. He took Sam Houston's hand "I'm glad for whatever reason we had this talk. Finally, I see it all. Never again will I doubt your friendship, Sam, or your loyalty to Texas. Fill her up again, Sam. My God," Stephen mighty nigh had tears in his eyes. "To think how fully I trusted him!"

Twilight came on and they went over to the tavern for supper for it had been a long time since Stephen felt so good—so free.

"Why don't we call on the Raguets, Stephen?" Houston said. "I'd like you to meet Mr. Raguet and of course, Miss Anna," with a glow.

"I'd probably better find a place for the night. It was a long ride."

"Oh no," Sam declared. "Mr. Raguet sees eye to eye with you— you know, getting what we want, but taking it a step at a time. Most of these donkeys, like the Whartons, want to jump into a war of a sudden, and, Stephen, you of all people know we are not ready for a war with Mexico."

"Would be interesting to hear what he has in mind," Stephen said.

The Raguet's home, the largest in Nacogdoches, was fairly near Frost Thornes, and Adolph Stearne, whom Sam Houston had cultivated with a passion. He aimed to marry Miss Anna, and these people were socially in a position to help him in this project of the heart. The interior was as lovely as the exterior. And Miss Anna was quite talented in music. From time to time, she coyly lowered her lids and raised them ever so slowly at Stephen, and Stephen, thinking she was trying to make Sam Houston jealous, rested his case. "Don't you think we ought to retire to a place where we may talk on things concerning the future of Texas?"

Dawn was breaking over the forest, chickens were crowing, and the animals were playing in the corral. Stephen, bleary-eyed, after a long night and hot coffee by the pot over details and strategy, began the long ride, verily happy for the first time in years.

Everybody knew that Sam Houston was in a state from love sickness over the pretty Miss Anna Raguet. Houston wrote her long letters and sent them by his friend Dr. Iron. Sometimes she replied, and sometimes she didn't. Houston was in a state. Finally, he heard that the doctor always remained, after delivering Houston's epistle, for dinner and perhaps an evening of cards, or music. These trips seemed not to tire Dr. Iron, with him springing off his horse as though he'd been only to the post office and back. So Houston, really not wanting to get singed a second time for love of a woman, began to lengthen the time between his messages. Whether he should get Houston on it or just let him sweat it out, he decided that his first duty was to get a force to move out to attack while the enemy was static waiting for reinforcements. So volunteers flooded in from Brazoria, Velasco, all parts near enough.

And again Stephen marveled at Texas, so big, so wide. In time he heard about the routing of the Mexicans who were then in the aggregate of five hundred under Ugartechea returning to "take" the cannon. And this last dispatch was to the effect that General Cos was expected at any moment to attack Goliad since it was a connecting link from Bexar to the coast, but instead while attacks upon Gonzales and Goliad went on, General Cos was making a dash to San Antonio with six hundred troops to assume command in full. Austin would have to move, and fast.

After attending to the various details, General Austin, with his volunteer army of about three hundred men, took up his line of march to San Antonio, October 13. With Stephen were his two nephews William Joel and Moses Bryan. In this group of courageous men were Milam, Travis, Bowie, Bonham Stewart and others.

It was April of 1835 when Thomas J. Rusk entered Sam Houston's law office. He deposed upon oath, stated and declared that he was a native of the United States of North America, that his age was twenty-nine years, that he desired to dwell under the wise and just government which offered the protection of its beneficent laws to honest and industrious men.

He was now a full-fledged Texan. "Where are the towns—if any?"

Houston replied, "Well, there's Victoria set up in 1824. In fact, one of the first three incorporated. Martin de Leon brought his colony of forty-one families to the site. He called it Guadalupe de Jesus Victoria. Real good luck, too. Became the first cattle capital, and it was where the very first cattle brands were used. You see, just about everybody raised them, some to a greater degree than others. So they had much confusion over who owned what. There were no fences, and the cattle would naturally stray off. After a few killings, I was about to say, they decided they'd put their brand on them. Then they wouldn't have to kill their next door neighbor, even if he did live fifty or a hundred miles away."

"I came through San Augustine, back there close to the Sabine," Rusk said. "It looked as though it might be old, also."

"They say that it was the first town in Texas. You know that for many years the Spanish had a mission amongst the Adais Indians pretty close to where Fort Jesup is perched upon that high hill in the Hills of Surprise. But the mission and presidio across the Caddo Trail from it have been abandoned. They didn't need a presidio afterwards, but thirteen provisional governors were stationed at that mission of Los Adais, governing Texas, and it over close to Red River in Louisiana. But you asked about the old settled towns, I believe. There was a settlement at the embougement of Goose Creek into Galveston Bay, first settled in 1824, had a little saw mill and boat landing."

"I think I'll like it," Rusk said. "You've been a tremendous help, especially about the cattle and brands and all."

"Phil Sublett and I are proposing to lay out another this year if all goes well. If not, next year. The Mexican government gave the people of Gonzales a cannon when the redskins were whooping it up," Houston said, laughing, with a certain holding back in it. "And we welcome you, Mr. Rusk."

The law of 1830 had closed the door to immigration, and given to Nacogdoches a new role as a smuggling center. Lafitte and his ilk would come up via Galveston Bay and hide in expansive forests.

But Stephen's colonists had been selected for their industry and integrity, and his own labors seemed incredible. He dealt with a central government at Mexico City and a state government at Saltillo, alike capricious, inexpert, often corrupt and always changing.

Stephen was the friend of the colonists whom hardships had disheartened and rendered distrustful. But being their military and civilian chief, their banker, broker, merchant and messenger, he was obliged to lead them against the Indians. He surveyed their lands, established jurisdictions, organized and administered a state. As a result, he remained a bachelor and submerged the best years of his life, a starved anchorite, depended upon by thousands of his people as he withdrew from the world, almost a hermit to the cause for which he lived. But he considered the still living of the "Old Three Hundred"—Anson Jones, William Wharton, John Wharton, Henry Smith, Sterling C. Robertson, Dr. Phelps, Bradburn, and William Travis. The others were farther away, had found broader lands and many successful cattlemen with fancy brands on their herds lived like barons. Then there were interesting and strong men not new to the wilderness, but newcomers to Texas; there were Sam Houston, Rusk, Fannin, Stewart, and others of whom he was justly proud. There were Sam Norriss and Hayden Edwards and his brother with mixed loyalties. They knew what they really wanted. They had been gone now for many years. It was said that Hayden Edwards was growing cane over on Red River, a neighbor of Davenport, who was experimenting with sugar cane, in hybridizing an island cane which was superior to that grown in Louisiana.

Most of those men, including Dr. Anson Jones, were Masons. Since they had already organized, it was his pleasure to join them. He hoped after the activities with such a great group of men, he would soon forget the many many months of his incarceration in the three different prisons in which he had been held in Mexico City.

This fleeting review was to Stephen a balance, what good had come of his father's life-death for Texas, and what bad. Did it balance? Would he come out the victor? Who could say?

So Stephen walked out on his gallery to watch the children of San Felipe de Austin, and again his heart ached to see them growing up like weeds, just getting bigger with no intellectual development at all. He turned back to the room where Gail Borden was working on the printing of his paper, in a part of Stephen's office.

"Gail," he said, looking at the handsome young face with so much admiration, "it seems that Santa Anna is headed this way. I hear the colonists west to the Guadalupe and San Marcos rivers and those also east to the Trinity and San Jacinto rivers are ready and armed to join up with the Brazos and St. Bernard aggregation. What do you think about meeting Santa Anna head on?"

"What else?" was the laconic reply. "I'll be done here in a minute, with the paper. Do you want some handbills printed up in a hurry?"

"Yes. While you print the call to arms, I'll dash down to fetch Little Bill Blanks to distribute them. And your boy can take the other direction." Stephen rushed out the door, and Gail Borden, feeling the urgency, tore out the paper type, and prepared the press for handbills. Gail smiled at Stephen, who still called Bill Blanks Little Bill. He was a grown man with a wife and still playing papa to his married sisters and little brothers, also grown. His busy hands set the type "CALL TO ARMS" and was waiting for the ink to dry on the primer sheet as Stephen and Bill came in. "How does it look, Steve?" he asked, holding it for a better angle.

"That ought to do it!" Stephen Fuller Austin exclaimed with his heart pounding fiercely from the running. And he began his own preparations. It had come. Santa Anna was burning every house including Barnett's fine residence. He can always build anew, he thought . . . the land was his. But would it be after Santa Anna's scythe had crossed the broad land? He felt a little sick and knew it was from this final stroke. What else could he do but to defend the land, protect the people, his people, and give until there was nothing left. He caught a glimpse of the man and boy dashing to their horses, like Paul Revere of old, and not so many years ago when he stopped to think about it. And what had become of Bill Blanks? Was it two-three years ago he had gone to San Antonio to check on a parcel of free land he found out about—and had never been seen since? He, too, had wanted more "elbow room." It was quite possible that the Karankawas had caught him, and a shudder at the thought of the cannibals feasting on poor, hardworking Bill.

"Since Sam May Williams has gone, Gail, I leave the business of whatever nature to you to administer. You are familiar with it."

"Don't worry about the business. Likely there won't be any until this matter of Santa Anna is resolved."

They had been warned. General Cos at Matamoros, conveying his final answer, that all the people of Texas must unconditionally submit to any reforms or alterations that congress had to make in the Constitution . . . that the country would be invaded whether the obnoxious individuals were given up or not . . . and that everything else would be regulated by the army. Cos was expected in San Antonio de Bexar on the sixteenth of September and would attack the colonies immediately. They were not ready for an invasion. Not ready for war, "war is our only recourse." He sent messages to all parts of the country "to prepare to defend yourselves, your rights, and your country. . . ."

James W. Fannin of Caney Creek wrote: Letters have been rec'd express from Compano informing the citizens of Matagorda that the armed vessel *Vera Crusanna* had arrived and was landing arms and ammunition and that they were to await two more vessels with 400 troops expected soon—General Martin Perfecto de Cos is on board and I suppose the expected force with what is at Bexar is to form a small body-guard with which he proposes visiting San Felipe.

Fannin and Joe Mims ran a sugar mill and cotton plantation on the quiet St. Bernard River, so unlike the turbulent Brazos, three miles west of the town of Brazoria. Fannin, a West Pointer, had been in Texas a little better than a year, and already felt as though his feet had just grown up out of the quagmire of a Texas swamp. He sent this intelligence to Columbia, Velasco, San Felipe and folks along the Brazos and St. Bernard rivers. "We need your speedy and efficient cooperation. We have determined here to raise a sufficient force to justify a reasonable belief that we can succeed, in an effort to secure at least the arms and ammunition and if to be found the troops. This is the plan for this vicinity," he said.

So far, so good, and everything finished off with a question mark. Austin wrote hundreds of letters, sent out handbills informing the colonists on what thin ice they all skated.

Then came the letter from William B. Travis, a fellow townsman absent from San Felipe a few days:

All eyes are turned toward you; and the independent manly stand you have taken has given the Sovereigns confidence in themselves—Texas can be wielded by you and you alone; and her destiny is now completely in your hands—I have every confidence that you will guide us safe through all our perils

This is not base flattery of a servile mind, but it is the reasoning of one ardent in his country's cause, and who wishes to unite his feeble efforts with those who have the power and inclination to lead us in safety to the desired end.

And Stephen was thankful for Travis's offer to defend Texas.

It seems there had been a demand for a cannon given them four years before to defend Gonzales against the Indians, especially the cannibalistic Karankawas. They usually lived on and near the island of Galveston, but roamed widely along the Gulf, and heaven help those who were unfortunate enough to be caught, and Gonzales had seen too much of them at that time, for a fact. But now, the people of Gonzales refused to give up the cannon. Cos demanded it.

123

CHAPTER TWENTY-THREE

In Mexico, Santa Anna was winning the revolution against Bustamente and his party. On August 3, General Teran, the military
commander of the Eastern Provinces which included Texas, took
command against Santa Anna. He was soon defeated in a battle by
forces under command of Montezuma, a strong supporter of Santa
Anna. Following this defeat, General Teran, desolate and grief-
stricken, committed suicide at Padilla, on the spot where on July 19,
1823, Iturbide was shot.

Stephen let his thoughts wander over the broad land and the
nature of it. There was Goliad, the home of the Aranama Indians
when Goliad came into being in 1749 . . . home to the Indians long
before recorded history. The mission and presidio called Santa
Dorotea. Goliad was where Colonel James Fannin and his outnumbered men were massacred after honorable surrender of 342
soldiers on order of General Santa Anna. That was on Palm Sunday, March 27, 1836. And La Bahia, presidio, Spanish "God, Gold
and Glory." The church was built first, then the presidio for the
padres' protection. Santa Maria del Loreto de la Bahia, also 1749,
was near the mission of Goliad.

Such a wayward spirit is the little San Antonio River, that the
Indians called it "Drunken-old-man-going-home-at-night." Stephen
saw again the beautiful Ursula on the arm of her beloved James
Bowie at the Governor's Palace. The low whitewashed adobe structure with ten rooms, was typical of colonial Spain with its carved
doors and low-beamed ceilings and mosaic tile floors. A Hapsburg
coat-of-arms was there dated 1772. When the government was removed from the mission de Los Adais, thence to Nacogdoches,
thence to San Antonio it brought all the officials of New Spain or
Philipines at that juncture. It was where Governor Salcedo had
been hacked to death by Gutterz and McGee in their try, as those
before and after. . . . Stephen was glad he had been able to visit
with the Bowies before she left with their two children to a visit
with relatives in Mexico City, for it was while there that the dread
epidemic of cholera struck, and rolled north, taking thousands of
lives, amongst them Ursula and her children. Jim Bowie was shat-

tered. He was a man who wanted to die. He was a soul lost—but was too religious to commit suicide as had Teran.

Stephen could see San Antonio, or Bexar, with his eyes closed, remembering it had been laid out by the king of Spain in 1730 with two plazas for recreation. Farsighted. Then he saw the Querotaro University founded in 1682—College of the Holy Cross—by priests, Father Francisco Hidalgo; Jose Diaz; Felix Isadore Espinoza; Nunez; Antonio de San Buenaventura Olverez; Martinez Marino; Juan Perez; de Vaca; Salazar; Massinettes. Margil de Jesus was chosen president of the College called Zatachinies to prepare missionaries for the field. It was here that Miguel Hidalgo of Dolores was educated. Miguel Hidalgo.

It may have been this train of thought, or his worry about Emily's children, but he was now concerned more than ever about the lack of public schools in Texas. Mexico! How could they deny our children when the oldest university on this hemisphere was in the City of Mexico and another in Lima, Peru!

It was August before Stephen again wrote in support of the convention and schools: There are no public schools or academies in Texas endowed or established by the state, but there are private schools in all parts and very good ones; and as soon as there is a local government to give form and protection there will be much progress in that direction."

Later in Matamoros, recovering from a severe illness, he wrote to Sam Williams not to sell the beautiful tract of land at the foot of the mountains east of the Colorado. . . . "I mean to go there and live there. It is out of the way, will do for an academy scheme, with which I can amuse myself and do good to others."*

The legislature of Coahuila-Texas assembled at Monclova, March 1, 1835, and closed its last session April 21, 1835. It opposed the Centralist or Military party and demanded that the constitution of 1824 be upheld.

With the two opposing parties long in conflict, memorials from each pouring into the National Congress, President Santa Anna, who had been elected leader of the Republicans, suddenly deserted

*The University of Texas, largest in the South, and the remains of Stephen Fuller Austin are here on this site.

his party and joined the Centralists. Saltillo immediately "declared" for Santa Anna and at the same time obtained the support of General Martin Perfecto Cos, commandant general of the Eastern Interior Provinces including Texas.

Owing to the fact that it was the Monclova legislature that had squandered the Texas lands, Cos determined to take advantage of the situation by heading a military force to dissolve the government at the capital city.

At the time, there were several Texans including Samuel M. Williams (Stephen's secretary), Francis W. Johnson, Ben R. Milam, James Bowie, John Cameron, Dr. James Grant, and others in Monclova on official and private business. They realized the very serious nature of the proceedings and determined to treat with the Governor Viesca and persuade him to close the session, and flee to San Antonio. Certainly, this man was a brilliant scholar and statesman, and so accompanied by his secretary of state, Dr. Grant, and Ben Milam, attended by a small escort of militia for guard, attempted to reach the border, but they were overtaken by a force of twenty-five men and forced to surrender. After a week of confinement at San Fernando they were removed to Rio Grande and on to Monterrey to "stand trial." Finally they all escaped and reached Texas sometime during the summer and fall. So there was confusion and instability and no one part of Texas heard the same reports as others, that there was talk at San Felipe they should organize a force to go to the rescue of Governor Viesca.

The men struck out and had reached short of La Bahia, when a voice from the dark grassy prairie slowly became a form with a rifle pointed at them. "Who are you?" for he had heard them talking in his own language. Ben's heart leaped for joy when he heard their reply, "American soldiers on their way to Goliad. But who are you?" The men closed around Ben Milam.

"I am Ben Milam," he answered. "I just escaped from a Mexican prison . . . dang nigh starved to death . . . cold . . . wet and tired."

"You come on with us, Ben." The foreman asked, "What became of the others? Sam May Williams, Francis Johnson, James Bowie, John Cameron, and Dr. James Grant." "Why, we'd been over to Monclova on business, had a small detachment when we saw what was happening. We tried to cross the border, "Ben Milam said, "but we didn't make it. First thing we knew, into their jug. I couldn't tell you what happened to the others . . . I figured if we could get out one at a time we wouldn't be missed so quick. Scattered like chickens after a hawk swooped down, I reckon." They lost no time in traveling as Ben reported. "Imagine sending us to Monterrey to stand trial—just like we been up to something!" he irately exclaimed.

Revolution was under way in Mexico. Skirmishes everywhere. But the most disastrous was the crushing of Zacatecas. About the time General Cos was dispersing the Monclova legislature, the dictator-president, Santa Anna, was crossing with 3400 troops to crush the last spark of liberty from the state of Zacatecas for it was a choice plum, the rich mining state of Mexico. On the plains of Guadalupe, Governor Francisco Garcia prepared to resist with 5,000 men and several pieces of artillery. Santa Anna demanded Garcia to surrender, which Garcia refused to do. Early the next morning, May 11, 1835, a fierce and bloody battle commenced which lasted for two hours. Santa Anna strutted off that bloody field leaving 700 dead and 2700 wounded. They plundered the capitol, took arms and ammunitions. This he did to Mexicans. To subdue them, he said. If he would do that to his own race, what would he do to Texans?—So the tale was told by the returning men from Monclova, and it spread like a prairie fire across the broad land.

CHAPTER TWENTY-FOUR

Henry Austin of Bolivar-on-the-Brazos wrote to Mary, his siter, in September . . .

Stephen has at last arrived. I rode all night through the swamp and rain to meet him at Perry's Peach Point Plantation. His arrival unites all parties. . . . Now we meet on middle ground. Strict Republican Principles—that is, to stand upon our constitutional and vested rights—reject the Centralismo Plan if offered to us and if they send a force to fight us to repel force by force. United we have nothing to fear.

127

The day came with all essentials for a dinner prepared and ball musicians obtained for Jane Long's Tavern, which also was her home.

Stephen arrived to deliver his "keynote speech" in which he reviewed his actions as their agent to Mexico in 1833, Mexican politics, the revolution, the change in government from federal to central. . . . "The people will soon be called upon to say whether they agree to this change or not.;' Then he raised his glass in a toast: "The constitutional rights and the security and peace of Texas—they ought to be maintained; and jeopardized as they now are, they demand a general consultation of the people."

There were sixty covers laid and they were three times filled by men alone. In the evening the long room was filled to a jam. At least sixty or eighty ladies danced the sun up and the Oyster Creek girls would not have quit then had not the room been wanted for breakfast. "Such enthusiasm!" Henry Austin exclaimed happily. Stephen listened to Henry with tongue in cheek. Henry, who had his children safely tucked away under Mary's wing, was having the time of his life. Poor Mary. Dear, dear Mary. . . .

Reasoning that San Antonio could be taken in four or five days, Austin told his men, "I'll remain as long as ten men will stick by me, because the salvation of Texas depends on the army being sustained and at the same time we must organize a government to sustain the army." Travis elected to remain at Bexar.

There had been much speaking by Sam Houston, Dr. Archer, and Pat Jack. But what little Stephen had to say, who on account of illness was just able to sit on a horse, concerned the necessity of sending back members to the meeting in November, to be in San Felipe.

Food, clothing, ammunition and supplies were gathered at convenient places. Carts, wagons, and teams were solicited for use in transportation. Several cannons were mounted and sent to General Austin. Henry Meigs of New York, who had married a first cousin of Stephen, wrote him in September that "The United States are looking to your course with deep interest. It is not possible to separate you from them long. Every political, religious and commercial tie exists between them and you."

They came—from Natchitoches Louisiana the Singing Bee Hunter and one company of dragoon to mention only one that is was composed mostly of French men who had a long history of hate toward anything Spanish or Mexican. These were not from Fort Jesup. The Mission San Francisco de la Espada, "St. Francis of the Sword" about eight miles below Bexar and his report: "I shall move with the army today to the Mission, and press the operations as fast as my force will permit. I have but four hundred effective men. General Cos has about nine hundred and is well fortified. We need reinforcements. I shall persevere here—my health is bad. There has been skirmishing daily but yet no loss on our side."

"The members of the convention except the commander and his staff leave here today to hold the convention on November 1 or as soon as they get a quorum."

Following his original plan to move slowly and cautiously as near Bexar as was possible, on the following day, General Austin dispatched Captains Bowie and Fannin with about ninety men, to select a position on the river for the army, nearer Bexar. The battalion reached Mission Concepcion about two miles south of the city and went into camp. Their position was reported to General Austin, who made ready to follow immediately. However, Bowie and Fannin's force had been spotted by the Mexican scouts, who reported the small number of Texans. The Mexicans hastened therefore to capture this body before the main army could reach there.

About three hundred cavalry under command of Ugartechea and a hundred infantry under Mariano Cos attacked about daybreak in a dense fog. But the sentinels gave the alarm, and the Mexicans were repulsed, leaving behind a brass cannon, a long six-pounder. About fifty were killed and as many wounded. The Texans lost one man, Richard Andrews of Mina.

Austin and his troops arrived in the middle of the day. He asked for and got the answers to such questions: Do you think we should storm Bexar, or wait and other such problems? General Cos had his orders to hold the Alamo. No matter what.

The plan for military defense of the country was presented and adopted. All members now turned to the important event of selecting a commander-in-chief of the regular army. As at Gonzales, when Austin was selected to command the volunteer army, there was splendid material in Texas to choose from—graduates of West Point, veterans of the War of 1812, famous Indian fighters, warriors, men of public office, of confidence, courage and conviction.

129

Among the number to be thought of was Sam Houston, delegate from Nacogdoches, and already chosen commander-in-chief of that district. He was unanimously elected commander-in-chief of all forces, both regular and volunteer. "To his will, wisdom, courage and unfaltering patriotism were to be entrusted the destinies of Texas." General Houston thanked the body for their expression of confidence "in his patriotism and abilities."

So it was that later Dr. Branch T. Archer, William Wharton and Stephen Austin were notified they were to leave immediately for the United States to obtain funds and other assistance for the war which seemed inevitable. Austin offered to mortgage his estate, as did James Fannin and Ben Fort Smith. Austin, at Bexar, prepared to leave for the United States, sent letters out that the men's loyalty was still unabated, but they had refused to storm the Alamo. He hated to leave a job not finished.

Burleson took Austin's place. Stephen had finished his duty as an army man, taking on the more demanding one of securing help. He must explain to his countrymen why Texas had taken up arms.

Santa Anna's agents were busy with the Indians, who numbered two thousand able fighters. Then Sam Houston sat at the Council Fire of the Bowl, war lord of the Texas Cherokee.

Colonel Gray arrived then at Washington-on-the-Brazos and in his saddlebag he was carrying two hundred thousand dollars in specie Austin had obtained in New Orleans. Colonel Gray entered the scene during a hot brawl between Smith and the council. Texas at that moment was without a government. Things calmed down at sight of the dispatcher.

"No, Houston is not here at the time . . . but I'm expecting him any day," Smith said. "I gave him a furlough which is up tomorrow. He'll show up." It was February 28, and the delegates were arriving.

"I'll freeze to death in this barn," Colonel Gray said, teeth chattering. He was warmer on the horse, he said, from the animal heat.

"Get more wood," he said to an orderly. "And see about some coffee for the colonel."

"Did our commissioners get away to the East all right?" Smith wanted to know.

Colonel Gray handed the governor a parcel from Stephen Austin.

A mud-splattered horseman flung himself to the ground and tore into the hall. "Where's General Houston?" Not even this cowboy paid any attention to the erstwhile governor. "The Alamo, sir!" he gasped, while holding a letter out to Smith. "I'd better open it."

On the twenty-fourth of February, the day after the siege began, Travis penned his appeal:

Commandancy of the Alamo,
Bejar, Feb'y, 24th, 1836.

To the People of Texas & All Americans in the World—

Fellow citizens and compatriots—

I am besieged by a thousand or more of the Mexicans under Santa Anna—I have sustained a continual bombardment & cannonade for 24 hours & have not lost a man—The enemy has demanded a surrender at discretion, otherwise the garrison are to be put to the sword, if the fort is taken—I have answered the demand with a cannon shot, & our flag still waves proudly from the walls—*I shall never surrender or retreat.* Then, I call on you in the name of Liberty, of patriotism & everything dear to the American character to come to our aid with all dispatch—The enemy is receiving reinforcements daily and will no doubt increase to three or four thousand in four or five days. If this call is neglected, I am determined to sustain myself as long as possible & die like a soldier who never forgets what is due to his own honor & that of his country.

Victory or Death.

William Barret Travis
Lt. Col. Comdt.

P.S. The Lord is on our side—when the enemy appeared in sight we had not three bushels of corn—we have since found in deserted houses 80 or 90 bushels & got into the walls 20 or 30 head of beef.

Travis

A hat was passed amongst the delegates for the courier

131

Smith to sustain him, and he rode hurriedly away, glad to be out of the wild shouting over Travis and the predicament he was in. Each had his own opinion of what ought to be done. And into this clamor rode Sam Houston, who had been sitting in council with the Cherokee. So it was decided for the soldiers to take up positions at the present as would best secure it from the cannon shot of the Cos's men, and only two men were for storming Bexar—which would have proved fatal had they done so. Austin's army was now situated at the Old Mill located about eight hundred yards north of the Alamo.

There is a small tunnel, a canal really, that passed from the Alamo a distance away and was hidden by brush and a few mesquite, at its outside entrance, and it was through this that scouts came and went—as long as Cos held it.

Relying on information, Captain Dimmit dispatched a detachment of thirty-five men under Westover to reduce and burn the Mexican fort. Citizens of Goliad and vicinity furnished twenty horses and those of Victoria furnished thirty beef. Small wonder they could be so generous, . . . it was the cattle kingdom, Victoria was.

Captain Dimmit reported to General Austin the result of Westover's mission: "The cannon, arms and ammunition at the post were taken. Seven enemy killed and about a dozen wounded. It was sixty-five Mexicans against fourteen of our men." Small wonder Texas grew more sure each passing day.

But the Consultation at San Felipe de Austin sat in session. The Texas troops returned to Goliad.

James W. Fannin was one of those unknown quantities, a Georgian about thirty-one years of age, educated at the United States Academy, West Point; he had landed in Texas as a slave-runner, had money and was a free spender.

The summer of 1835, Fannin became a most ardent adherent, spending time and funds recklessly. At Concepcion he shared the command with James Bowie. Sam Houston, recognizing in this West Pointer a man who could be of great assistance to the cause, offered Fannin an appointment as inspector general of the army with the rank of colonel. The strategy devolved and the siege was pulled back to La Bahia and Gonzales. "Furlough the men to their homes but remain on call. Be ready to return at a moment's notice.

When we are strong enough, then with force, reduce San Antonio!"
Houston said, "It's better to do well late than never!"

Washington-on-the-Brazos was as much pure wilderness as could be found; about a dozen cabins and shanties made up the town of one street which was but an opening cut through the woods, its stumps still standing. The food supply was down to cornbread and fat pork. It was to this that Colonel Gray splashed through the mud to reach, for in his saddlebag he carried a letter for Houston from Austin.

A weary Houston arrived for the convention two days later. But as he neared Washington-on-the-Brazos, his mind wandered. He saw with spotlight clearness his wasted life, and now that he had reached the age of forty-three, he determined to shape up his affairs and look ahead.

The delegates worked on through the night with the cold numbing their feet and legs in the fireless shed which was their convention hall, and soon the wind whisked out of the north bringing the thermometer down to thirty-three degrees. But it was labor not lost. They had wrought a Declaration of Independence without one dissenting vote and signed it on March 2, 1836. Eleven signers were native Virginians; nine were from Tennessee; nine from North Carolina; five from Kentucky; four from South Carolina; four from Georgia; three from Mexico; two from Texas; one from Yucatan; two from Pennsylvania; two from New York; one from Massachucetts; one from New Jersey; one from Ireland; one from Scotland; one from England; and one Canadian.

Miserable and cold, the men were also hungry. They went out to the tavern for breakfast and while dining on eggs and pork and cornbread, by the warmth of the wide hearth, were a happy and talkative crowd.

"Well, now that we've declared freedom from Mexico, you'll have to see to it that it sticks, General Houston," declared Lorenza de Zavala. There was the whole responsibility upon Houston's shoulders—and this was his opportunity to face ahead. The president elected was David G. Burnet; Lorenza de Zavala, vice president; Sam Houston commander-in-chief of the armies. Into these happy considerations rode J. W. Smith, courier from Travis to the convention. He brought an urgent call for help and said that he would defend the Alamo and die like a man should help fail to reach him in time. It was the last appeal.

"My God!" exclaimed Sam Houston, springing to his feet. "He was ordered to blow up that death trap and escape. My orders have been disregarded."

Robert Potter also moved; being short, he jumped upon a box: "The convention will immediately adjourn, arm, and march to the relief of the Alamo!"

"Utter madness!" Houston shouted to be heard. "Too little, too late! We'd never get there in time!"

What manner of creature was Travis anyway—that he would risk the lives of one hundred and sixty-plus men? Why, common sense would preclude his remaining there in the face of sure death. Santa Anna commanded five or six thousand men! "Go on with your work," he said with some bitterness. "I'll leave for the front. If mortal power avail, we'll relieve the brave men in the Alamo!" He strode from the hall and mounted his horse. He was wearing a Cherokee coat and vest of buckskin. With him rode the faithful Hockley and three volunteers, rode out to meet Santa Anna and his army of thousands.

There had been the Battle of Gonzales October 2 and the Battle of Goliad October 9 in 1835 and on October 28, skirmishes of Bowie and Fannin at Mission Concepcion with the enemy. Then came the consultation at San Felipe November 1-14: plan for provisional government, with Henry Smith the first American governor and Sam Houston commander-in-chief of the army. There had been three commissioners; Austin, Dr. Archer and Wharton, to leave immediately for the United States for assistance in their fight. So while winter hung on in a most devastating manner, the Texans had declared for independence. That was in March 1-17, 1836.

Sam Houston, Hockley and a few companions rode through the cold rain. "We better catch up with General Ward and stop him before he runs into a trap," Houston said as they reached Goliad. They found Jim Bowie with only a handful of men but Houston was stunned.

"Get to the Alamo. Demolish it. Blow up all fortifications, remove all cannon, then blow up the Alamo, then get the hell out of there!"

"As you wish," Jim Bowie said but the expression on his face brought out further explanation from Houston.

"I would go myself, or would have marched straight there, but the Matamoros rage is so high. I must see Ward's men!"

Ward was a good man, all things being equal. He had come from

Georgia commanding a well-equipped battalion. Houston's concern was a proclamation nailed to a door, signed by Fannin, calling for volunteers to march on to Matamoros and promising that the troops should be paid out of the first spoils of war, taken from the enemy. So Houston pushed on to Refugio to get hold of Ward's men. Dr. Grant, too, had to be forestalled at any price. Arriving at Refugio, Houston found nothing of supplies and not a soul. The place was deserted. They rested there that night, aiming to leave at the crack of dawn. It was then that Johnson galloped in exclaiming, "The General Council has deposed Governor Smith. And Fannin is now commander-in-chief." Johnson sprang from his weary horse still declaiming, "Fannin's in charge of Ward's men and supplies; Matamoros would be taken. Mexico should be smitten with fire and sword."

Jim Bowie, Colonel Bowie, led his small company to the Alamo, leaving Sam Houston standing in the rain, stunned, outraged beyond words. Finally he said to Hockley, faithful Hockley, "To hell with them. I'm shaking the sand of Texas off my feet. You are free to do whatever seems right for you—and the men." And leaving them there he straddled his horse and called back, "But I shall set Texas free!"

Hockley turned to his companions, "Fannin must have known something we didn't. Who told him he was commander-in-chief? Oh well, we may as well sleep here. No use trying to catch up to Houston. He's been stripped of all authority. Great Ceasar, what a mess!"

Certainly, Sam Houston had had his share of unpredictable experiences—his wedding to Eliza Allen, their separation after only twelve weeks; giving up his governorship and taking a steamer to parts unknown, taking the blame for his problems upon himself. He might have been a bitter man, but Houston seemed always to come back mightier than before. As he had turned then as a lad to his friends with the Iliad under his arm, again after his troubles with Eliza Allen, now, humiliated, angry, and dismissed, he would return again to the Cherokee, to the wigwam of Oo-loo-te-ka, principal chief of the Western Cherokee.

CHAPTER TWENTY-FIVE

Ben Milam was dead and they buried him where he fell. But they had routed General Cos, and sent him back to Mexico. In February 1836, the lookouts sighted advance segments of Santa Anna's army on the outskirts of San Antonio. Inside, within the walls of the plaza and the San Fernando Cathedral, the Texans were under the joint command of Lieutenant Colonel William Barret Travis, a twenty-eight-year-old lawyer from South Carolina, and Colonel James Bowie. The Texans retired behind the walls of the Alamo, in number about 150 men. To this force then came David Crockett, who in his early life had been one of the first families of Fulton, Arkansas, laid out by the Austins, Moses and Stephen, as a rest stop for the colonists they planned to bring into Texas. Now these same men were fighting for this new land they called home.

Hastily they built up earthworks and secured broken areas of the ancient wall. Travis said, "Dr. Sutherland and John Smith . . . go to Gonzales for help. Explain to Fannin how it is here. Grant has stripped this fort of everything he could carry off."

"Yes, sir," Dr. Sutherland said, and the two disappeared to the southeast, toward Gonzales, with exchanges of cannon fire sizzling through the air overhead.

The Mexican officer wanted to have words with Travis. "We demand unconditional surrender of the Alamo garrison!" His demand was answered by a cannon shot. Then Santa Anna appeared and soon the red flag of "no quarter" was flying from the tower of San Fernando Cathedral. To the death. The enemy was already upon them, six thousand strong.

The plaza was a conglomeration of uniforms: Crockett in his deerskin tunic and pants, and coonskin cap with the furry tail dangling, and Travis in his military uniform with high boots and high-formed cap with visor with a sword belt and sword of Damascus steel and James Bowie wearing a flat-topped wide-brimmed hat, a protection against the hot Texas sun, and his fringed buckskin tunic and pants, a relic of his youth along the Mississippi River, Bayou Sarah and Vidalia. Jim Bowie sprang upon a gun platform, with his foot catching in a crack, causing him to fall head first to the ground. "This is a hellovaway to fight a war!" he exclaimed. He was quickly taken up and made comfortable on a cell cot in the Alamo. "Thirteen good cannon out there and not a danged one of 'em knows how to handle one of them effectively!" He would leave his cot and get back to his post, and rising, fell to the floor. He had been stricken with typhoid fever the first hour of the engagement. But Davy Crockett was picking off the enemy with expert marksmanship. Thirty he counted as he pulled the trigger. Those not killed retreated back across the bridge. Then they would try to tell Santa Anna something. The Mexican flag of 1824 was hoisted to the top of the roofless Alamo . . . they were fighting for the restoration of the Republican constitution. Santa Anna had it abolished when he changed sides. "Don't shoot until you have one in the sight. Save your ammunition. Make every shot count, "Travis counseled his men.

Day followed day with Travis searching the rolling terrain for a sight of Fannin, or the couriers to Gonzales, and seeing nothing but nothingness that flows on and on, Texas is so broad a land.

Other couriers were dispatched to Goliad, and finally, Seguin related that Fannin thought it not feasible to send troops or to go to the Alamo at all. So Seguin, and one of his men, made a dash for Gonzales to seek help from that post. But Captain George Kimball and thirty-two of his men were already on the way to the Alamo and on March first were safely guided into the Alamo by John Smith, amid cheers from Travis's men. And the third of March, Colonel Bonham, returning from a mission for Travis, riding hard and eluding the Mexican sentry, reported to Travis that he could expect no help at all from Fannin. It seemed to be the end of all hope, and those thirty-two brave men Kimball had brought would suffer the same fate as the others.

Also on the night of the third, Smith, the courier, crawled along the acequia, the little canal which almost completely circled the convent and hospital outside of the plaza wall. He was carrying the last appeal that Travis made, the messge to the delegates of the Texas Convention then meeting at Washington-on-the-Brazos, where independence was being declared. Later that night, Travis, desperate, called his weary men together, and taking his sword from the scabbard, indented the brown sand with its point. "I must tell you that we are facing the most crucial moment of our lives. It appears so hopeless, that I am now giving you a choice of stepping across the line and joining me in certain death—or of taking the chance of escaping by going over the wall." A mercenary, by the name of

Moses Rose, a Frenchman, said, "You don't pay me for dying, Colonel Travis . . . only fighting. I take my chance!" and over the wall he went. The others? Well, they walked across that line with brave smiles on their weary faces. To a man. And there was James Bowie, too sick to stand, let alone walk, dying of typhoid pneumonia, said, "Carry me over, boys. I'll shoot as long as the bullets hold out." If there had been entertained a doubt as to the rightness of his decision, it was obliterated now. It was a supreme hour for them all.

The Mexican cordon was tightening, and their cannon had breached the north wall. The Texans stood in position at their posts, sleeping as they could, while keeping watch on the Mexicans who were lying on the ground. Not a shot was fired all night. Everybody slept, in one fashion or the other, and Travis said to Jim Bowie, "It's the lull before the storm." And Jim, very sick, replied, "Yep. It'll be hand to hand in here, come daylight." But his pale fingers slid along the Bowie knife Rezin had made for hm, and his index finger caressed the tip, which was razor sharp on both sides. As long as I last. . . ."

"My God, Jim!" Travis said in agony of spirit, "that we must sacrifice ourselves to hold Santa Anna engaged until Houston can raise an efficient army to do battle with that two-faced Mexican!"

"That's all right with me, Will . . . life hasn't been worth a damn to me since I lost my family, nohow," Jim said. "But you? So much to live for. Why, you're almost a kid with your life ahead of you."

"I have a wife and daughter in Alabama . . . and my son's in school here in Texas. Separated . . . have been for many years." And Jim looked with sorrow on his friend.

"I knowed there was something wrong there, but I was never one to be prying into other people's business. Jane is pretty, ain't she?" And Travis, young, handsome, with glazed eyes, turned away.

As dawn appeared gray over the valley, the Mexican bugles broke the silence, and the church bells were ringing in Bexar "Jesu decus Angelicum" for it was Sunday morning, March 6. The Mexicans knelt quickly crossing themselves, for they, too, might never see the sun set, and arose hastily, for the bugles' "deguello" *no quarter* rent the air. Out of the darkness Santa Anna's troops, using ladders, scaled the walls of the Alamo. The first wave fell to the Texan shot and cannon. A second emerged over the rim, and they, too, were raked off, but the third clambered over each other and hit the ground, firing as they ran. General Duque was stomped to death by his own men in their headlong flight from the Texan guns.

The angelus lauds ringing out the remembrance of the Annunciation were not heard now—at least not by William Barret Travis, who lay dead behind his cannon near the northwest corner of the plaza wall.

Despite their heavy losses, the Mexicans broke into the Alamo, bayonetting cell to cell, clubbed and knifed, and then they saw Jim Bowie lying on his cot with two pistols aimed at the door. After the round was used, a bayonet found its way into Jim Bowie, who welcomed death.

Davy Crockett and his Tennessee riflemen fell on the grounds facing the chapel, strewn Mexican bodies all around. Bonham died at his post on the south wall. Carnage. Pure carnage. Santa Anna had lost 670 men out of the first wave of 800. The guns fell silent. Texas had lost on the Sunday morning 182 officers and men, but Mexico counted its loss at fifteen hundred. Would Sam Houston use the time Travis had provided?

David Crockett was one of those leaders who had given up a brilliant career to leave Arkansas and join hands with Travis, Bonham, and the others. Already a veteran of the Creek campaign under Andrew Jackson and a congressman from Tennessee, he had a reputation of fearing not even the Devil. He was a backwoodsman with a droll sense of humor. And like Sam Houston he went to Congress clad in buckskins and a coonskin cap. Davy had brought along his trusty rifle he called Betsy to help out against the Mexicans. Even so, he was a little old for that sort of thing. He was almost fifty years old. He did his best and died with the others. Oh yes, it was Thirteen Days to Glory!

Mrs. Dickinson told of his playing his fiddle for the sick and discouraged, and his telling a joke or two to bring up the lagging spirits. They waited, and yet there came no help to the Alamo. Who could reach them in time? Who with a handful of farm hands face up to seven thousand well-trained Mexicans? Who indeed? They found his old fiddle and Old Betsy, which had been fired as long as the bullets held out. Santa Anna thought to erase them by piling all the dead into a funeral pyre and setting fire to it. But all it did was set fire to the Texans. "Remember the Alamo!" "Remember Gonzales!" "Remember Goliad!" became their battle cry. Fannin and Crockett and Travis, and Stephen Austin knew that in Brazoria a heart would be crying. . . .

Santa Anna, never one to take unnecessary risks, had watched the conflict from afar. Now he made his impressive entrance to view the bodies of the dead officers, Travis, Bowie, and Crockett. With much display, he ordered, "Build a funeral pyre . . . and gather the dead Texans and burn them." Then, Santa Anna saw the white woman, Mrs. Dickinson, her children and two other Mexicans. "You may go, Senora, go and tell Sam Houston that the Alamo has fallen, that the Napoleon of the West has conquered it." He sent her on to Gonzales with the other innocents caught in the Alamo.

Santa Anna strutted—he had won the battle. And Sam Houston was saying, "He may have won the battle, but we'll win the war!"

CHAPTER TWENTY-SIX

For days now the Karankawas had been prowling along the coast, finally coming on to Peach Point. Stealthly they searched the barn, the stables and the smoke house. There was just the odor of dried manure and stray feathers where chickens had once been. The gin was silent, and the sugar mill. All the plantation was as though an epidemic had wiped it out. The Karankawas wore no clothing, save a small apron or a G string. They ceased their prowling and stood at the tall brick entrance way, and just within it. Certainly, those men approaching from the Brazos River were Indians, but they had never seen this strange people before. They were all big men, but only one wore a silver bar through his nose.

Chief Tarshar, with many of his braves, had finally ventured to survey the land of Texas. Actually, he felt there was not much of an alternative. Colonel Brooks, their agent, had been against their selling their million acres, but now informed them they must sell. Tarshar was threatened. He would have no blacksmith nor blacksmith shop; he would have no gunsmith nor gun shop. Colonel Brooks was bearing down. So first they went out to the Guadalupe and Colorado rivers, and not liking it out there, decided on the Brazos. Peach Point was the first plantation Trashar found on the river and, not knowing how far it was to the Gulf, the Big Water, pulled in and tied up to a willow. Obviously, something was wrong with all the white eyes fleeing eastward toward the Sabine, Emerging up over the bank of the river, he saw the Karankawas just standing there . . . the naked giants, and not a white person to be seen anywhere.

"What are you doing at Peach Point?" Tarshar asked, for surely they had no business there. By grunts and sign language they talked.

"What are you doing in our country. Where do you come from?"

"From across the River of Cypress. But you've not told me what you are doing here in this plantation."

"It's none of your business," their leader said, drawing up and pulling his long-bladed knife. Each found a partner, and some had two. Disemboweling seemed to be the ticket, with them standing up fighting as though they'd get in one more lick before they fell. Real carnage took place splattering blood over the brick pillars, breaking off branches of Emily's choice shrubs, and tearing up the oyster shell drive. They fought like well-fed men, not hungry, as Tarshar at first thought. And they died. Two Caddo were mortally struck in the chest, dying instantly.

The Karankawas had never seen heads shaved up the sides with a roach from the forehad to the nape of the neck, and such tattooing! Suddenly, their leader sprang back, seeing the battle lost, and cried, "These are strange men. Perhaps even gods. Flee to your island!" They fled, leaving their dead where they fell. Those severely wounded had a quick knife drawn across their jugular vein. Their chief bowed low, and promised never to enter that land again, if only the man from another world would permit their going and not kill them.

After a quick search, Tarshar knew that the Mexicans had already raided Peach Point. He knew then what his next move was to be.

At Caney, Mrs. Fannin was making a stew. After this, there was nothing else to cook up. Six families had piled in on her as the safest place to escape Santa Anna and his army out in the swamp, miles from anywhere. They had their children with them, and the children swung onto their pets, cats and dogs. In heaven's name how would they manage? The wagon of supplies Fannin had promised to send had not shown up. She knew he himself would not be returning to Caney, for he had cut short a furlough at home to meet the volunteers and arms and ammunitions at Velasco. He had left her well supplied for one family. But six?

Fannin had been a rich man, but adventure to Texas had drained him to a perilous degree. Just at that time, Stephen Austin, Dr. Archer and William Wharton enroute to Washington and points East met him there. It was after their men had gone to this place and that for Texas, that news of Santa Anna's approach had preceded him.

Mrs. Perry had fled and, not knowing where else she might find safety, she remembered the Fannins' plantation on Caney. Then it was the third or fourth day there along with the five other women and their children at Caney, that two Indian braves and their chief appeared, each bearing a young buck across his shoulder. Chief Tarshar could speak her language, having learned it from Larkin Edwards on Red River, who had been the Caddoes' interpreter for many years. Now he bowed in Larkin's best manner, and said, "My compliments, Madam." He stood tall and smiled down at Mrs. Fannin. "I know of your trouble, that your men are gone to war. Allow us the pleasure of presenting you these fine fat deer, for which we have no use."

Mrs. Fannin stood on the steps of her gallery, purely awe-struck and open-mouthed, until Emily joined her. She said, "Why, it's Chief Tarshar! I'm sure of it. My brother Stephen Austin has told us so much about you. I feel I already know you." She turned to Mrs. Fannin, "May I present Chief Tarshar, head chief of the Caddo Federation—Mrs. Fannin."

The handsome Indian again bowed, so that they saw the silver tube through which his long black braid had been drawn, and the red feather. His earrings and amulets made little tinkling sounds as the tiny bells on his moccasins. Six feet and better, thought Emily. All man. All heart! She thanked Tarshar for the deer and explained there was not one amongst them who knew how to handle them.

"You've but to accept them, Madam," he said, showing his teeth like a row of pearls, as he smiled. "My braves will do the rest, Where?"

Mrs. Fannin had prayed for succor, but who could have imagined that it would come from this direction? She was laughing through her tears as she went on the path around the house to the kitchen yard. There, between two trees was a board-table or bench and she pointed to it. "You'll just never know how much this means to us, Chief Tarshar," she said, while the braves slipped knives beginning at the foot and slitting the hide upward and in the middle, where the animal had been gutted and up the other leg and so on until they could peel the deer hide off of a piece. So deftly and so swiftly done.

There it was all finished, quartered, and hanging up high from the dogs on iron hooks she found for them. "Just leave half a side, the ribs part. We'll feast tonight. Won't you stay?"

And again remembering how Larkin would have done it, "Thank you, no. We must get back, all together. There's one other thing I must see about, before leaving for the Caddo prairies."

"Mr. Fannin was sending us a wagon of supplies, but they've not reached us. . . ."

"I understand," Tarshar said. And as he was leaving, Emily Perry stepped up and walked along the path with him.

"What ever brings you to the coast, Chief Tarshar? That is, if you don't mind telling me."

"The Caddo have been offered a large tract of land somewhere in Texas—wherever I decide to settle. I'm exploring, you might say."

"Oh," Emily exclaimed clasping her hands together. "I recall brother hoping you would come to Texas to live. He thinks as farmers there are none better. But that was years and years ago. Before . . ."

"Before, Madam?"

"Yes, before our trouble with the Mexicans. General Santa Anna is trying to beat us into submission."

"Which way was the wagon of supplies coming from?" Tarshar asked.

"From Velasco."

"We'll go in search," Tarshar said, not telling of the Karankawas he had found prowling around Peach Point. Nor of the bitter hand-to-hand fight they had fought and won.

"Traveling by boat?" Tarshar shook his head. "Here is my horse. Take it, and Mrs. Fannin has a couple you can use." Emily hoped Mrs. Fannin would agree. This was no time to be on a fence.

Three hours later Mrs. Fannin was cooking the deer meat, and Emily was making bread when they heard the sounds of wagon wheels. She recognized it as being from the mercantile in Velasco, but the horses were the same as the Indians rode off on, and one of them was driving. "Let us get the wagon emptied up first, please, Madam," Tarshar said, "for we have a chore to do."

Emily, glancing at her own animal, saw a bundle canvas-wrapped

143

across the horse's back. The animal was skittish and wanted the thing removed. The braves went silently about their business, unhitching the ladies' horses from the little buckboard, and her own and taking all three to the barn.

"Before I tell you what we found, I must tell you there's nothing to worry about, not now. But we found on landing at your plantation, about twenty-five Karankawas who were in the act of pillaging. But we demanded to know what they were doing so far from Galveston Island. They became furious, and all at once attacked us—of course, a thing they shouldn't have done."

"You chased them off?" Emily exclaimed, her eyes bugging at the thought she might have been there when they decided to come to Peach Point.

"Some—the rest we killed." Tarshar let thought flow on what he now must relate to this beautiful and sensitive woman.

"I'm glad." She stood facing Tarshar. "What happened to the driver of the wagon?"

"The Karankawas ate him. All we brought to be buried are bone and his head they'd cut off." And Emily reeled over in a dead faint.

CHAPTER TWENTY-SEVEN

Gail Borden was born in Norwich, New York, November 9, 1801. His parents were of New England descent and in 1814 emigrated from New York to Covington, Kentucky, then to Indiana, but in 1822 Gail went south to Mississippi in the hope of improving his health There he taught school and worked as the county surveyor and United States deputy surveyor. In 1829 he went to Texas. There he was elected delegate to the convention that in 1833 petitioned the Mexican government for separation of Texas from Coahuilla. He was also in charge of the official surveys of the colony, compiling the first topographical map of Texas.*

The land office at San Felipe de Austin was under his charge up to the time of the Mexican invasion, replacing Sam May Williams.

*The following year, Gail Borden moved to Galveston. In time he became famous as the inventor of the process of condensing milk.

Early in 1835 with his brother Thomas Borden he established the newspaper, Telegraph and Texas Land Register at San Felipe. When Santa Anna's army was seen coming directly toward San Felipe, Gail tore his presses from the floor and dumped them into the bayou. But now he was busily engaged in printing handbills directing the people and carriers to ride day and night to get them to the various settlements.

"You'll never find it!" the boy helper exclaimed, rushing about grabbing up paper and other materials needed in the printing of a newspaper.

"Oh, yes I will," Gail declared, swiping his hands one palm against another. "I tied a scuppernong vine to it!"

"Hadn't I better get these sheets we've already run off to the settlements?" the lad Jim Smith asked Gail with one eye on the door through which he could see the approaching Mexicans and Borden.

"Too late, Jim. No doubt they'll burn the town. Let's grab whatever we can of Stephen's papers and get the hell out of here!"

"Like Pa allus says, we're just a mile ahead of the sheriff!" Jim's hands moved like lightning, scraping off the counter. Gail emptied up the old desk Stephen had used since he had built the log cabin, back in 1822. Gail was spluttering, "Most methodical person I ever saw." He raised up, took a quick glance at the slowly moving Mexican army, and said, "Get the horses . . . yours is already saddled, but saddle mine. We'll have to move fast now."

Jim swooped up whatever victuals were at hand on spits in the brick fireplace, and crammed the food in a gunny sack he used for carrying the papers. Headed away from San Felipe, Gail Borden took one last long look at Austin's headquarters. "I'd like to remember it as it is this day," he said. "Tomorrow it'll be just ashes."

CHAPTER TWENTY-EIGHT

General Edmund Pendleton Gaines of Fort Jesup in Louisiana had dashed across the Sabine as news filtered in, all of it bad. But Gaines had acted without authority and faced a reprimand and possible courtmartial and being ordered back to his commandancy at

145

Fort Jesup. Now he was armed with orders, poorly veiled, to get himself and his dragoons into Texas at the earliest moment. All during his enforced static position, he remembered the words of Milton, who wrote on his blindness: "they also serve, who only stand and wait." It alone could give him what any ambitious man would want, to serve in his heart and mind, even when his hands, as it were, were tied. When Houston's letter came, or rather Austin's with some lines from Houston appended, his mounted dragoons with heads held high with flags waving, bugles blowing, emerged from the high gates of Fort Jesup onto the San Antonio Trace headed west. It was not a great distance, some thirty miles to San Augustine.

Stephen Austin had written Houston a hasty note: It is very desirable that General Gaines should establish his headquarters at Nacogdoches. Use your influence to get him to do so. And if he could visit us here in Columbia and give the people assurance of the good faith of General Santa Anna in the offers and treaties he has made you and with this government, that would also be helpful. Colonel Gray was the courier.

Houston accepted Austin's note. Then he penciled an asterisk after "treaty" and wrote on the margin, "I made no treaty." At the foot of Austin's note he wrote these additional lines: "General I refer this letter to you and can only add that such a step will . . . save Texas. Your friend, Sam Houston." and sent it on to Fort Jesup.

What bitterness should excompass a soul? Austin did what he thought best for Texas—in the light of the situation. But Sam Houston was also an ambitious man, even as General Gaines, who desired nothing more than to fill his chest with medals and the history books with Gaines!

General Houston, heading his army, such as it was, had left Gonzales March 13, after assisting the families there to flee to safety. The Alamo still smarted. By mid-morning the army was organized: Edward Burleson, colonel; Sidney Sherman, lieutenant colonel, and Alexander Somervell, major. Before he could fall back, he made a report to the Military Committee in session at the convention, with details of the fate of the Alamo, and of his order to Colonel Fannin to go to the aid of Bexar. "The order to Colonel Fannin will indicate to you my conviction that with our small unorganized force, we

cannot maintain sieges in fortresses, in the country of the enemy."
He had given orders to Neill to blow up the fortifications of his
post and fall back to Goliad. He was fearful lest Fannin and his
men at La Bahia suffer the same fate as the Alamo.

The spring rains had begun, the streams swelling, the prairie like
a sea, with no line of demarcation of river save a meandering line of
open space between heavy forest. Women and children, deprived of
their men, scattered in all directions like chickens frightened by
hawks. Nacogdoches to the east . . . always east.

Mr. Johnathan Ikin, an English capitalist, had come to San Felipe
de Austin in response to a bid from Texas for four million dollars.
He witnessed one of the speediest decisions in memory, for it was
with the greatest haste the delegates headed toward Harrisburg
where their aim was to set up their new government. Lorenza de
Zavala rode a small mule, while by his side, the Mr. Ikin sloshed
through the mud, not risking the ornery mare who had rather slip
and slide, than walk like Zavala's gray mule. There was uppermost
in his mind that such a transient government, the most unstable he
had ever seen, in a state of flux, would not be a good risk. After all
four millions had been hard come by! It was pouring down.

They reached Harrisburg soaked to the skin, whereupon Mrs.
Harris's metal was tested. She could provide beds for the President
Burnet and Vice President de Zavala. The other dignitaries—a misnomer, she decided, if there ever had been one—dried by the great
open fireplace, were permitted to roll themselves into blankets and
there sleep on the floor. She had, however, fed them well. It was
then that young Lorenza de Zavala embraced his father and, attended by a French valet, breasted the storm and the fleeing colonists for he was headed out to find Sam Houston and his army.

CHAPTER TWENTY-NINE

The Secretary of War, Thomas J. Rusk, received a letter by courier from General Sam Houston. It read:

It was a poor compliment to me to suppose that I would not
advise the convention of any necessity that might arise for

their removal . . . You know I am not easily depressed but before my God, since we parted I have found the darkest hours of my life. For forty-eight hours I have not had an ounce of food, nor have I slept. I was in constant apprehension of a rout—yet I managed as well or such was my good luck that the army was kept together.

At Gonzales if I could have had a moment to start an express in advance of the deserters, all would have been well, and all at peace east of the Colorado. But the deserters went first, and, being panic struck, all who saw them breathed the poison and fled. Oh, why did the cabinet leave Washington-on-the-Brazos?"

Volunteers came in, poorly equipped and without artillery, but anxious to fight. Houston maneuvered down river, and his scout, Deaf Smith, brought in a Mexican who informed them that General Sesma was approaching with seven hundred and fifty men with two field pieces. Sesma camped on the west side, two miles above the right wing of Houston's army, and sent reinforcements. Without a thought as to what his men thought, for Houston was ever his own man, he ordered, "Retreat!"

"Retreat!" his baffled soldiers shrieked.

"The army will march at sunset!" Houston said.

Six miles from the river the army bivouacked without fires and grumbled themselves to sleep. At dawn they were again marching. . . .

"Close up!" Major Ben Fort Smith of the staff asked Captain Mosely Baker, "What do you think of Houston's strategy, if that is what you call it and not desperation?"

This gave Baker a good reason to let everybody know just how he felt about it, for in a loud voice he said, "I think little enough, and unless reasons for the retreat are forthcoming, Sam Houston'll be deposed from command before this day is over!"

Such a threat just worked a hardship on all the soldiers. And Captain Baker had no time for investigations. Houston marched the men so relentlessly with thirty weary miles behind them, the men dropped too tired to care. They had covered the whole distance between the Colorado and the Brazos and bivouacked a mile from San Felipe de Austin.

Through Houston's mind, seeing San Felipe de Austin in the distance, was the scene of his departure. He remembered saying, "Get on with organizing a government. I'll leave this moment to aid Travis." Still he could not fathom Travis at all. The men from Gonzales fled the convention without ceremony, others in sheer and utter confusion got reeling drunk, but with all there had been a well-knit delegate with a stubby beard who had to stand on a bench to be seen and heard and who calmly directed that the first order of business was a government. The Constitution was slapped together by midnight and the bearded man, David Burnet, was elected provisional president. There were two bulges in his coat; one was his Bible, the other his pistol. His background left little to be desired. The delegates, for the most part, had heard about this man, who thirty years earlier had left New York to see the world. He was with Miranda's romantic but rash descents upon Venezuela and had roamed with wild Indians in the little-explored West. He was a sober man who neither drank nor smoked, which gave him, no doubt, they thought, his robust health. His vice president was Lorenza de Zavala, formerly of Yucatan, and his cabinet was elected also. At four o'clock in the morning, March 17, the New Administration was sworn in, and the exhausted men retired for breakfast. Now was a time for sober consideration of their position, and a number of the delegates were thusly occupied, when a fugitive dashed into San Felipe de Austin shouting the groundless rumor that Santa Anna's cavalry had crossed the Colorado. The members dispersed in all directions. There was general panic, for their families were exposed to the ruthless Mexicans! It was a runaway, Sam Houston thought, recalling the scenes along the road. Carts, wagons, carretas, anything that would carry were compelled to labor, with whole families walking. . . . He had no need to ask the reason why. He could see it in their faces. Night and day in a continuous stream they passed over the Brazos.

Houston's scout returned from the settlement of San Felipe. "The convention has removed to Harrisburg, sir;" he said, "and the most of the colony has fled also." Houston was just furious. He drew from his saddlebag, writing material, and wrote a letter to the secretary of war, Rusk.

In the distance Sam saw the affluent Bernard Plantation, home of Colonel Groce, "Texas's Cotton King," and the Brazos River lying between. This most turbulent stream had been made savage by the spring rains. Questions arose in Houston's mind, until there at the

149

wharf he saw Groce's boat *Yellow-Stone* taking on cotton. He pressed this vessel into service to get his army across, and at many other times. Colonel Groce and the Bernardo Plantation were at Sam Houston's disposal. "Cattle, I'll supply you with all the beef you can use." Colonel Groce was Sarah Groce's father, father-in-law to William Wharton, under whose standard Sam Houston had formerly labored. There may have been a connection, maybe not. It could be that Groce himself had wanted to be free of Mexico since he shipped most of his cotton not to Vera Cruz, but to Liverpool— and paid and paid and paid.

In a few days, as things began to shape up for Houston, he sent a courier to Harrisburg with his detailed report:

> The Mexican armies were scattered over a wide expanse of territory, far from their base of supplies. I could have successfully attacked General Sesma on the Columbia, but it would have been but a straw. My game is Santa Anna himself. My men were anxious to fight, not seeing the ultimate goal, and were provoked with me at my order to retreat. Captain Baker reported he had been fired upon at San Felipe. One man was killed, John Bricker. There was no other incident in that quarter. San Felipe was set afire, but the people escaped heading east. I trust Harrisburg will not share the fate of San Felipe. . . .

CHAPTER THIRTY

In February 3, 1836, General E. P. Gaines asked for arms and ammunitions and a request to the Secretary of War Cass, which was sent on to the Quarter Master General Thomas Jesup, for immediate appropriations, "for barracks, quarters, storehouses, hospital, stables, etc., for materials for the same at Fort Jesup, Louisiana in the amount of $25,000. He explained that the fort had been set up in 1822. Quarter Master General Jesup, pleased that the cantonment Jesup had become a fort, sent on the request.

The major part of the Third Infantry had constituted Colonel

Many's army, but for General Gaines and his immediate needs was sorely inadequate. So in January of that year he had already ordered five companies from Jefferson Barracks, St. Louis, Missouri. Five companies of the Third Regiment and eight companies of the Sixth were to advance at once to the Sabine River and bivouac at Camp Sabine, General Wilkinson's former camp of 1806.

Fort Jesup was a square mile of land surrounded by extensive stone and wooden barracks. Much of it was suddenly replaced, and Fort Jesup took on the appearance of an active post. When letters and rumors and the obvious panic of the residents of Texas passed before Gaines's eyes, it was aggravating to say the least that his orders had not come to cross the international border. But when Esubio, brother of Manuel Flores, sauntered in for a talk, he said, "I've just come from the Cherokee. . . . They aim to raise the Indians against Texas. I intend to attack and set fire to Nacogdoches!" Gaines bristled. He had heard enough to stir any man's heart to action.

He wrote a memo:

> These facts and circumstances present to me the important question, whether I am to sit still and suffer these movements to be so far matured as to place the white settlements on both sides of the line, wholly within the power of the savages, or whether I ought not instantly to prepare the means of protecting the frontier settlements and if necessary, compelling the Indians to return to their own settlements and hunting grounds. I cannot but decide in favor of the last alternative which this question presents; for nothing can be more evident than that an Indian uprising, or war, commencing on either side of the line will as surely extend to both sides as that a lighted quickmatch thrust into one side of a powder magazine should extend the explosion to both sides. With this in view Flores has recently passed up the valley of Red River producing considerable excitement among the Caddoes.

Materials arrived daily, and work progressed at Fort Jesup. By March the soldiers had little to do but parade or drill or care for their horses, which were new more or less. Now they were being called cavalry. Horses were to be bought at Stewart's plantation,

"Grand Ecore," and it was Dr. Stewart himself who came along with the charro to Fort Jesup. This was why Stewart found himself on the road to locate the army of Sam Houston.

But winter hung on and March rain was as cruel as the February snow and sleet. Fort Jesup was behind Dr. Stewart now and the river of cypress, Sabine. General Gaines had held him back and the news kept coming to General Gaines—all of it bad. There were La Bahia and Goliad, and Santa Anna, flushed with the blood of the Texas-Americans he chose to call "land thieves," was marching across the Gulf country like a prairie fire. General Sam Houston was falling back, retreating, falling back and retreating and the men were deserting and the rain, and the rain, and the rain . . . but Houston finally reached his goal.

The streams were swollen and covered the wide expanses with water, so that Stewart let his horse find its own way, keeping his eye on a distant oak grove. Families with whatever they could get on their mules or carts, for most of the wagons were in service, were fleeing Santa Anna on horseback or on foot, and Stewart splashed through their trackless direction. "Turn back!" they cried, but not stopping. They could not know what he was carrying in his mind a most important message from General Gaines to General Houston. Should he fail as others had failed, with interceptions always a threat, the message would die with him. Sam Houston must know that the United States stood behind him—for God's sake, give him word! He must know that there awaited him more guns and ammunitions than Santa Anna could ever raise, and Houston's word was all he needed to give.

All day Stewart rode through the rain. Sometimes it came in blinding sheets, veiling the way. Then it would squeeze off and wait and gather strength and come on again harder than before. In the distance he saw a lone oak tree, with nothing but softly rolling plains. He headed for it. He eased off his horse stiff-legged and wrapped the bridle around a low branch, and untied his blanket and took his yellow slicker he had worn and laid it wet side down on the high roots of the oak, and, rolling himself in the blanket, was asleep as soon as his body was fully on the ground. He wondered when he awakened how long he had been there. The clouds had drifted away toward Louisiana and a pink glow told him to head to it, for that would be west. He could barely straighten up for he had been in the saddle much longer than his usual time, even when his patients were a long way down Red River.

He started out again following the red glow, not knowing he had lost his way, and came upon a small group of men by the side of the road from Nacogdoches to the sea. They were camping not far from Liberty. "Hello there," he called, not wanting to be shot at, and when the bodies had faces, Stewart said, "I took a pinking to be a sunset. I've been asleep." A man stepped toward him from the spit over which half a cow was cooking. The man pushed his hat back from his face and looked directly into Stewart's eyes. "Man, don't you know it's dangerous to be rambling around like you're doing?"

"Well, actually, I'm not rambling. I'm looking for General Sam Houston's camp." Dr. Stewart surveyed his situation. Enemy? Which side?" I must have missed the road. But never have I seen such terror as the people fleeing Santa Anna. Is he that close?" Stewart held the horse's bridle, not knowing when it would be expedient to spring upon him. "I ought to have been there yesterday!"

"Well, that's Harrisburg burning," the man said. "Our impermanent capital. Ain't that a helluvanote?"

"You'll find him, I reckon, down at Colonel Groce's plantation. He keeps the general in beefs. And speaking of beef, fork that stump, pard, we're about to eat. This here's Deaf Smith, and that's Wharton, and I'm Anson Jones . . . the rest of the boys joined up with us are from San Felipe. That pinking you saw to the west, may or may not have been San Felipe burning. Nothing much left, they tell us, but ashes."

The man, Anson Jones, must be the famous doctor he had heard so much about in his own special treatment of malaria, and his form took on many shapes as the firelight played on him, his face, his back, a shoulder, as he cut off slabs of meat from the spit, ladled beans from a dutch oven on the coals and the tin plate flickered and the tin coffee cup. Stewart was that hungry nobody could believe it, and his jaws worked on the hot beef and his stomach drew it down half ready. While he ate he heard without listening: "Man, you fellows were smart to get into Columbia before Santa Anna made his swath across there. I'll bet Bell's Prairie's a mess. Didn't have no trouble getting into the Masonic hall?"

Stewart saw that Deaf Smith's eyes followed from one speaker to another, and he was reading their lips in this small light!

Anson Jones patted his saddle bag, "She's right here . . . every dot and tittle." He was proud of something, Stewart could see, but getting records from a building before the Mexican army swept through was not what Stewart would have done. "Wharton and I got outta there in the nick of time!"

"Colonel Many at Fort Jesup speaks well of Mr. Deaf Smith," Stewart said. It was introduction enough for the men. He was a messenger from General Gaines to General Houston. "Holy Maker!" Jones was taking Stewart's hand and damned near wrung it off he was that glad.

Anywhere east people went to escape the enemy, and the Mexicans kept rolling. There was no time for eating, for resting, and with every new deserter came the same cries, "Run . . . run for your lives. Santa Anna's army headed here!" Small wonder that the people were in panic.

He directed for procurement of horses, supplies, beefs and artillery. Anything that would shoot! Having crossed the LaVaca, Houston made camp on the bank of the Navidad Rio, with sleet peppering down. "If our people would act in concert," he said, "we could expel every Mexican . . . and with fifteen hundred we can defeat all that Santa Anna can send to the Colorado."

Two mud-splattered gentlemen sprang from their horses—one was carrying his saddlebag—and mounted the stairs of the Masonic Temple two at a time. In less than five minutes, for time was precious, they were back on their horses headed north. Columbia had few enough defenders, and they were either going or readying to go and paid no attention to Wharton and Jones. They spoke to no one but Dr. Anson Jones who smiled in a knowing way, and patted the saddle bag bulging with records and things pertaining to Masonry. They raced over the ferry of the Brazos, and headed up the coast, hoping to find Houston's trail. Santa Anna was a clever man. And a Mason. "We better head north so's not to miss him," Jones said.

They reasoned Houston must be retreating to Nacogdoches, where he knew General Gaines would be waiting. Following heavy impressions certainly an army of foot soldiers, they pulled up and speculated on what the sign meant. Houston could not be aiming for Nacogdoches for at the fork of the road, the tracks turned south, toward the bay. Stewart went immediately to General Houston, who was giving his men a last important word: "A decisive battle is near at hand in which some of you will be killed, but victory is certain."

Sam Houston turned then, and seeing Dr. Stewart, whom he had known for a long time, shook hands and said, "General Gaines send you?" and Stewart replied, "Yes. He wanted you to know that he was waiting armed and fully prepared to fly to your aid. This time, sir, he has permission from Washington City. They directed General Gaines' to go to the aid of General Houston with all possible speed. But General Gaines is already this side of the Sabine, and is waiting for your orders."

"Well, Dr. Stewart . . . you wait here. I'll know soon enough. Then I'll send General Gaines a message, and thank you for coming." Sam Houston mounted his beautiful gray-white horse, and Dr. Stewart rejoined Dr. Anson Jones, Dr. Ewing, and Wharton who was about to get behind a cannon.

The skirmishing that day amounted to little, each rather feeling for the strength of the other. And Jones observed, "The Caddoes Gaines considers dangerous, not because they are strong and warlike, but because they have a perfect knowledge of the topography of the country. They can easily lead the more western tribes to the cabin of every frontier settler. He fears them more as guides than warriors. They have caused General Gaines and Colonel Many no end of apprehension. That is why Gaines mounted his reinforcements."

"He told me," Stewart opined, "that mounted soldiers were superior, regardless of their purpose. So he purchased horses, and more horses. I had just delivered him a string, when he pressed me into service. Of course, I was perfectly willing to come. I lost a brother at the Alamo . . . he followed Davy Crockett out there."

CHAPTER THIRTY-ONE

Houston and his army arrived and went into camp on a high knoll on the plantation of Charles Donoho, and aimed to remain there for the other segments to catch up. Colonel Groce had sent beefs to the Texans each day, had rendered any service of which he was capable.

Houston expected the same kind of assistance from Donoho. But Donoho stormed Houston's camp with "and don't you dare to cut down any of my timber for your fires!"

And Houston said in his mind that he would have to agree with the jackass. "All right, Mr. Donoho. I promise we shall never cut down one of your trees."

Mr. Donoho was satisfied and returned to his house. General Houston remarked casually, "See the fences, boys? They're not trees now, are they? And of course, we'll just have to have a fire!"

The soldiers, relaxed and laughing at foxy old Sam, took hold of the fence posts, and soon Mr. Donoho had no fence along that stretch of his land. But a great fire blazed away and hot coals cooked their bread of flour mixed with lake water and wrapped around sticks. Houston said, "I feel like dancing tonight."

"With each other out here on the grass? Come on, General."

"No, in Donoho's parlor."

"But he ain't asked us . . . sir," the young Texan drawled.

"That's all right. We're protecting him, the ingrate!" Houston replied. "One of you fellows get over to the refugee camp and fetch the women . . . and six of you ought to be able to set the furniture out in the yard. We got to have space to swing our partners in."

Sam Houston decided that amongst his men he had enough fiddlers and guitarists . . . there was the fife and drum. "It ought to make a hell of a good band," he said in his mind. So he called the musicians.

Mr. Donoho sighed, and welcomed the girls from the refugee camp all primped and shining, and watched the soldiers moving his fine furniture out under the stars with outward calm. He had already seen what bucking Sam Houston meant when he saw from his window his oak posts going up in in smoke. He said to Mrs. Donoho, "It's better to join him than fight him. We'd be sure to lose everything, if not."

The dance lasted all night. Houston was so impressed by a number he heard that he decided it must be played to bring up his men's spirits to fever pitch. "Will you come to the bower I have shaded for you?" On the other side, Houston's thoughts were on the lovely Miss Anna Raguet, who had tied his sash and sent him off to war, little dreaming that his trusted messenger Dr. Iron would wed her. Why don't you speak for yourself, John . . .? But Sam was in that

156

haze which might be called the twilight zone, where Miss Anna was concerned.

Houston had word that San Felipe lay a bed of ashes, the little log capital Stephen called home, and a sense of humility over-shadowed all else. Stephen had so sincerely welcomed him to Texas, to San Felipe, and Jim Bowie, the damned of the living who could not stand the loss of his lovely Ursula and his two children to cholera. If ever man wanted to die, it was Jim Bowie. He would always wonder about the expression on Jim's face when he ordered Jim to the Alamo to blow it to kingdom come, and get the hell out of there . . . had he delivered that message? Had he decided this was the quickest way to release his soul from its constant torment? Only God knew the answer.

Wharton exclaimed, "To hell with sleeping tonight. Let's get on down the road. What did you say your handle was, pardner?"

"Stewart. I don't think I said who I am . . . but I'm a doctor and I live in Natchitoches . . . General Gaines had a two-fold reason for sending me instead of Colonel Many or Lieutenant Bonnel, who wouldn't be able to help out, medically speaking. But I'm sure you have enough doctors without me."

"Never enough, Dr. Stewart," Anson Jones said. "Especially now!" Like a rapier Santa Anna was gleaning the old, the young, sparing the women and children, but he was determined to rid Texas of the Americanos who were attempting to take Texas from Mexico by force. That must never happen. But Deaf Smith was talking in his low deep voice, "We'll have company to the general's camp."

And Anson Jones said, "Before God!"

These activities were akin to law, this broad land, Stewart said in his mind. It was the only law and order possible in a region where settlements and society had gone in advance of the institutions and instrumentalities of organization. Men were receptive to leadership. Dr. Stewart thought about and mourned the death of his younger brother who followed the blood trail into Texas and died at the Alamo with the Singing Bee Hunter and the anxious lads of Natch-itoches.

"Come on, boys," Dr. Anson Jones called as the men had set their plates down, empty. "There's not a moment to lose!" The response was that instantly all had forked their horses and were flying across the prairie with a showing of oyster shells, and Stewart knew they were approaching the coast. In a matter of hours they had reached Houston and his army already encamped in a wooded area near the bay.

"Well, I'll be damned!" Wharton exclaimed. He's on the way to Harrisburg."

"And not a word to General Gaines!" Dr. Jones said. "Oh happy day!"

"Whatever he's up to, you can bet your last dollar that he's got it figured out. Imagine heading into a storm!" Wharton said.

It was to gain a certain sloping terrain from which he could see the approach of the enemy that Houston camped. Nearby were Groce and Zavalas and many of Houston's friends strung along the bayous and river, where a bridge crossed Vince's Bayou, and over which both armies must pass. "There'll be beef enough," Jones said, to which Wharton replied. "Yeah . . . Houston believes in sharing."

They came upon camp in the shape of a half moon. It was in readiness, with Sidney Sherman commanding the left wing; Burleson the center with infantry; and Lamar on the right with artillery. Houston was riding his great gray-white mare up and down, checking, rechecking. This must not fail. Sam Houston was laying his all on this altar.

"It'd take a draft horse to hold him—even that one looks sway-backed!" Wharton said facetiously.

"How can you make jokes when neither of us knows if there'll be a Columbia come tomorrow?"

"Yeah. I been thinking about that, Anson. Being a Mason sure as hell's calling for more than a man feels like giving!"

Down nearer the bay Santa Anna had his encampment—set and waiting for Houston and his sorry bunch they called an army. Obviously, General Santa Anna did not anticipate the fury that was to come.

All day both armies had small skirmishes, feeling out each other. Houston took time out for a sandwich and cup of coffee. Wharton and Jones cleaned their guns while they talked to Houston. He was squatting Indian fashion while he ate. "I've sent Deaf Smith and Henry Karnes over there to wreck the bridge, it being the only means of escape, theirs, and ours too, you might say. As Travis said, it's Victory or Death!"

That night they all slept, American and Mexican. But the next morning about nine o'clock a Mexican force was seen winding across the prairie to join the main body of Santa Anna's army, when at that moment Karnes and Smith came in. "Mission accomplished! Harrisburg is ashes!" Smith and Karnes had been whacking away all night to cut Vince's bridge down, and now they retired back of "The Twin Sisters," a gift of cannon from Tennessee.

"Charge!" Houston commanded, riding his great gray-white mare and the cannons, "The Twin Sisters," filled with rusty nail, cut wire, horse shoes—anything, blasted away with brutal accuracy into the Mexicans. And they, taken by surprise, were momentarily in a state of shock. But they suddenly came alive, firing from all quarters. One was a telling shot, aimed at General Houston, but felling his horse instead of him. Houston was mounted again instantly on another, and he directed, commanded and rode hard, so that his men caught the spirit of him, their leader. And then a ball went through his ankle and into his mount, which stumbled to its knees and quietly closed its eyes.

Houston realized that he had been hit, but a numbness, not pain, was all he felt as he straddled his third horse, and as he passed and repassed his three arms of soldiers, he was followed by a trail of blood. Very soon now he would not be able to see the enemy, nor his own men. What was happening to him?

General Sam Houston opened his eyes, discovering that he was lying upon the ground and that Dr. Ewing had cut his boot off with a Bowie knife and was pulling small splinters of bone which issued in many directions from a shattered ankle. Dr. Ewing said, "General?" and Houston replied, "Yes, sir, I'm awake . . . what happened?"

"To be brief, you've had a foot shot off, or soon will be off. I can't possibly salvage such a shattered bone. I'm sorry. I'll have to get you to New Orleans just as soon as possible, not only to see if they can save your foot, but your very life is in danger."

"It's so quiet, Dr. Ewing!" Houston said, rising upon an elbow.

"Why, the battle lasted but about half an hour. It has been over and the Mexicans routed for ever so long. You had quite a nap!" The doctor was bandaging the ankle mostly to stop the bleeding and filled Sam with some of Varner's strong liquor.

The escaping Mexicans headed into the quagmire and the tall salt grass along the estuary, the tall grass which lived on neither land nor sea, but earth in the making, where many died.

Santa Anna, enjoying a siesta in his luxurious tent, smacked his jaws in anticipation of the complete subjugation of the stupid gringos. He had them now, right in the palm of his hand. There was nothing of pressure—he was calling the shots, so his soliders were about their usual camp duties, some butchering beefs, some cooking, others watering the horses, and they were pretty well scattered about. General Cos and his contingent were resting after their forced march to meet Santa Anna for the big and last battle with the Texans. They had stacked their arms against a tree, little suspecting attack. When they heard the alarm it was too late. The ragamuffins were hurdling their barricade like a good steed in Virginia.

Santa Anna sprang upon his horse, seeing few men standing up fighting but many sprawled upon the ground, and took out for Vince's Bridge, thinking that General Castrillon was a fool to display such cool bravery in trying to rally his force. Certainly, Castrillon would die there, and his men with him. Indeed, Santa Anna figured a good run was far better than a bad stand! But Santa Anna did not know that his escape was cut off, that Vince's bridge had been cut down. Ah, that tall marsh grass . . . it would be a good place to hide until he could gather his thoughts and make some plans. He realized he was in a trap, and a trap of Houston's own making.

Dr. Anson Jones cried out, his arm pointing, "There's General Almonte with several hundred men surrendering in a body!"

Wharton exclaimed following Jone's point, "Yeah. I wonder what happened to General Gaines and his dragoons?"

"He was supposed to stand at Houston's back!"

"He sure was. Gaines'll stand at Houston's back til his belly's beat blue!"

"It never was his idea to let Houston have it . . . you know he was danged near courtmartialed for jumping the gun, earlier."

"If we don't find that Santa Anna, and he falls on us again, say in a year or two, why we can just say adios to fifteen years of as hard labor as I've ever done. How many towns has that devil already burned down?" Wharton had really had his fill.

"Now, you just don't forget if the people had given up that cannon the Mexicans loaned them during an Indian uprising, we'd likely as not ever riled Santa Anna. After all, it was theirs."

Jones said, thinking back a good many years, "You know he's not such a bad little guy when you know him. Stephen Austin says he has been a true friend to the colonists, and him, even a Mason!" Jones patted his saddlebag. "There's sure one thing ain't nobody ever going to know about!"

"What's that?"

"That the records of the first masonic lodge in Texas rode gallantly through the Battle of San Jacinto, just like the rest of us!" Both men eyed each other. "Yeah . . . let's keep it a secret!"

CHAPTER THIRTY-TWO

The next day General Cos with his force came in. Altogether there were seven hundred and fifty Mexican prisoners, in one way or another. They were being guarded by Texas soldiers.

There were six hundred dead scattered about over this woman's land, and the stench was getting unbearable. She had already demanded the removal of the bodies. "We'd better get off before she gets a shotgun after us," Houston said while the fever burned and his eyes glazed. He still refused to leave for New Orleans. "But first, dispose of the bodies. How many did you say we lost?"

"General, we lost two killed outright. We got about twenty-three wounded. Some real bad. It looks like four or five just can't make it."

Six passed away that night. The next morning, they were all buried in a common grave, barely a stone's throw from the ancient oak tree under which Houston lay, his saddle for a pillow.

"You better take the wounded across there to de Zavala's plantation," Houston said. "I'm sure the Senora de Zavala won't mind looking after them until they're able to go home."

Out there amongst the oaks, young Lorenza de Zavala was searching for the body of General Castrillon, a boyhood friend of his father. Houston saw the young soldier who had joined him accompanied by a French valet, stoop down and when he stood up, he was holding the general's body. He turned toward the de Zavala cemetery, and there, quite alone, he buried the body. Houston was deeply touched by this scene, for such tenderness Houston had rarely seen. "Who ever said war was hell knew what he was talking about." In the morning, if he lived. . . .

It was a long night for Sam Houston. With every heart throb, the excruciating pains shot through—and his opium was almost all gone. But early the next morning of the twenty-second, James Sylvester and Joel Robinson, scouting for escapees along the bay, found a little Mexican sleeping on a hillock, probably a muskrat mound, dressed as a common soldier. "Wal, a prisoner's a prisoner. They all gotta be fed. But I swear, I just ain't got the stomach for bayonetting him this early in the morning!" So he prodded the soldier, awakening him from sound slumber, and motioned him to rise and get ahead. All the way back not a word was spoken, and the only sound was the crunching of feet on reed.

They reached the compound where the hundreds of prisoners were and hats went up and tears poured and Ave Marias, but the loudest voices, "El Presidente! El Presidente!" purely startled the two scouts.

"Well, I be doggoned!" Robinson said, grinning from ear to ear. "Santa Anna hisself!" and "What do you know."

But El Presidente ignored the rousing welcome, the tears, the hands crossing themselves in gratitude for their beloved Presidente's having been spared to them. And straightening as if a ramrod were up his back, he demanded of his captors, "Take me to your General Houston!"

Young de Zavala had returned from the Zavala cemetery, and now for some time Houston had been employed watching a crowd of "Tories" gathered across the San Jacinto on a hill immediately back of Lynchburg. These Tories were traitors, interfering with the war. "Captain Kokernot, take a force over there and rout that bunch. They're just of nuisance value!"

Houston sent a message to President Andrew Jackson, telling of his victory at San Jacinto. Sam Houston might be suffering the torture of the damned in body, but his spirit soared to heights unknown. Miss Anna Raguet, be impressed!

After writing out his report he must needs leave for New Orleans. There were 600 muskets, 300 sabres and 200 pistols. Several hundred mules and horses, and near $12,000 in specie. Couriers were sent out in all directions with "Tell them to come home and plant their corn." Then Santa Anna walked bravely to him.

"I am General Antonio Lopez de Santa Anna, president of Mexico."

General Houston said, welcoming Santa Anna, "I'm slightly debilitated General Santa Anna. There's been an accident."

Ignoring Houston's sally, he said, "I place myself at the disposal of the brave General Houston."

He places himself. He's the commander-in-chief of the Army of Operations. Damned if ever I saw such a gutty little devil! Houston

162

kept a poker face. He must not show how gratifying it was to see the Mexican general. He raised himself upon an elbow, "As you can see I cannot stand. But I'm very glad to see you." He would never mean anything more.

Now Lorenza came to report to Houston and act as interpreter if needed, which was not likely, for Santa Anna was a linguist. Recognizing Lorenza de Zavala as his old friend's son, the Mexican's face lit up. "Ah, my old friend's son!" But Lorenza had just buried one very dear to him and his family, his father's boyhood friend. He bowed. His attitude was cool. Had General Castrillon not given his life filling Santa Anna's shoes while this man raced to safety? Houston could almost feel the spit that belabored the lad's mouth.

Santa Anna would not be snubbed. "That man may consider himself born to no common destiny who has conquered the Napoleon of the West. It now remains for him to be generous to the vanquished."

Houston levelled his eye on Santa Anna. "Like the four hundred you massacred? Or Fannin, or Travis at the Alamo?"

"Believe me . . . I allowed them thirteen days to escape, but they would not. I sent warning after warning . . . I could do no less, for Stephen Austin is my friend of many, many years. But they would not go!"

"Thirteen days to glory!" Sam Houston said.

"But about Fannin and his four hundred who surrendered expecting to be treated as prisoners, some consideration. But what did you do? You stood them up against a wall and shot them. Do you really expect clemency?"

General Santa Anna went pale. "Oh sir, do you have a bit of opium?"

Houston revived him, and then, the Mexican feeling composed, they began serious dialogue. "No, no," Houston replied. "It's not in my domain to discuss treaties with you. I just want you to get your goddamn Mexicans across the Rio Grande and keep'em there!" Santa Anna stiffened, but, wily strategist that he was, relaxed. After all *he* was the prisoner.

An armistice was then proposed which provided for the evacuation of Texas. Santa Anna wrote the orders to Filisola and other generals in the field, and sent them—or rather Houston sent them out by Deaf Smith to see that they were truly delivered.

"Restore the general's baggage to him. Set it up nearby. All his personal things." The prisoner withdrew under cover of his guard, to dress himself in proper uniform. Later, over a bottle of cognac provided from the prisoner's own stores, he sat on the ground by Houston's side, while Houston waved the guard to stand back.

After a while when the blood warmed and flowed Houston asked, "What makes you want to be a dictator, General?"

"Ah, Senor Houston . . . it will be a hundred years before my people are able to govern themselves," Santa Anna replied sadly— as if it were something he did not wish to recognize as a fact.

"I don't think so," Houston said.

"But si, Senor General, a man with any brain in his head would have seen my predicament—a prisoner of the Gringo," a smile almost benevolent, "would never have so spiritedly cried, 'El Presidente! El Presidente!'" There were real tears in his eyes.

Why was Santa Anna not shot as the angry Texans wanted, demanded? Well . . . Santa Anna was a Mason.

Houston, in his official report of the battle, which he sent to the president of the republic, gives a lively firsthand picture. He wrote:

At half-past three o'clock in the evening, I ordered the officers of the Texan army to parade their respective commands.
. . . Our troops paraded with alacrity and spirit, and were anxious for the contest. Their conscious disparity in numbers seemed only to increase their enthusiasm and confidence, and heightened their anxiety for the conflict. Our situation afforded me an opportunity of making the arrangements preparatory to the attack without exposing our designs to the enemy. The first regiment, commanded by Colonel Burleson, was assigned to the center. The second regiment, under command of Colonel Sherman, formed the left wing of the army. The artillery (two cannons donated to the Texas cause by the citizens of Tennessee, and affectionately called "The Twin Sisters") under special command of Colonel George W. Hockley (Faithful Hockley), inspector-general, was placed on the right of the first regiment; and four companies of infantry, under the command of Lieutenant Colonel Henry Millard, sustained the artillery upon the right.

Our cavalry, 61 in number, commanded by Colonel Mirabeau B. Lamar, whose gallant and daring conduct on the previous day had attracted the admiration of his comrades, completed our line. Our cavalry was first dispatched to the front of the enemy's left, for the purpose of attracting their notice, whilst an extensive island of timber afforded us an opportunity of concentrating our forces, and deploying from that point, agreeably to the previous design of the troops. Every evolution was performed with alacrity, the whole advancing rapidly in line, and through an open prairie without any protection whatever for our men. The artillery advanced and took station within 200 yards of the enemy's breastwork, and commenced an effective fire with grape and canister.

Colonel Sherman, with his regiment, having commenced the action upon our left wing, the whole line, at the center and on the right, advancing in double quick time, rung [sic] the war-cry, 'Remember the Alamo!' received the enemy's fire, and advanced within point blank shot before a piece was discharged from our lines. Our lines advanced without a halt until they were in possession of the woodland and the enemy's breastwork—the right wing of Burleson's and the left of Millard's taking possession of the breastwork; our artillery having gallantly charged up within seventy yards of the enemy's cannon, when it was taken by our troops.

The conflict lasted about eighteen minutes from the time of close action until we were in possession of the enemy's encampment, taking one piece of cannon (loaded), four stand of colors, all their camp equipage, stores and baggage. Our cavalry had charged and routed the enemy upon the right, and given pursuit to the fugitives, which did not cease until they arrived at the bridge (Vince's Bayou). . . . The conflict in the breastwork lasted but a few moments; many of the troops encountered hand-to-hand, and, not having the advantage of bayonets on our side, our riflemen used their pieces as war-clubs, breaking many of them off at the breach. The rout commenced at half-past four, and the pursuit of the main army continued until twilight. . . .

Houston wrote his report four days after the battle in which he was painfully wounded, one of the few casualties. Only 9 Texans were killed or mortally wounded and 30 more wounded less seriously. Of the Mexicans, according to Houston's report, 630 were killed, 208 wounded and 730 taken prisoner. Among the last was Santa Anna himself, who was captured in disguise on the following day.

While he was alone, Houston picked up an ear of corn and began nibbling on it, and a few kernels fell to the ground. The young guard stooped down and, retrieving them, said, "I'll take these back and plant them on my farm. I'll call my corn, Houston Corn."

"Not so, lad. You must call it San Jacinto Corn!" Houston said, ripping off a handful and giving it to the soldier. (To this day San Jacinto corn is planted and enjoyed throughout Texas.)

General Sherman divided the spoils of war to soldier and sailor while Houston prepared to board the schooner for New Orleans. Dr. Ewing doubted if Houston would reach there alive. His voice was very weak as he bade his soldiers farewell. "It will be fame enough to say you were a soldier at San Jacinto," he said.

CHAPTER THIRTY-THREE

Fortunes changed in Texas at this time—what seemed expedient yesterday was not so today, but on the fourteenth of May, after the government was set up in Velasco on the eighth, it seemed there were two treaties; one private, and one public. The first was to the effect that Santa Anna embark for Vera Cruz and there in his own country "acknowledge the independence of Texas."

President Burnet appointed two scouts, Hardeman and de Zavala, to accompany the prisoner on his way. The *Invincible* made ready to sail for Vera Cruz June 3, but winds of chance blew over the land. Wild excitement and cries of indignation rose among soldiers and citizens, and suddenly two hundred and fifty men swarmed the *Invincible*. And there was Green commanding, "Hand over Santa Anna!" Feeling was running high in the States, and these men hastened to Velasco when the news reached them. But Burnet shouted, "Never!"

"Wal, President Burnet, it's your life, or his'n." Green aimed his gun at Burnet, who was now completely surrounded by these men Americans just full of fight.

"Now see here," Burnet said more calmly, "it's not my idea—seems it's the only way we can get recognition from Mexico. Get them off our necks."

"Oh me!" Green smirked. "You talk like a fool, man. Soon's ever that rat's foot lands on Mexican soil he'll gather a stronger force than ever and be right back here. I say, let's kill him, now!"

"You could be right," Burnet agreed, sounding quite logical "Put that thing away. You got me outnumbered. Take him!"

So Santa Anna, under guard of Captain Patton and a detachment of soldiers, was taken across the river to the warehouse of McKinney and Williams. Several times the Mexicans tried to let him escape and died for their trouble.

Columbia went wild. "Hang him!" was the most common cry. "Stake him over an ant hill!" was also popular—a favorite method of torture amongst some tribes of Indians. There certainly was need for action, thought Dr. Phelps as he listened to the clamor.

Santa Anna, the prisoner, was aghast at the compatriots' attempts to release him. But it was the Texans who guarded him who had had their fill of it and were at last ordered to put Santa Anna in chains. This indignity was noted by the Masons. Dr. Phelps now set about restoring a bit of it to the prisoner. "Sooner or later, the Mexicans will get him out, and likely as not over the dead bodies of our guards!"

"Where do you want to take him, Dr. Phelps?" President Burnet asked with tongue in cheek. Where, pray, was there a more secure prison than that warehouse?

"To Orozimba, of course," Dr. Phelps said. Orozimba was twelve miles up the Brazos River in a deep forest with a broad lake on one side and a swamp on the other. "You know where my plantation is—how impregnable? No one in his right mind would try to escape from it."

Sam Houston was in New Orleans having his shattered ankle treated; Stephen was on his way back from the east; Burnet, glad to wash his hands of it, agreed to let Dr. Phelps have him.

Santa Anna rode the twelve miles up the dirt road, with only a sprinkling of oyster shell, the common spread for the Gulf Coast roads, up the Brazos through a beautiful country, with thousands of wide-branched oaks and orchids of many colors swinging; there on the meadows blue bonnets spread a welcome carpet of lavender-blue and beyond these open areas, fat cattle roamed. The azure of a Texas sky, as wide and broad as to the treetops, Santa Anna could see, so different from the deserts of Mexico. "No," Dr. Phelps said, "moss is not a parasite; it is an air plant of the pineapple family. The trees that are dead, died of old age, or were hit by lightning, or one of our supreme hurricanes knocked them down."

"Like Port La Vaca?" Santa Anna asked. "Nothing remains of that once perfect beach settlement. Ah, Senor Dr. Phelps, hurricane destroys me!" They jogged on toward Orozimba.

Presently, Santa Anna spoke, "It was worth fighting for, senor." But he did not specify if he meant Texas or Mexico. But Dr. Phelps

167

knew he was talking about Texas . . . wonderful Texas.

Mrs. Phelps made the prisoner as welcome as she dared, with others watching, especially the house servant, Maud, who actually ran the house and everything in it.

Several days later, Dr. Phelps escorted Santa Anna to the biggest oak tree in his garden, and not wanting to risk escape, chained Santa Anna to the oak. "Sorry to do this . . . but should you escape they'd shoot me down like a dog, with even less compunction!" Phelps mounted his horse to ride over the fields, to see how it was, and late that afternoon, the doctor returned. It was a vast plantation requiring many hours to cover just the cotton fields, for cattle fattened on the rest.

He rounded the bend from the river, casting his eye for a sight of the prisoner, having worried the day long, and springing off his horse, he exclaimed, "They finally got him. What a fool I was to leave him alone!" He knelt beside the prostrate body, lifted his eyelid, and thought he might have returned in time, for the scent of laudanum took the doctor's breath away. "Quick, help . . . somebody . . . anybody. Help!" he rose to his feet and shouted. It being that time of day when the field hands were coming in, he instantly had several strong men to lift Santa Anna into the house, not that he was that heavy, being a small man, but he was dead weight. Mrs. Phelps, seeing at a glance the prisoner on his bed, ashen, took the order of the doctor already running toward Maud's domain. "Hot water, soda, salt," she said, casting her eye toward the cupboard. She was reaching for salt, also. Maud, casting a belligerent glance toward the agitated Mrs. Phelps, muttered, "I do declarr. Why you atryin' to save his life? All de trouble dat man cause. Humph!" Her hands on her hips she squared up with, "Jes' save dem vigilantuses, or whatebber dey is, de trouble!"

"Now stop talking like that, Maud!" She whirled down the hall and suddenly whirled back again. "Did you say vigilantes?" and Maud in great importance replied, "Yessum!" But Maud, holding the pot of boiling water, hoped that her foot would hit something, just right.

Late in the twilight when night insects began their sawing and clouds of mosquitoes swung across Orozimba from their daytime retreat, Santa Anna opened his eyes. The doctor had scarcely left his side all the while, after the soda and the vomiting, kept cool compresses on the prisoner's head and throat. "Ah, Senor Dr. Phelps,

. . . I have made such a debacle of things . . . I did not need to burn the ranchos or the settlements. How many mothers have no place tonight? How many leetle ones have no food? Husbands gone, food gone, home gone? What despair they have! Time for reflection, I found it was too much even for me!"

"So you attempted suicide?" Dr. Phelps had been annoyed with the recurring thought it might be because he would deny the rope he so richly deserved. But here was this man, remorseful to such degree!

"An army officer does what he thinks expedient at the time. . . . It is well known that you saved the life of Mrs. Dickson, her infant and her personal servant . . . that you had your own stores unloaded by the side of the road, and put them in the cart and sent them on their way. What I can't understand, is whatinhell she was doing at the Alamo, knowing full well they didn't have the ghost of a chance."

"Ah, Senor Phelps . . . Mrs. Dickson . . . she is like my people, when the women follow their men, no matter what, or where. I was touched by such devotion."

Mrs. Phelps, pushed a stray curl from her face, "Cast your bread upon the water. . . ."

"As Padre Muldoon says . . ." Santa Anna was tired, "Good night."

Stephen landed at Velasco June 27, 1836. He had completed his services as commissioner to the United States and now entered Texas as a private citizen. He wrote many letters from Velasco, one of which was to Henry Austin. He had visited with Mary, had been accused of being married to Texas, and so the facts of life had slowly crept into his consciousness. If that was the way Mary felt about it, there was little he could do at this late day to change her. Henry was still in New Orleans, no doubt, Stephen thought, having a gay old time. He wrote: "I wish all of my name or connection to stay in Texas and abide the issue be it what it may. Your children ought to and must remain in Lexington, but you ought to be here. . . ."

He was tired and disappointed with Mary's observation, and it seemed that now he had no focal point, no aim, no goal. He visited with Josiah Bell, his oldest friend, who resided now in Columbia, and from Bell's home, he rode a mule the twelve miles to Dr. Phelps's plantation, "Orozimba," where he spent three days in deep conversation with the prisoner, Santa Anna. He never lost sight of the fact that in his first struggling years in Texas Santa Anna had been a friend. His talks were, to him, at least, profitable, for there were in Columbia many citizens who most strongly desired to see the Mexican get his just dues! Not only in Columbia, though they offered the nearest threat, but the length and breadth of Texas. Then there was Mirabeau Lamar, who laughed at the word *treaty*. And Robert Porter agreed.

Stephen Austin was anxious to have the conflict resolve itself. He wanted so very much for Texas, independence and recognition by both the United States and Mexico. To this end, while visiting Josiah Bell in Columbia, he made the visits to Orozimba daily for three days and held long talks with Santa Anna in Spanish.

"Henry Morfit," he said to the prisoner, "was sent down here to scan the situation and give his opinion of whether recognition be advisable, and he sent word back to President Jackson that not at this time. . . . Why, now is when we need recognition!"

"I have no idea how much good it might do, or harm," Santa Anna said, "but I could write a letter to President Andrew Jackson asking him to mediate." Santa Anna rested against his prisoner's oak. July was so very hot. Following a severe winter, with too short a spring, summer fell upon them with a vengeance. But it was the last visit that Austin would pay to Santa Anna. Stephen had already mentioned it. "I'll have to get to Velasco to have an audit of my vouchers." Presently Santa Anna heaved a sigh, wiped the wet from his face and smiled at his old friend, Stephen Austin.

"If you will be so kind as to fetch me paper and pen, I shall be glad to write the letter for you. You may take it along as you go, send it by special courier, or however you please."

Mrs. Phelps supplied the material, a turkey quill, foolscap, and ink pot.

CHAPTER THIRTY-FOUR

Peach Point and Emily's family were soothing to Stephen but he knew there was no escaping an accounting of his journey. "Just begin at the beginning," James Perry said and leaned back in his

170

favorite chair with his pipe. His long legs crossed, he began blowing smoke rings.

Stephen began: "By the last of March we had arrived in Washington. I went on to New York to get money, and from there I went to Philadelphia, and other eastern cities. Dr. Archer left for Richmond, Virginia, but William stayed on in Washington, having known the president from way back when, to beg borrow or steal some consideration for Texas. Later on, William joined me in New York, where he showed me a letter he had received from our New Orleans agent, Bryan. I'll give you the high points as well as I can remember them. 'Advices from Matamoros which can be depended upon represent the advancing army of 8,000 strong waging a war of extermination. A thousand men blockading San Antonio, and a thousand more in reserve. Grants men who surrendered refused quarter and murdered in cold blood. Our army concentrating on the Rio Grande.' "

"The storm that had approached from beyond the Rio Grande . . ." Mr. Perry remarked, dumping the ash from his pipe. Emily brought in the tea service and Stephen waited until the clatter of tea cups silenced.

"Then I had the letter from you, written from Lynchs Ferry the first week of April telling of the run-away scrape. . . ."

"It certainly wasn't funny, my dear brother. I went ripping out of Peach Point like a whirlwind, taking the children with me."

"I can well imagine," Stephen said. "I remember you wrote, 'A dark time for Texas . . . but I still have hopes.' "

"Hear you gave a bang-up speech in Louisville, Stephen," Mr. Perry remarked. "News of Wharton's address in New York City also. They must have caused the hair to rise to have had such wonderful response. Money and men and supplies came flooding the warehouse."

Stephen had the grace to get red in the face. Emily remarked, "I don't see how you get so much done, as shy as you've always been!"

"Well, you might say, I'm just a mother lioness, and somebody's after my cubs!" Stephen grinned slowly, a lazy smile. "We finally got back to Washington. We found all the newspapers and letters we should have received there, in New Orleans. Well, not all."

"But that was, must have been May! Why, already General Houston had, on April 26, I believe, notified General Gaines at his camp on the Sabine of his victory at San Jacinto. I know that General

Gaines immediately dispatched a special courier, Lieutenant Ethan Allen Hitchcock, to get the information to President Jackson.

"Hitchcock made it to the capitol in record time and delivered Houston's letter May 17, 1836. We left on the twenty-seventh for home. But Wharton thought, being a friend of Jackson's, he could influence him in the direction of Texas." He added after a moment, "Recognition and Independence for Texas."

"And so you are home . . . with June almost over. How is Mary putting up with you putting off the wedding?" But Stephen wouldn't even try to reply to so pertinent a question. Germane, yes. Personal? Yes. Some of his business? Yes. He didn't even himself know the answer.

"Houston and Governor Smith both opposed the expedition to the west," Mr. Perry said. They had so much to talk about in order to bring each other up to date on the news, but Mr. Perry did not again ask Stephen about Mary Holly. "After the siege of San Antonio a remnant of Citizen's Army, possibly three hundred troops, stayed on with Neill. Among them was a wealthy Scotsman, name of Dr. James Grant. He was a resident of Parras, Coahuilla for many years with his Mexican family. He was a liberal and against Santa Anna and the centralized system. It seems we've all done a right about-face where Santa Anna is concerned. Anyhow, Santa Anna confiscated Grant's property and expelled him from the country. So he landed in Goliad with Governor Viesca, Dr. Cameron and others."

"I remember him," Stephen said. "I was of the same opinion—that by uniting with the liberals of Mexico we might throw Santa Anna and his despots out!"

"The night before you left for the East, Stephen," Mr. Perry went on, "you intercepted a letter that said ten thousand Mexicans under Santa Anna were on the march to Texas."

"I still had to leave them there, but Neill was a good man. Getting money and men and supplies seemed at the time of much greater value to the cause than staying there."

"That's for sure. It was purely selfish motives that prompted Dr. Grant to attempt the capture of Matamoros. He left Bexar by way of San Felipe. He stripped every fortification in the country, San Antonio too, taking all but eighty men, horses, blankets, supplies, and medicines. It left the post defenseless. He left there December 30 and camped at Goliad, where Johnson joined him."

"James Fannin left Bexar for a visit with his family on the Bernard, but it was cut short due to the arrivals from Louisiana, Georgia, and Alabama. We met them at Velasco when we were leaving."

Stephen and James Perry continued their talk as they walked about Emily's colorful garden. June was displaying its finest dress for his welcome home. So many chickens and hogs and cattle. Mr. Perry had a way with cattle. "How are my cattle doing? You're keeping them back of the bayou, I hope. They're half-brothers, I mean Eliza's. I suppose they've increased enough by now that we can sell off some?"

"They are doing very well indeed. Of course, Santa Anna took off some for his army . . . I was just glad that he didn't burn down the house."

"I haven't seen Eliza in a long time—too long. I want to see my little namesake, Stephen Fuller, too. I guess I'll ride over there in the morning."

"I wouldn't if I were you. Emily wouldn't let me tell you, but little Steve is dead."

"Oh no!" Stephen cried, feeling muchly as if he'd been kicked in the stomach by a mule. "I must hurry there tonight."

"I wouldn't if I were you," Mr. Perry said, sounding, even to himself, like a wheel turning.

"She's married again," he said finally. "And while she may be glad to see you, night time wouldn't be the right time."

CHAPTER THIRTY-FIVE

In Velasco, Stephen told the other commissioners about Morfit's delaying tactics. Wharton stormed the news. "I'll be damned!" he shouted. "After all we tried to do in Washington and elsewhere!"

William Wharton that December 20, 1836, Envoy Extraordinary and Minister Plenipotentiary of the Republic of Texas, had spread his credentials before Secretary of State Forsythe. Lacking an official seal, Sam Houston had stamped the documents with the impress of his cuff links. Mr. Wharton was handsomely groomed and presented an elegant reflection on Texas and Texans in his presentation. For this elegance he had paid himself, as well as his passage to Washington—Wharton was a wealthy man, and important to Texas. On the carriage to Washington, he had read the president's message and found nothing of annexation in it. As to recognition there was a mere acknowledgment that Texas was independent of Mexico. "Recognition at this time . . . would scarcely be regarded as consistent with that prudent reserve with which we have heretofore held ourselves bound to treat all similar questions. . . ."

Mr. Forsythe said, "Mr. Wharton, that clamor for annexation has embarrassed the United States. In view of the ruckus stirred up by the abolitionists, would it not be better if the matter were taken care of under the administration of a Northern president?"

William Wharton was not a native Tennesseean for nothing, nor a friend of Andrew Jackson of long standing. He saw no reason why Van Buren should have the glory for the years of silent effort of Andy Jackson, and thinking along this line, he bade Mr. Forsythe goodday, while his feet and his thoughts headed down Pennsylvania Avenue.

President Andrew Jackson welcomed his old friend William. He had been very ill, and still had very little strength, with age and problems and failing. He yearned for his home.

There too, a red hot ember still burned for Texas, but with every argument Wharton put, Jackson would smile and say, "Let Van Buren . . . Leave it to Van Buren" and would shake his head in definite finality. Wharton now reviewed the report of that Henry Morfit, sent with best of intentions, no doubt, but now, like a thorn in the flesh of Texas.

Soon after the New Year, the Mexican War was ended and in March a treaty was signed. Mexico's claim to Texas was relinquished; a tract of land, Upper California, New Mexico, Arizona and parts of Colorado, Nevada and Wyoming, for $18,750,000 ceded to United States. It was not too much to pay Mexico. Now they were from sea to sea.

These three, now going over their vouchers, had become good friends, Wharton had not been guilty as Sam Houston would have believed; Dr. Archer and Stephen were as brothers, now that his own brother was gone. They had come together at Velasco, and all their vouchers were piled out in front of them for the auditor to examine. Wharton looked across the table at Stephen in the silence when nothing was heard but the shuffling of papers and said, "I say, Stephen, we'd like to submit your name for the presidency of the Texas Republic!" Wharton thought this a novel idea and it would be a bombshell. But not so.

"I've had many letters suggesting that I enter, from the States as well as all over Texas. But you know, William, I am not well. Of course I'm not blaming Burnet for calling a convention election in September. No one seems to pay any attention to him anyway. That matter of the *Invincible* and Santa Anna—they ought to have had their measure taken right on the boat!"

"Yep," grinned Dr. Archer, who agreed with anything Stephen said. "That was pure insubordination—that's what it was!"

"Insubordination, like hell!" Wharton shrieked, and jumped from his stool, prancing like a jinny. "If I'd been president and those fellows had stormed me and taken my prisoner at gunpoint, they'd have swung from the highest yardarm!"

"Can't you forget you're a Mason, William—just this once?" Stephen suggested without raising his voice. "We've a country to save!"

The room was again quiet. There were only the sounds of their now heavy breathing and boots scraping on the puncheon floor and the crinkle noise of paper in a charged atmosphere. Stephen leaned his head over the table, resting it on his folded arms. There was this strange migratory government first established in his colony of San Felipe de Austin by himself—the first and only for years and years . . . and he was proud of his settlement and of his Old Three Hundred. It had been October 10, 1835, when the officials fled to Harrisburg after Houston left to join Fannin, or Travis, or wherever he would find his army. This government was set up in the "Capital of Refuge" and the faithful newspaper, *The Texas Telegraph and Register*, was ready to go to press on that April 12. A printer peering out the window shouted that the Mexicans were setting fire to the place. All the while his hands were busy yanking the press free and he ran with it to the bayou. "Rest in peace," he told it as it sank to the bottom. But now it had been brought from its watery grave and kept hot these days with handbills and record and all sorts of printing since the great victory after San Jacinto. Then the bird roosted in Columbia, but he had heard about a town plotted at the confluence of the Buffalo Bayou and San Jacinto rivers. His mind drifted . . . after whom, whose name would it bear? Burnet? LaMar? Houston? Austin? It didn't really matter. What did was his vouchers and his getting back from Velasco to Peach Point so that Emily would not make herself sick worrying.

It was through this faithful press that Stephen made his decision known:

> I am influenced by the governing principle which has regu-
> lated my actions since I came to Texas, fifteen years ago,
> which is to serve the country in any capacity in which the
> people might think proper to employ me. I shall not decline
> the highly responsible and difficult one now proposed, should
> the majority of my fellow citizens elect me. My labors and
> exertions to settle this country and promote its welfare are
> well known. My object has been the general good, and the
> permanent liberty and prosperity of Texas.

These were distributed. There was almost no campaigning.

CHAPTER THIRTY-SIX

With Stephen rode Dr. Archer to visit the army in Victoria. While there both men came down violently with swamp fever. Dr. Archer dragged himself, half delirious, to his home on Eagle Island. Stephen crawled onto his horse with help from a soldier, being almost dead and falling off his horse several times only to mount again with the last vestige of his strength. But he was so completely spent with a high fever and shaking so with ague that as he rounded the driveway through the high brick entry, he fell onto the oystershells in a faint. The men folks at Peach Point lifted Stephen and put him to bed on the first floor. It was a pleasant room, with a window and a view of the north side of the garden. Certainly it was a most opportune time for Emily to say, "I told you so!" but there was only love in her lovely face as Stephen finally opened his eyes. She called for a fresh nightgown and Alice hurried away to fetch it. "You are wringing wet, Stephen," she explained. "We'll have to get you into dry clothing now . . . but the fever is broken."

Late that afternoon he watched the long-legged white cranes meandering along the river and heard the unbelievable honking of geese in and out of the wild rice along the Gulf. Many, he knew, lived here all the time, especially the cranes, but the geese would only spend the winter, then go off to the north to wherever they called home. It was then that Stephen saw, beyond the heavy shrubbery, the log cabin he had asked Mr. Perry to have built for him. "I see it out there, Emily. My house."

"This is your home, Stephen, for as long as you wish to call it so." She sat by his side and smoothed the shock of unruly hair from his high forehead. "Peach Point is your home. But, dear brother. I'm worried about you. You've been engaged to Mary Holly for ever so long. . . . Stephen, are you going to let Henry's six children delay your marriage much longer? Henry Austin knows when he's got a good thing going. . . . But to deprive his sister a life of her own is not fair, either to her or to you, when children you and she might have are denied! Of course, it's really no business of mine. I shouldn't have mentioned it. . . ."

"Time, Emily. You realize naturally that Sam Houston will be the president of the republic. He has earned it. At that time I shall be free to move in the direction you are concerned over. But I'm only entering my name in the race to please some of my friends who are pressuring for it."

"Oh," she exclaimed, greatly relieved. "I'm so glad you'll be home so we can plan it all . . ." and her voice faded away down the long hall from which many voices of many children came. Laughter, and shrieks of terror, which Emily closed off after her. "I've brought you some soup. Perhaps tomorrow we'll let you join the family at dinner. Rest now, while I think over some excellent weddings I've attended. We do want your wedding to Mary to be the outstanding social event of the year. No, years!" she laughed triumphantly. Emily left him.

All Stephen had ever had in the way of a home was that two-room log cabin in San Felipe: office in one, bachelor's quarters in the other. Must he live forever vicariously with children of other men? He turned his face toward the east, toward the front window, while his heart cried out for Mary, for the lilting music of her laughter. Oh, Mary, how much I need you, my darling. . . . But Henry Austin was having a gay old time in New Orleans knowing that Mary was taking the best of care of his children. When he was able to get out of that bed, he'd write Henry. He'd tell him straight out how he felt about it. Diplomacy be damned!

Stephen had made an appealing address in the Second Presbyterian in Louisville. He said in part: "The people of Texas have taken up arms in self-defense, and submit their cause to the judgment of an impartial world, and to the protection of a just and omnipotent God. . . ."

Seated in the audience was Albert Sydney Johnston, who listened intently. After the speech, Mr. Johnston gave Stephen a most substantial check, which he followed himself to Texas. He purchased a plantation later which he called "China Plantation" but while the first days and weeks passed, he was busily engaged in assisting the colonists in every way he could.

Stephen wrote Mr. Perry: "The hearts of this people are with us. Nothing is now needed but union at home and an absolute and immediate declaration of independence—I hope it is already made by the convention and an express dispatched with it for the commissioners."

Mary Holly did and was doing all she could to help the cause. But Stephen was unhappy with his visit with her. Henry's children were romping all over the house and followed them into the garden. He really wanted to break Henry's neck.

CHAPTER THIRTY-SEVEN

In September Houston became president; Mirabeau B. Lamar, vice president. There were also elected to Congress fourteen senators and twenty-nine representatives. They voted to adopt the constitution drawn up in March, that power of amendment should be by convention elected for that purpose. And they were in favor of Texas being annexed to the United States.

Stephen knew that Emily would be glad that he had not become president, and to quickly give her peace of mind, he wrote to Mr. Perry; "I have been solicited to go into the new cabinet as secretary of state, or to go as minister to the United States. I have declined.

. . . The land office is to be closed; besides this, my health is gone. I must rest to nurse my constitution and try and restore my strength. . . ."

Columbia was not of itself magnificent, but all around it, there were great plantations; affluence oozed through the swamps and bayous and prairies with cattle, hogs and chickens; cotton was also grown and ginned, and sugar cane and corn with grist mills. It was because of their isolation from the beaten path that most of these palatial plantations escaped the torch. And so Columbia was now enjoying good conversation, banquets, barbecues, balls, and every sort of good fellowship. This was Stephen's element. He was a man who loved art, music, dancing and colorful ball gowns, so that his spirit was revived and his body as well. He considered perhaps he had been hasty in refusing to serve. He again wrote Peach Point: "I have decided, upon reflection, to always serve Texas in any way or manner when called upon by the people to do so . . ." He then wrote to President Sam Houston: "Your Excellency is fully aware of the debilitated state of my constitution and health, and also of the labors which devolve upon me in the land department. I however accept of the appointment and am ready to enter upon the duties of the office, with the understanding that I be allowed the privilege of retiring should my health and situation require it. . . ."

November was windy and cold, with the sickening promise of another nasty winter. Stephen was back in Columbia and he listened to Sam Houston's message to the Texas Congress with more than passing interest. The big problem before them was to find a suitable site for their capital. Houston said: "The present position of our government is one of the greatest inconvenience and absolute embarrassment."

Stephen reflected on this topic which Houston was handling with some delicacy, that the privy was like floating on a lake and too far distant for one suffering dysentery. A crooked smile wreathed his sober face—there had been many who hadn't made it. Houston continued: "We have accommodations for no branch of the public trust. Congress itself is scarcely provided as a body with sufficient buildings—no rooms are set aside for committees of your body. No offices for the chief departments of the executive branch of the government . . . the personal accommodations for all are very deficient." Laughter above a murmur. "I would call your particular and immediate attention to this subject and am compelled by my station to suggest that business cannot profitably proceed unless Congress adjourns to some point where better accommodations. . . ." Yells and laughter filled the room and "Yeah, yeah, yeah!"

"Well," Houston grinned, "do I take this as a voice vote?" Another storm of agreement and "Yeah, yeah, yeah!"

President Houston saw the man rise, and recognized John Kirby. "Now, there is a town at the confluence of White Oak and Buffalo Bayous. My brother Augustus and I have plotted a new town where we propose to construct a commodious building and have it ready for the Second Congress." John Kirby sat down. The new town would be near the center of the most of the activity and with a stream, the San Jacinto River and Buffalo Bayou access to Galveston Bay. It was a natural, the delegates cried, and it was accepted. They would call their new city, Houston. (April of 1837, it became the capital of Texas.)

Stephen's health was not good, but seemed to be improving. He wrote his dear Mary a long letter—at least it started out to be a long letter. It began: "Houston goes into office under favorable auspices and harmony and union is the order of the day. . . ." His mind began wandering, his eyes, too, seeing the marvelous shrubbery Emily had banked along the property. His heart cried out for a home of his own with this, the only woman he ever loved, but he realized her first consideration was Henry Austin's six children. She would not, could not begin life with Stephen under these circumstances. Dear Mary. He glanced over those first few lines he had written. To his love? Politics? And again he was in the summer house of Mary's lovely home basking its great white-pillared pile under ancient magnolias. He had been enroute to Washington, New York, or wherever his work would take him. Lexington was glorious at that time of year. Azaleas, rhododendron, and yellow jasmine fought for supremacy in the spacious garden. They were holding hands as lovers do who have been separated by hundreds of miles, but with all this intimacy, there seemed to be a gulf between them. "It can't be just the children, Mary!" he said. "You know I should welcome them as my very own."

"Oh, dear Stephen . . . you recall Father Muldoon? Well, he's married to his Church. But you? You're married too—in much the same way. You see, you'd be a bigamist!" Her lilting laughter could not hide the despair.

"That's a strange analogy, Mary," Stephen said perplexed. "Paradoxical."

"There's really nothing paradoxical about it, my dear. You're married to Texas!"

Yes, Houston was entering his office auspiciously . . . and Stephen's hand reached out and ripped the letter to shreds.

Stephen had reflected on all that had gone before . . . when Samuel May Williams first came to him as his secretary, how when he was in prison Sam carried on faithfully. Sam had been a poor man in those days, and like himself, had at several times through the years been reduced to linsey-woolsey, or just plain cotton, giving of themselves and their fortunes, be they ever so small. They had ridden mules to help the colonists and Sam never blinked an eye, but went along with him in everything. Now he recalled how embittered he had been toward Sam Williams for the land deal and the Galveston Bay and Texas Land company, which Stephen had never quite understood, even with a public notice Sam had given the newspapers. Stephen got up, had his horse saddled, and rode out to Quintana to see his old friend and secretary to tell him he felt no animosity and ask whether they could not be friends again. In a way it had been a companionable and dear friendship. Stephen missed Sam Williams.

But when Stephen arrived at the store, he was told that Sam had kicked the soil of Texas from his feet and now lived in Baltimore. Stephen went back and wrote to Sam: "Sam, please come home. It is November, and I have a deep apprehension that I shall not be long in this world. . . ."

Stephen was kept busy. All of November he worked answering queries and demands from the people scattered over the broad land. But one day, as he stood at his window looking out upon the Independence Oak, that three-trunked ancient specimen, he caught sight of some men riding with a purpose toward the landing. On closer observation, he saw that it was Major W. Patton, Colonel Hockley—Old Faithful—and Colonel Bernard Bee, and between them rode Genral Santa Anna. Oh, yes . . . he remembered now. They had gone to Orozimba to get the Mexican general on horseback, and now were in truth headed for Velasco, enroute to Washington,

D.C., so that Santa Anna could confer with President Andrew Jackson. He walked out to the gallery and raised his hand in salute. It was the last time Stephen Austin would lay eyes on this, his protector, his salvation in numberless ways when he mothered the infant called Texas. Stephen turned back into his cold office, and sighed, "Ah, history . . . I fly the immortal flag." But he was not thinking of himself—but of Travis, Bowie, Bonham, Crockett and Stewart.

From Baltimore came Mr. Samuel May Williams, straight to Galveston, and there began the erection of a magnificent house in Greek Revival that in a time when costs were at a minimum, exposed Sam as a very wealthy man. Even in a city where pretentious homes were the norm, Samuel May Williams's house was pointed out as the most magnificent in the city of Galveston or anywhere on Galveston Island. But Stephen Fuller Austin did not hear of it— Stephen who had apologized that he had erred in his condemnation of Sam Williams. The palms grew well around the estate, and the banana trees lined the walks with their purplish blooms . . . where azalea and oleanders made a fairy land of the garden. Sam Williams's garden!

CHAPTER THIRTY-EIGHT

On October the third of 1836, an independent nation met in convention at Columbia. Housing was and had been a problem. From the first day it had been a problem. The delegates decided, since it was a lovely day, to hold their convention outside, under the "triple oak" by the side of the road, or main street of Columbia. Under this oak the first cabinet of the republic was sworn in. Stephen Fuller Austin, secretary of state; Henry Smith, secretary of treasury; Thomas Rusk, secretary of war; Sam R. Fisher, secretary of the navy; James P. Henderson, attorney-general; Robert Barr, postmaster-general; with William H. Wharton, minister to the United States.

The duties of secretary of state were involving Stephen more heavily each passing day. There were men from all over the country demanding audience. Hundreds of letters poured in, most of which needed to be answered. At night he would fall into bed, and lately it was to dream. Every night this past week the dream was so repetitious that Stephen was becoming alarmed. Certainly, it must be that old mule of Rob's he rode into Columbia every day. He sent the mule out to Peach Point and bought himself a fine horse. But the dream came on. Always the same dream. It was old Rob, his negro servant who had been with him many years and had been dead for at least three. Old Rob would come and stand over his bed with his battered hat wringing from his long thin fingers. "I've built you house . . . no window and jes' one door. Built it in a day's time."

As winter drew a chill blanket over Texas, Stephen felt the aching cold whistling through the chinched logs, and he would rise from his desk and stand before the fire, and turn and warm the other side, and then return to work. The very sight of that pile of letters discouraged him. They found him there, with his head upon his arms, a pen of turkey quill in his fingers. Stephen had double pneumonia.

There arrived at the office then, Mr. Perry in his beautiful black barouche to have Stephen home with Emily and the children for the Holy Days. Dr. Archer had been working over Stephen, whom he loved like a brother as everyone knew, and looked gaunt as he opened the door for Mr. Perry. "What's the matter with you, Archer?" he said with a smile that became a frown as his eyes slid across the room to the bed. "For heaven's sake, man . . . is Stephen sick?"

"Pneumonia . . . in both lungs. As you hear, every breath is torture."

"How long has he been like this?"

"Two days. I've been right here every minute of the time."

"And you look it. Is there no one whom you could trust to stay with him for a few hours?"

"I cannot leave him." Such brevity.

"I have come for him in the barouche. Could we take him home?"

"As long as there is life in Stephen, I shall entertain hope. But as for moving him at this stage, it would be sheer folly. Certain death."

There was a flutter of eyelids, and Stephen's lips were moving. Mr. Perry leaned from one side, Dr. Archer from the other to hear what Stephen was trying to say. He had heard them talking! "Go back and tell my dear sister that I love her . . . all of you. I'll come when I'm stronger."

"She loves you, too, brother . . . we all do . . . and we'll be waiting." To Dr. Archer he said, "Could I relieve you for a while, Dr. Archer?"

"No indeed. I shall never leave him. But you feel free to return and deliver his message."

On Christmas day, Stephen was delirious, and remained so until he roused two days later. The room was full of people, wanting to help, for certainly, Stephen Austin had been like Moses who led them to this Promised Land. "He is waking, now, Dr. Archer. You must get some rest. We can look after him." But when the friend looked into Archer's eyes, they were full of tears. "You must be just wore out!"

But Stephen was talking, lucidly, clearly, plainly. "Texas is recognized. Archer told me so!" A triumphant smile settled over his features, and he turned his face toward the wall, as Death closed his eyes.

The Republic of Texas went into mourning. Stephen's remains lay in state in Columbia for two days, while thousands of friends came in the bitter cold to pay their last respects.

A gray pall hung over Columbia. The blacksmith shop was silent. The machinery of business stopped. The main road was a sea of horses, buggies and barouches, from plantations fifty miles away. Dr. Phelps of Orozimba, the Whartons of Eagle Island, Velasco, Washington-on-the-Brazos, San Felipe de Austin . . . so many came and from so far. There was Sam Houston, who headed the funeral procession and all members of the Texas government, officers of the army and navy, sorrowing relatives, and they formed a long line of silent souls to Bell's Landing and Josiah Bell, a very old friend and first of the "Old Three Hundred," two miles away. The coffin was taken aboard the *Yellowstone* for the eighteen-mile journey down the "Arms of God" under command of a funeral escort, headed by George Poe. At Perry's Landing, they were met by the First Infantry and the cortege conveyed the remains to the Perry Cemetery. Here, they had built a sepulchre, for the ground had been frozen hard for many weeks, made of brick, with no window and just one door. It had been made in a day's time.

"As a testimony of respect to his standing, undeviating moral rectitude, and as a mark of the nation's gratitude for his untiring zeal and invaluable services, all officers, civil and military, are requested to wear crepe on the right arm for the space of thirty days. All officers commanding posts, garrisons or detachments, so soon as information is received of this melancholy event, cause twenty-one guns (one for each county in the republic) to be fired, with an interval of five minutes between each; and also have the garrison and regimental colors hung with black during the space of mourning for the illustrious deceased." This was Sam Houston's message to everyone concerned throughout the land.

The Republic of Texas went into mourning, and thousands came in the bitter cold to view his remains, which lay in state for two days in Columbia. They brought pine branches from which the snow had been shaken, and holly with red berries . . . it was all they had in the way of flowers, but his bier was all but hidden by their offerings. Certainly, their love went with them.

Emily had memorized Houston's proclamation: "The Father of Texas is no more. The first pioneer of the wilderness has departed. General Stephen Fuller Austin, secretary of state, expired this day at half-past twelve o'clock, at Columbia. December 29, 1936." It was bittersweet.

From Velasco the cannon saluted Stephen, while his body slowly moved into the sepulchre, with no window and just one door, made in a day's time.

Emily's eyes swam with a strange happiness. "Mr. Perry, Stephen would have wanted it to end this way," she said softly.

POSTLUDE

On the afternoon of March 3, 1837, his last day in office, Old Hickory yielded, sending to the Senate the nomination of Alcee La Branche of Louisiana to be charge d' affairs to the Texas Republic. It was confirmed.

The hands of the White House clock were converging upon the stroke of twelve, midnight, when Andrew Jackson and William

Wharton, standing in the dismantled study, raised their glasses to "Sam Houston's Republic!" the ill and feeble president toasted. "It should open the way to American dominion over the shore of the Pacific Ocean."

For Andrew Jackson the reign was over. William Wharton thought "Yes, but from its very inception it has been Stephen Fuller Austin all the way." But he said nothing, knowing Jackson's great love for Sam Houston. What did it matter? History, in the long years ahead, would know whose republic it was.

In 1839, five tired, dusty horsemen reported back to President Mirabeau Lamar, that they had located the ideal site for the capital, on the north bank of the Colorado River, not knowing that the same site had been chosen by Stephen Austin twenty-five years earlier. "And the place where I'd like to spend eternity." What Master Hand guided the men? Who indeed had recalled that Stephen had wanted this as a final resting place? Today a great university keeps him company—and he, knowing, scans the blue of Texas sky from his pedestal, as his young Texans learn life's glorious lessons.

In memoriam in retrospect: Santa Anna was all anxiety for his country. He offered his services to Maximilian and landed at Vera Cruz, where the French promptly arrested him. Later deported in the year 1872, he was allowed to come home to Mexico City, where he died almost penniless, 1876. All that dismal time, he had been ignored . . . even during celebrations honoring the very battles he had fought and won. He was the forgotten man. Yes, this generation was like the Israelites, and the pharaoh who knew not Joseph.

There must have been times when he might have envied Stephen Fuller Austin, who died at age forty-three, at the height of his glory . . . loved and beloved by his countrymen. What more could a man desire?

Museum and Monument, San Jacinto, Texas

The stela:
Inscribed in stone in eight panels, reading from the southeast corner around the monument's base, are the essential facts of the Texas Revolution. The text of the inscriptions follows:

The early policies of Mexico toward her Texas colonists had been extremely liberal. Large grants of land were made to them, and no duties or taxes imposed. The relationship between the Anglo-Americans and Mexicans was cordial. But, following a series of revolutions begun in 1829, unscrupulous rulers successively seized power in Mexico. Their unjust acts and despotic decrees led to the revolution in Texas.

* * *

In June, 1832, the colonists forced the Mexican authorities at Anahuac to release Wm. B. Travis and others from unjust imprisonment. The battle of Velasco, June 26, and the battle of Nacogdoches, August 2, followed; in both the Texans were victorious. Stephen Fuller Austin, "Father of Texas," was arrested January 3, 1834, and held in Mexico without trial until July, 1835. The Texans formed an army, and on November 12, 1835, established a provisional government.

* * *

The first shot of the revolution of 1835-1836 was fired by the Texans at Gonzales, October 2, 1835, in resistance to a demand by Mexican soldiers for a small cannon held by the colonists. The Mexican garrison at Goliad fell October 9. The battle of Concepcion was won by the Texans, October 28. San Antonio was captured December 10, 1835, after five days of fighting in which the indomitable Benjamin R. Milam died a hero, and the Mexican army evacuated Texas.

* * *

Texas declared her independence at Washington-on-the-Brazos, March 2. For nearly two months her armies met disaster and defeat; Dr. James Grant's men were killed on the Agua Dulce, March 2, William Barret Travis and his men sacrificed their lives at the Alamo, March 6, William Ward was defeated at Refugio, March 16, and James Walker Fannin and his army were put to death near Goliad, March 27, 1836.

* * *

On this field on April 21, 1836, the army of Texas commanded by General Sam Houston, and accompanied by the Secretary of War,

187

Thomas J. Rusk, attacked the superior invading army of Mexicans under General Santa Anna. The battle line from left to right was formed by Sidney Sherman's regiment, Edward Burleson's regiment, the artillery commanded by George W. Hockley, Henry Millard's infantry and the cavalry under Mirabeau B. Lamar. Sam Houston led the infantry charge.

* * *

With the battle cry, "Remember the Alamo! Remember Goliad!" the Texans charged. The enemy, taken by surprise, rallied for a few minutes, then fled in disorder. The Texans had asked no quarter and gave none. The slaughter was appalling, victory complete, and Texas free! On the following day General Antonio Lopez de Santa Anna, self-styled "Napoleon of the West", received from a generous foe the mercy he had denied Travis at the Alamo and Fannin at Goliad.

* * *

Citizens of Texas and immigrant soldiers in the army of Texas at San Jacinto were natives of Alabama, Arkansas, Connecticut, Georgia, Illinois, Indiana, Kentucky, Louisiana, Maine, Maryland, Massachusetts, Michigan, Mississippi, Missouri, New Hampshire, New York, North Carolina, Ohio, Pennsylvania, Rhode Island, South Carolina, Tennessee, Texas, Vermont, Virginia, Austria, Canada, England, France, Germany, Ireland, Italy, Mexico, Poland, Portugal and Scotland.

* * *

Measured by its results, San Jacinto was one of the decisive battles of the world. The freedom of Texas from Mexico won here led to annexation and to the Mexican War, resulting in the acquisition by the United States of the states of Texas, New Mexico, Arizona, Nevada, California, Utah, and parts of Colorado, Wyoming, Kansas, and Oklahoma. Almost one-third of the present area of the American nation, nearly a million square miles of territory, changed sovereignty.

OFFICERS AND MEN OF THE TEXAS ARMY
WHO PARTICIPATED IN BATTLE OF SAN JACINTO,
APRIL 21, 1836

A

Adams, Thomas Jefferson
Aldrich, Collin
Alexander, Jerome B.
Allen, John Melville
Allison, John C.
Allison, Moses
Alsbury, Young Perry
Alsbury, H. A.
Anderson, Washington
Andrews, Micah
Angel, John
Anson, Orin D.
Armot, W. S.
Armstrong, Irwin
Arnold, Hayden
Arocha, Jose Maria
Arocha, Manuel
Arreola, Simon
Atkinson, Milton B.
Avery, Willis

B

Bailey, A.
Bailey, H. W.
Bain, Noel M.
Baker, D. D. D.
Baker, Joseph
Baker, Mosely
Balch, H. B.
Balch, John
Bancroft, J. R.
Banks, Reason
Barcinas, Andres

Bardwell, Solomon B.
Barker, George
Barkley, J. A.
Barr, Robert
Barstow, Joshua
Barton, Elder B.
Barton, J. A.
Barton, Wayne
Bateman, W.
Baxter, M.
Baylor, Dr. John Walker
Bear, Issac H.
Beard, Andrew Jackson
Beason, Leander
Beauchamp, John
Beebe, John N.
Begley, John
Belden, John
Belknap, Thomas
Bell, James Madison
Bell, Peter H.
Bell, Thomas Henry
Bennett, J. L.
Bennett, William
Benson, Ellis
Benton, Alfred
Benton, Daniel
Bernardi, Prospero
Bernbeck, W. C. F.
Berry, Andrew Jackson
Berryhill, W. M.
Billingsley, Jesse
Bingham, M. A.
Bird, James
Birt, S. P.

Bissett, R. B.
Blackwell, Thomas
Blakey, L. S.
Bledsoe, G. L.
Blue, Uriah
Bollinger, E.
Bollinger, Peter
Bond, Henry
Booker, Dr. Shields
Boom, G. E.
Borden, John P.
Borden, P. P.
Bostick, S. R.
Bottsford, Seymour
Bowen, W. R.
Box, John Andrew
Boyd, J. C.
Box, Nelson
Boyle, William
Bradley, Issac B.
Bradley, James
Brake, James
Branch, E. T.
Breeding, F. S.
Breedlove, A. W.
Brenan, William
Brewer, H. M.
Brewster, H. P.
Brigham, B. R.
Brigham, Moses W.
Briscoe, Andrew
Brookfield, F. E.
Brooks, Thomas D.
Brown, David
Brown, George J.
Brown, Oliver T.
Brown, W. C.
Browning, G. W.
Bruff, C. C.

Bryan, Luke O.
Bryan, Moses Austin
Bryant, B. F.
Buffington, A.
Buford, T. Y.
Bullock, D. M.
Bunton, I. W.
Bust, Luke W.
Butts, Augustus J.

C

Caddell, Andrew
Cage, B. F.
Calder, R. J.
Caldwell, Pinckney
Callicoatte, John B.
Callihan, T. J.
Campbell, Joseph
Cannan, W. J.
Carmona, C.
Carnal, P.
Carpenter, J. W.
Carper, Dr. W. M.
Carr, John
Carter, Robert W. P.
Cartwright, M. W.
Cartwright, W. P.
Caruthers, Allen
Casillas, Gabriel
Casssidy, J. W.
Chaddick, Richard H.
Chaffin, James A.
Chapman, H. S.
Chavenoe, M.
Cheairs, John F.
Cheevers, John
Chenoweth, John
Chiles, Lewis L.
Choate, D. Jr.

Christie, John
Clapp, E.
Clark, James
Clark, John
Clark, William
Clarke, C. A.
Clarkson, Charles
Clayton, J. A.
Clelens, Josh
Clemmons, L. C.
Clemmons, W. H.
Cleveland, H. N.
Clopper, ——
Coble, Adam
Cochran, J. D.
Coffman, E. G.
Coker, John
Cole, B. L.
Cole, David
Coleman, R. M.
Collard, J. S.
Collins, Willis
Collinsworth, J.
Colton, William
Conlee, Preston
Conn, James
Connell, S.
Connor, James
Cook, J. R.
Cooke, F. J.
Cooke, Thomas
Cooke, W. G.
Cooper, M.
Corry, T. F.
Corzine, H.
Cox, Lewis
Cox, Thomas
Craddock, J. R.
Craft, J. A.

Craft, R. B.
Craig, H. R.
Crain, R. T.
Cravens, R. T.
Crawford, Robert
Criswell, W. V.
Crittenden, R.
Crittenden, W.
Crosby, Ganey
Crunk, N. S.
Cruz, Antonio
Cumba, James
Cumberland, G.
Cunningham, G.
Cunningham, L. C.
Curbiere, Antonio
Curbiere, M.
Curtis, Hinton
Curtis, James, Sr.

D

Dale, E. V.
Dallas, W. R.
Dalrymple, J.
Darling, Socrates
Darr, George
Darst, E. C.
Darst, R. B.
Davey, T. P.
Davidson, J. F.
Davis, Abner C.
Davis, G. W.
Davis, J. K.
Davis, Moses H.
Davis, Samuel
Davis, Travis
Davis, W. H.
Dawson, M. N.

Day, William
Deadrick, D.
Deadrick, F.
Deadrick, G. M.
Denham, M. H.
Denham, Colden
Dennis, T. M.
De Vore, C.
DeWitt, J. C.
Dibble, H.
Dillard, A.
Dixon, J. W.
Doan, Joseph
Doolittle, Berry
Doubt, D. L.
Douthet, James
Dubromer, Dr. Tobias
Duffee, William
Dunbar, William
Duncan, John
Dunn, Mathew
Durham, W. D.
Dutcher, Alfred

E

Earl, William
Eastland, W. M.
Edgar, J. S.
Edingburg, C. C.
Edson, A. B.
Edwards, Isaiah
Edwards, T. C.
Egbert, J. D.
Eggleston, Horace
Ehlinger, Joseph
Eldridge, J. J.
Ellenger, Joseph
Elliot, J. D.
Elliot, P. S.

Ellis, W. L.
Enriquez, Lucio
Erath, G. B.
Evetts, J. H.
Ewing, Dr. Alexander W.
Eyler, Jacob

F

Faris, H.
Farley, T. M.
Farmer, James
Farrish, O.
Farwell, J.
Fennell, G.
Ferrell, J. P.
Ferrill, W. L.
Fields, Henry
Finch, M.
Fisher, W. S.
Fitch, B. F.
Fitzhugh, Dr. John P.
Flick, John
Flores, Manuel
Flores, Martin
Flores, N.
Floyd, Joseph
Flynn, T. A.
Foard, C. A.
Fogle, Andrew
Foley, S. T.
Forbes, John
Ford, S. P.
Forrester, C.
Foster, A.
Foster, J. R.
Fowle, T. P.
Fowler, S. J.
Fowler, T. M.
Franklin, B. C.

Frazer, H.
Freele, J.
Fry, B. F.
Fullerton, W.

G

Gafford, J.
Gage, Calvin
Gainer, J. N.
Gallaher, E.
Gallatin, A.
Gammell, W.
Gant, W. W.
Gardner, G. W.
Garner, John
Garwood, S. J.
Gay, Thomas
Gedry, Lefroy
Gentry, F. B.
Giddings, G. A.
Gilbert, J. F.
Gill, J. P.
Gill, W.
Gillaspie, L. J.
Glidwell, A.
Goheen, M. R.
Goodloe, R. K.
Goodwin, L.
Graham, J.
Graves, A. S.
Graves, T. A.
Gray, James
Gray, M.
Green, B.
Green, G.
Green, T.
Greenlaw, A.
Greenwood, J.
Greer, T. N. B.

Grice, J. B.
Grieves, D.
Griffin, W.
Grigsby, J. C.
Gross, Jacob
Gustine, Dr. Lemuel

H

Halderman, Jesse
Hale, J. C.
Hall, J. S.
Hall, John
Hallet, John Jr.
Hallmark, W. C.
Halstead, E. B.
Hamilton, E. E.
Hancock, G. D.
Handy, R. E.
Hanson, T.
Hardaway, T. M.
Hardin, B. F.
Harmon, C. M.
Harmon, John A.
Harness, W.
Harper, J.
Harper, P.
Harris, A. J.
Harris, J.
Harris, James
Harris, Temple Overton
Harrison, A. L.
Harrison, Elzy
Harvey, David
Harvey, John
Haskins, T. A.
Hassell, J. W.
Hawkins, W. J.
Hawkins, W. W.

Hayr, James
Hays, W. C.
Hazen, N. C.
Heard, W. J. E.
Heck, C. F.
Henderson, F. K.
Henderson, Hugh
Henderson, Robert
Henderstrom, Augustus
Henry, C. M.
Henry, Robert
Herrera, Pedro
Herron, J. H.
Hickox, F. B.
Higsmith, A. M.
Hill, A. B.
Hill, H.
Hill, I. L.
Hill, J. M.
Hobson, John
Hockley, G. W.
Hogan, J.
Hogan, T.
Holder, P. A.
Holman, S.
Holmes, P. W.
Homan, H.
Hood, Robert
Hope, Prosper
Hopson, L.
Horton, A.
Hotchkiss, R.
Houston, Samuel
Howard, W. C.
Howell, R. F.
Hueser, J. A.
Hughes, T. M.
Hunt, J. C.
Hyland, J.

I

Ijams, Basil G.
Ingram, Allen
Ingram, John
Irvine, J. S.
Irvine, J. T. P.
Isbell, J. H.
Isbell, W.

J

Jack, W. H.
Jackson, W. R.
James, Denward
Jaques, Isaac L.
Jennings, J. D.
Jett, James M.
Jett, Stephen
Johnson, B.
Johnson, G.
Johnson, G. J.
Johnson, James
Johnson, John R.
Johnson, John
Johnston, T. F.
Jones, Allen B.
Jones, Dr. Anson
Jones, David J.
Jones, E. S.
Jones, G. W.
Jordan, Alfred S.
Joslin, James

K

Karner, John
Karnes, Henry W.
Kelly, C. O.
Kelso, Alfred

Kenkennon, W. P.
Kennard, W. S.
Kent, Joseph
Kenyon, A. D.
Kibbe, W.
Kimbro, W.
Kincheloe, D. R.
King, W.
Kleburg, R. J.
Kornegay, D. S.
Kraatz, Lewis
Kuykendall, M.

L

Labadie, Dr. N. D.
Lamar, Mirabeau B.
Lamar, Shelly W.
Lamb, G. A.
Lambert, W.
Lane, W. P.
Lang, G. W.
Lapham, Moses
Larbarthrier, C.
Larrison, Allen
Lasater, F. B.
Lawrence, G. W.
Lawrence, Joseph
Lealand, James
Leek, G. W.
Leeper, Samuel
Legg, Seneca
Legrand, E. O.
Lemsky, F.
Lessassier, A.
Lester, J. S.
Leuders, F.
Lewellyn, J.
Lewis, A.
Lewis, A. S.

Lewis, J. E.
Lightfoot, W. T.
Lightfoot, W. W.
Lind, John F.
Lindsay, B. F. Jr.
Loderback, J. D.
Logan, W. M.
Lolison, A.
Lonis, G. W.
Loughbridge, W. W.
Love, D. H.
Love, R. S.
Lowary, J. L.
Lupton, C. W.
Lyford, John
Lynch, N.

M

Magill, W. H.
Maiden, Isaac
Maldonado, Juan
Malone, Charles
Mancha, Jose Maria
Manning, J. M.
Manuel, A. C.
Marner, John
Marre, Achelle
Marsh, Alonzo
Marshall, J. L.
Martin, J.
Martin, P.
Mason, C.
Mason, G. W.
Massey, W.
Maxwell, P. M.
Maxwell, T.
Maybee, Jacob
Mays, Ambrose

Mays, T. H.
McAllister, J.
McClelland, Samuel
McCloskey, R. D.
McCorley, P. B.
McCormick, J. M.
McCoy, John
McCoy, W.
McCrabb, John
McCrabb, Joseph
McCullough, B.
McFadin, David H.
McFarlane, J. W. B.
McGary, D. H.
McGary, Isaac
McGay, Thomas
McGown, A. J.
McHorse, J. W.
McIntire, T. H.
McIntire, W.
McKay, Daniel
McKinzie, Hugh
McKinza, A.
McKneely, S. M.
McLaughlin, R.
McLaughlin, S.
McLean, M.
McMillan, Edward
McNeel, P. D.
McNeely, B.
McStea, A. M.
Menchaca, Jose A.
Menefee, J. S.
Mercer, Eli
Mercer, E. G.
Mercer, G. R.
Merritt, R.
Merwin, J. W.
Miles, A. H.
Miles, Edward

Millard, Henry
Millen, W. A.
Miller D.
Miller, Hugh
Miller, J.
Miller, W. H.
Millerman, Ira
Millett, Samuel
Mills, A. G.
Mims, B. F.
Minnitt, Joshua
Mitchell, A. S.
Mitchell, James
Mitchell, Nathan
Mitchell, S. B.
Mixon, Noel
Mock, W. N.
Molino, Jose
Money, J. H.
Montgomery, A. M.
Montgomery, John
Montgomery, R. W.
Moore, Robert
Moore, Robert D.
Moore, Samuel
Moore, W. P.
Mordorff, Henry
Moreland, Isaac N.
Morgan, Hugh
Morris, J. D.
Morton, John
Mosier, Adam
Moss, John
Moss, M. M.
Mottley, Dr. Junius W.
Murphree, David
Murphy, Daniel
Murray, W.
Myrick, E. P.

N

Nabers, Robert
Nabers, W.
Nash, J. H.
Navarro, J. N.
Neal, J. C.
Nealis, F.
Neill, J. C.
Nelson, James
Newman, W. P.
Noland, Eli

O

O'Banion, J.
O'Conner, P. B.
O'Conner, T.
Odem, David
O'Driscoll, Daniel
O'Neil, John
Orr, Thomas
Osborne, B. S.
Ownsby, J. P.

P

Pace, D. C.
Pace, J. R.
Pace, W. W.
Pace, W. C.
Park, J. B.
Park, W. A.
Parker, Dickerson
Parrott, C. W.
Paschall, Samuel
Pate, W. H.
Patterson, J. S.
Patton, St. Clair
Patton, William
Patton, W. H.

Pearce, Edward
Pearce, W. C.
Peck, Nathaniel
Peck, Nicholas
Peebles, S. W.
Pena, Jacinto
Penticost, G. W.
Perry, Daniel
Perry, J. H.
Peterson, W.
Pettus, E. C.
Pettus, John Freeman
Petty, G. W.
Peveto, M., Jr.
Phelps, J. A. E.
Phillips, Eli
Phillips, Sydney
Phillips, Samuel
Pickering, John
Pinchback, J. R.
Plaster, T. P.
Pleasants, John
Plunkett, John
Poe, G. W.
Powell, James
Pratt, T. A. S.
Proctor, Joseph W.
Pruitt, Levi
Pruitt, Martin
Putnam, Mitchell

R

Rainey, Clement
Rainwater, E. R.
Ramey, L.
Ramirez, E.
Raymond, S. B.
Reaves, D. W.
Rector, Clairborne

Rector, E. G.
Rector, Pendleton
Redd, W. D.
Reed, Henry
Reed, Nathaniel
Reel, R. J. W.
Reese, C. K.
Reese, W. P.
Rheinhart, Asa
Rhodes, Joseph
Rial, J. W.
Richardson, D.
Richardson, J.
Richardson, L.
Richardson, W.
Ripley, Phineas
Robbins, John
Robbins, T.
Roberts, Zion
Robinson, G. W.
Robinson, J. W.
Robinson, Jesse
Robison, Joel W.
Rockwell, C. B.
Rodriquez, A.
Roeder, L. Von
Roman, Richard
Rounds, L. F.
Rowe, James
Ruddell, John
Rudder, N.
Rusk, David
Rusk, Thomas J.
Russell, R. B.
Ryans, Thomas

S

Sadler, John

Sadler, W. T.
Sanders, John
Sanders, Uriah
Sanett, D. A.
Sayers, John
Scallorn, John Wesley
Scarborough, Paul
Scates, W. B.
Scott, David
Scott, W. P.
Scurry, R. A.
Seaton, G. W.
Secrest, W. H.
Secrest, F. G.
Seguin, Juan N.
Self, George
Sergeant, W. L.
Sevey, Manasseh
Sevey, R. E.
Shain, C. B.
Sharp, John
Shaw, James
Sherman, Sidney
Shesten, Henry
Shreve, John Milton
Shupe, Samuel
Sigmon, Abel
Simmons, W.
Slack, J. H.
Slayton, John
Smith, B. F.
Smith, Erastus
Smith, George
Smith, James M.
Smith, John
Smith, John
Smith, John
Smith, John
Smith, J. N. O.
Smith, Leander

Smith, Maxlin
Smith, R. W.
Smith, William
Smith, William C.
Smith, William H.
Smith, William M.
Snell, M. K.
Snyder, A. M.
Somervell, A.
Sovereign, J.
Sparks, S. F.
Spicer, J. A.
Spillman, J. H.
Stancell, J. F.
Standifer, J. L.
Standifer, W. B.
Stebbins, C. C.
Steel, M.
Steele, A.
Stephens, A. R.
Stephenson, J. A.
Steveson, R.
Stevenson, Robert
Stewart, Charles
Stewart, James
Stilwell, W. S.
Stouffer, H. S.
Stout, W. B.
Stroh, Philip
Stroud, J. W.
Stump, J. S.
Sullivan, Dennis
Summers, W. W.
Sutherland, George
Swain, W. L.
Swearingen, V. W.
Swearingen, W. C.
Sweeny, T. J.
Sweeny, W. B.
Swift, H. M.

Swisher, H. H.
Swisher, J. M.
Sylvester, James Austin

T

Tanner, E. M.
Tarin, Manuel
Tarlton, James
Taylor, A. R.
Taylor, Campbell
Taylor, E. W.
Taylor, John B.
Taylor, Thomas
Taylor, W. S.
Thomas, Benjamin, Jr.
Thomas, A. P.
Thompson, C. P.
Thompson, J. B.
Thompson, J. G.
Threadgill, Joshua
Tierwester, H. H.
Tindale, Daniel
Tindall, W. P.
Tinsley, J. W.
Tom, John Files
Townsend, S. B.
Townsend, Stephen
Trask, O. J.
Trenary, J. B.
Tumlinson, J. J.
Turnage, Shelby C.
Turner, Amasa
Tyler, C. C.
Tyler, R. D.

U

Usher, Patrick
Utley, Thomas C.

V

Vandeveer, Logan
Van Winkle, J.
Vermillion, J. D.
Vinator, James
Viven, John
Votaw, Elijah

W

Wade, J. M.
Waldron, C. W.
Walker, James
Walker, Martin
Walker, Philip
Walker, W. S.
Walling, Jesse
Walmsley, James
Walnut, Francis
Wardziski, Felix
Ware, William
Waters, George
Waters, William
Watkins, J. E.
Watson, Dexter
Webb, George
Webb, Thomas H.
Weedon, George
Welch, James
Wells, James A.
Wells, Lysander
Weppler, Philip
Wertzner, C. G.
Westgate, Ezra C.
Wharton, James
Wharton, John Austin
Wheeler, Samuel L.
Whitaker, M. G.
White, John Carey
White, J. E.

White, Levi W.
Whitesides, E. S.
Wilcox, Ozwin
Wilder, Joseph
Wildy, Samuel
Wilkinson, Freeman
Wilkinson, James
Wilkinson, James Jr.
Wilkinson, John
Wilkinson, Leroy
Williams, Charles
Williams, F. F.
Williams, H. R.
Williams, M. R.
Williams, W. F.
Williamson, John W.
Williamson, Robert McAlpin
Willoughby, Leiper
Wilmouth, Louis
Wilson, James
Wilson, Thomas
Wilson, Walker
Winburn, McHenry
Winn, Walter
Winters, J. F.
Winters, J. W.
Winters, W. C.
Wood, E. B.
Wood, William
Woodlief, D. J.
Woods, Samuel
Woodward, F. Marion
Woolsey, Abner W.
Wright, G. W.
Wright, Rufus
Wyly, Alfred Henderson

Y

Yancy, John

Yarborough, Swanson
York, James Allison
Young, William F.

Z

Zavala, Lorenza de, Jr.
Zumwalt, Andrew

BIBLIOGRAPHY

Bushnell, G. H. S. *Ancient Arts of the Americas.* London: Thames and Hudson, 1965.
Pre-Columbian Art of the Americas.
del Castillo, Bernal Diaz. *Discovery and Conquest of Mexico, 1517-1521.* Edited by Irving A. Leonard. New York: Farrar, Straus and Cudahy, c 1800.
de Madariaga, Salvador. *The Heart of Jade.* Fontana Books, 1944.
Life as it was lived by Montezuma, Mexico. A novel—a glittering tale of the Last of Aztecs.
Freeland, G. E., and Adams, J. T. *America and the New Frontier.* Sacramento, California: C. Scribner's Sons, 1936.
A review.
Glasscock, Sally. *Dreams of an Empire.* San Antonio, Texas: Naylor Co., 1950.
The story of Stephen Fuller Austin and his colony in Texas.
James, Marquis. *The Life of Andrew Jackson.* Camden, New Jersey: Bobbs-Merrill Co., 1937.
"Border Captain" and "Portrait of a President."
James, Marquis. *Sam Houston.* Garden City, New York: Halcyon House, 1929.
An unbiased review of the life and times of Samuel Houston.
Journal of American History Circa 1908.
Concerns the Creek and other tribes in North America.
Journal of American History Circa 1909.
Plantation life in ante bellum days.
Monument, Texas. San Jacinto Museum of History.
The Battle of San Jacinto, the heroes of the Battle.
Prescott, William H. *Mexico.* Vols. 1 and 2. New York: Peter Fenlon Collier, 1843.
And the life of the conqueror Fernando Cortes.

Scroggs, William O. *History of Louisiana.* Camden, New Jersey: Bobbs-Merrill Co., 1953.

The story of Louisiana.

Shakespeare, William. *Julius Caesar. The Complete Works of Shakespeare*, vol. 6. New York: Collier and Son, 1901.

Texas Travel Handbook. Texas Highway Department.

Concerns towns and the founders of Texas.

Von Hagen, Victor W. *The Aztec: Man and Tribe.* New York: Mentor, 1958.

Aztec civilization. City of Mexico. An archaelogical history of a people who created a rich and intricate culture in primitive Mexico.

Von Hagen, Victor W. *World of the Maya.* New York: Mentor, 1960.

A history of the Mayas and their resplendent civilization that grew out of the jungles and wastelands of Central America.

Further background for this work grew from the fact that the author of this work was educated in the schools of Harris County—the base of action in most cases, and knew several families of direct lineage of the heroes, one being the Stewart of the story.

Today Peach Point is a tourist attraction—a hurricane having blown the mansion away. The log cabin which Stephen Austin used as his office remains, as does the cemetery.

```
R0142141460   TXR    T
                     B
     25.00           AU7R


RASBURY, RUTH GRANDSTAFF
    BROAD LAND
```